"Sarah lived to be a hundred and twenty-seven years old. She died at Kiriath Arba (that is, Hebron) in the land of Canaan, and Abraham went to mourn for Sarah and to weep over her."

—Genesis 23:1–2 (NIV)

Extraordinary Women OF THE BIBLE

HIGHLY FAVORED: MARY'S STORY
SINS AS SCARLET: RAHAB'S STORY
A HARVEST OF GRACE: RUTH AND NAOMI'S STORY
AT HIS FEET: MARY MAGDALENE'S STORY
TENDER MERCIES: ELIZABETH'S STORY
WOMAN OF REDEMPTION: BATHSHEBA'S STORY
JEWEL OF PERSIA: ESTHER'S STORY
A HEART RESTORED: MICHAL'S STORY
BEAUTY'S SURRENDER: SARAH'S STORY

Extraordinary Women OF THE BIBLE

BEAUTY'S SURRENDER
SARAH'S STORY

Mesu Andrews

Guideposts

Extraordinary Women of the Bible is a trademark of Guideposts.

Published by Guideposts Books & Inspirational Media
100 Reserve Road, Suite E200
Danbury, CT 06810
Guideposts.org

Copyright © 2023 by Guideposts. All rights reserved.

This book, or parts thereof, may not be reproduced, stored in a retrieval system, or transmitted in any form or by any means, electronic, mechanical, photocopying, recording, or otherwise, without the written permission of the publisher.

This is a work of fiction. While the characters and settings are drawn from scripture references and historical accounts, apart from the actual people, events, and locales that figure into the fiction narrative, all other names, characters, places, and events are the creation of the author's imagination or are used fictitiously.

Every attempt has been made to credit the sources of copyrighted material used in this book. If any such acknowledgment has been inadvertently omitted or miscredited, receipt of such information would be appreciated.

Scripture references are from the following sources: The Holy Bible, King James Version (KJV). New American Standard Bible (NASB). Copyright © 1960, 1962, 1963, 1968, 1971, 1972, 1973, 1975, 1977, 1995 by the Lockman Foundation. Used by permission. The Holy Bible, New International Version (NIV). Copyright © 1973, 1978, 1984, 2011 by Biblica, Inc. Used by permission of Zondervan. All rights reserved worldwide. www.zondervan.com. Holy Bible, New Living Translation (NLT). Copyright © 1996. Used by permission of Tyndale House Publishers, Inc., Wheaton, Illinois 60189. All rights reserved. Contemporary English Version (CEV). Copyright © 1991, 1992, 1995 by American Bible Society. Used by permission.

Cover and interior design by Müllerhaus
Cover illustration by Brian Call represented by Illustration Online LLC.
Typeset by Aptara, Inc.

ISBN 978-1-959634-30-0 (hardcover)
ISBN 978-1-959634-32-4 (epub)

Printed and bound in the United States of America
10 9 8 7 6 5 4 3 2 1

Extraordinary Women OF THE BIBLE

BEAUTY'S SURRENDER
SARAH'S STORY

DEDICATION

To my amazing mama, Mary Cooley, who, like Abraham's wife, has a will of iron and a faith that covers her family in prayer day and night. She, too, waits with great anticipation to meet the One she's loved so long…but is gripped tightly by those on earth who love her deeply.

ACKNOWLEDGMENTS

I'd like to thank my sweet friend Melanie Dobson, who worked in concert with me to form Sarah's story as she wrote Hagar's account. It was fun to chat with a partner about these two *extraordinary* women of the Bible and imagine what their relationship might have been like before, during, and after the Bible's short record of their interactions. We tried very hard to "stay out of each other's story" and write only as much of the other woman's experience as was necessary to tell our extraordinary woman's story. If we've somehow overlapped or contradicted, please know it was simply two creative minds that unintentionally diverged!

Huge thanks, also, to my beta reader, Sherril Odom, who lends her amazing expertise as well as her unwavering love and support on so many of my projects. She's been a friend, coach, and dear sister in Christ for years now. I'm not sure how I'd write a book without her!

To my precious husband, I'm not even sure where to start. Since his retirement, he's become business manager, brainstorm partner, editor, proofreader, and chief cook and bottle washer. Somewhere amid all those roles, he finds time to be the best husband, dad, and grampy in the world. I love you, Roy Allen.

And, last but certainly not least, thank you to the wonderful team at Guideposts—the publishing team as well as the other authors included in the Extraordinary Women of the Bible series. It has been an honor and privilege to work with each of you!

Cast of CHARACTERS

Abram/Abraham • Sarah's husband and half brother, Isaac's father, and Elohim's chosen covenant bearer

Dirar • a servant given by Ishmael to Isaac's camp after their mothers reconcile

Ephron • son of Zohar, the Hittite

Hagar • Sarah's long-ago handmaid who bore Abraham's firstborn son, Ishmael

Isaac • Sarah and Abraham's miraculous son and heir of Elohim's covenant

Ishmael • Hagar and Abraham's son, heir of El Roi's (Elohim's) promises made to Hagar during His personal visitation to Hagar in the wilderness

Keturah/Ketty • Sarah's handmaid (fictional role), Abraham's second wife (Genesis 25)

Sarai/Sarah • Abraham's wife and half sister, Isaac's mother, and the woman chosen by Elohim to bear the heir of Elohim's covenant

Zohar • the Hittite who owns Kiriath Arba (Hebron), the land on which Isaac and Sarah have lived for more than two decades

Glossary of TERMS

abba • Hebrew word for father/daddy
abu • Canaanite word for father/daddy
ammatu • Canaanite word for mother/mommy
imma • Hebrew word for mother/mommy

NOTE TO READER

*The words of the wise are like goads, their collected sayings
like firmly embedded nails—given by one shepherd.
Be warned, my son, of anything in addition to them.
Of making many books there is no end, and much
study wearies the body.
Now all has been heard;
here is the conclusion of the matter:
Fear God and keep his commandments,
for this is the duty of all mankind.
For God will bring every deed into judgment,
including every hidden thing,
whether it is good or evil.*
—Ecclesiastes 12:11–14 (NIV)

Writing biblical fiction is a serious task. With it comes the responsibility of representing God's Word with truth and integrity, and I take that responsibility very seriously. The author of the verses above encourages us to use wisdom like *goads*. Goads are used to provoke or stimulate a reaction. I want my words to *goad* readers to run to their Bibles and say, "Is that really in there?"

But the verses above also warn us not to *add* anything to "them." What "them" is the teacher in Ecclesiastes speaking of? As we read the final verses of Ecclesiastes 12, it seems he may have meant to ward off additions to his own precious "book," not wishing anyone to edit his work (any author cringes at a tough edit). Yet he says, "Of the making of books there is no end." I don't believe the author of Ecclesiastes expected his book to be the last one written, to end all debates, or to squelch imagination. His warning came with a *heavenly* bridle, not a man-made one: "God will bring every deed into judgment, including every hidden thing, whether it is good or evil."

Because I have a healthy fear of the Lord, I come soberly to each new writing project. First, I read the related scripture passages repeatedly for weeks before beginning extensive historical research. External resources help me understand culture, archaeology, climate, and geology for Israel, surrounding nations, and/or the specific time period. The Bible reading always comes first, however, to ensure I gain a solid foundation of biblical *truth* before building with historical facts.

Fiction comes as the third component. Using the Bible as the firm and immovable foundation and historical facts as solid building materials, creative fiction becomes the mortar that fills any holes or unknowns and holds the story together. Faithful Guideposts editors help decide what fiction is acceptable, and, together, we consider the clues in scripture to create a seamless and believable story that stays consistent with the truths in God's Word.

But don't be surprised if it *goads* you to pick up your Bible and say, "Is that really in there?" I've also included an Author's Note at the back of this book to explain some of the historical research that helped me understand Sarah's cultural context. Now, turn the page and dive into the extraordinary world of *Beauty's Surrender: Sarah's Story*.

CHAPTER ONE

[Abram] said to his wife Sarai, "I know what a beautiful woman you are."
—Genesis 12:11 (NIV)

Kiriath Arba (Hebron), Sarah's Tent
2nd Ajaru (April), ca. 1901 BC

Sarah wore the golden headband *Abba* Terah crafted for her, with its gold chains hanging down, each one dripping with precious stones to create a sparkling veil. "You are more beautiful than any sunrise, my bride." Abraham repeated the words he'd spoken on their wedding day, but they sounded dreamy and distant. He looked at her differently now than when they were children or even during their adult years of shared faith.

Abba Terah stood beside them and spoke the marriage blessing over his eldest son and only daughter. They would leave Ur tomorrow with his grandson, Lot. The four of them had agreed to follow Elohim's call to Canaan while their only remaining family, Abraham's brother and Sarah's half brother Nahor and his wife, Milkah, planned to remain in Ur to oversee the family's gemstone-cutting business.

"The Lord our God made Great-*Imma* Eve from Great-Abba Adam's rib and presented her to him," Abba Terah said. "When El Elyon brought the woman to her husband, Great-Abba Adam said to his wife, 'You are now bone of my bone and flesh of my flesh.' So you, Sarai, shall cling to Abram, and he will protect you all the days of your life. And you, Abram, shall cling to Sarai, and she will bring you peace. In following God's commands in all these things, the two of you will become one flesh."

Abraham peered down at her and moved the tinkling golden veil aside. When he leaned down to kiss his bride—

Sarah gasped awake and whispered, "The bride changed to Keturah." She attempted to sit up, but her body felt buried beneath a mound of stones, weighted to the mat. She lay still, confused and staring at the central peak of her large, square tent, hearing only the sound of a sputtering oil lamp.

Elohim, were You speaking to me through that dream? Or had she eaten something that disagreed with her at last night's meal?

Why would Abraham ever marry Sarah's handmaid, Keturah? The woman was beautiful, but she was like a daughter to Sarah. Abraham completely ignored Ketty on his infrequent visits to Kiriath Arba. Sarah had purchased the girl from desert traders when she was only nine summers old. Ketty was now past her thirtieth year, having refused every betrothal Sarah suggested in order to serve until death parted them.

Sarah's last maidservant, Hagar, came to mind with new fondness. Perhaps the happy events of the past three days had seeped into her dream. Had Sarah mixed up Hagar with Keturah? Sarah had been shocked when her long-ago maid, and Hagar's son, Ishmael, had come to Kiriath Arba seeking reconciliation after thirty-two years of exile. Years before, Sarah and Hagar had been more than mistress and slave. They'd been friends, so close Sarah had given Hagar to Abraham as his wife—though never in a ceremony like in her dream. Was the dream spurred by Hagar's visit, and Sarah could simply blame nighttime imaginings for placing Ketty in her wedding veil?

Squeezing her eyes tight, Sarah whispered, "Or did You really speak to me in a dream, Elohim, as surely as You miraculously worked in Hagar's heart to forgive me?"

She remembered the moment she'd seen her approaching the altar beneath the trees of Mamre, where she offered wisdom to pilgrims each day. Sarah had bolted to her feet, startling Keturah and the others who had come to ply her with questions in the shade of the giant oaks. She raced toward Hagar and fell to her knees before the woman she'd once called friend. Their relationship had changed when Hagar realized she was pregnant, but Abraham and Sarah still raised Hagar's son, Ishmael, as their own to become their legal heir—until Sarah bore Isaac. At his weaning celebration, she'd ordered Abraham to send both the maid and her son away. Though still convinced separating Ishmael from her son was God's will, Sarah asked Hagar's forgiveness that day under the giant oaks of Mamre for the hideous way she'd banished them. Hagar had extended grace beyond imagining, and she'd promised to extend Sarah's deepest apology to Ishmael—who waited at the base of Judean hill country, still nursing his wounded heart. *El Roi, the God Who Sees, please open Ishmael's heart to the same sweet forgiveness his imma and I have tasted.*

No other God could so thoroughly soften human hearts. Throat tight, she whispered to Elohim again, "Would You soften my husband's heart to marry another of my maids?" The thought was too ridiculous. Ketty was like a sister to Isaac. Did Abraham even know her name? When he visited Kiriath Arba twice a year for the shearing festivals, Keturah spent most of her time with the other women in camp and left Abraham and Sarah alone to enjoy the privacy of her tent. Isaac watched over her like a shepherd with a wounded lamb, never letting his abba nearer than a stone's throw to his beloved sister for fear a harsh word might bruise her spirit. Ketty was much stronger than Isaac knew, and his abba was far kinder than he imagined.

But if the dream was from Elohim, none of that would matter. "You would convince them all," she whispered again into the coming dawn. *Ketty might bear Abraham children.* The thought pierced her. Eyes closed, Sarah inhaled a sustaining breath. She was running a race that hadn't even been marked out yet. She wasn't even sure the dream was from Elohim. But if it was from Him, could she bear the thought of a woman giving Abraham more children—possibly *many* children? What would happen to Isaac, who was to be the sole heir of the covenant? Her heart rate sped, considering the tangled complications that might arise, but she gave herself a mental shake. *Stop this, Sarah. You're harnessing a donkey before you've bought a wagon.*

She reached for the bronze bell on the low table beside her to call for Ketty. Why did her arms feel like cedar logs? Perhaps she'd ask the girl to add juniper and honey to the warm goat's milk this morning.

Hand poised over the bronze bell, she stared in horror. Was she still dreaming? A nightmare? Raised blue veins crisscrossed beneath translucent skin as thin as a butterfly's wings. She made a fist and released it. Knuckles, painful and swollen, looked like rounded knobs on a tree branch years after pruning.

When she'd gone to bed last night, she still possessed the only gift her imma ever gave her—the heavenly beauty of Great-Imma Eve. Abba Terah's second wife had died relatively young, but her beauty had been as legendary as the first woman created from Adam's side. Sarah had maintained her youth throughout her 127 years—in both appearance and strength—and though her hair was as white as snow, her body was that of a woman less than half her age. It was the reason pilgrims traveled from clans of every tribe and tongue to hear the gentle wisdom of a great imma at the altar Abraham had built under the trees of Mamre.

This morning, she wasn't even sure she could get out of bed— let alone make the walk from camp to the altar. *The altar.* Would anyone care that she'd retained the wisdom that age afforded if her appearance was no different than any other old woman? It had been the miracle of her beauty that drew desperate people to hear the extraordinary wisdom Elohim had taught her.

Instinctively, she reached up to touch her face. Had it changed as drastically as her hand? Struggling to roll onto her side, she braced herself on one elbow and reached for her bronze hand mirror. But then she hesitated. Did she want to see the face that might stare back?

She must. *Elohim, give me strength.*

Slowly, she lifted the mirror and saw a stranger in the reflection.

CHAPTER TWO

Terah took his son Abram, his grandson Lot son of Haran, and his daughter-in-law Sarai, the wife of his son Abram, and together they set out from Ur of the Chaldeans to go to Canaan. But when they came to Harran, they settled there.
—Genesis 11:31 (NIV)

"Adonai, my God." The words came out on a breath as she rolled onto her back and the mirror fell at her side. "So, this is what dying feels like," she whispered. She'd always wondered how Elohim would take her. And when. Would she die alone or with family around her? Her throat tightened. *Please, Elohim. You know it takes two days to fetch Abraham from Beersheba. There's so much unspoken between us.*

Abraham was still the most handsome man on earth—in Sarah's eyes. Though he'd aged naturally and was ten years her senior, she preferred the weathered skin of her shepherd to the perfumed kings she'd encountered. Abraham's rugged frame kept pace with his flocks, and twice each year he dashed up Kiriath Arba's rocky hills like a stag for the shearing festival. His laughter had charmed their Canaanite neighbors from Dan to Beersheba, drawing them to him like bees to almond blossoms.

Images from this morning's dream flashed before Sarah's eyes. Abraham—as he looked now—with Keturah in wedding garments and Isaac reciting the wedding blessing over them instead of Abba Terah. Sarah blinked, and the image fled. This wasn't a dream—it was a vision. *Elohim, You are speaking to me! To me!* But did He realize how impossible it would be for Abraham, Isaac, and Keturah to agree on such a marriage?

"As impossible as reconciliation with Hagar and Ishmael?" The question came as an answer, not from her own thoughts but a challenge from Above.

Her lips curved into a wry grin. Though her body remained weak, the inner frailty fled with the certainty that Elohim had clearly spoken. The so-called wisdom she shared with pilgrims beside the altar was simply the scraps of wisdom gathered over 127 years of living within the shadow of El Shaddai. But to hear His voice—how long had she waited for a personal visitation? Like the one Hagar had experienced so many years ago. Or the many clear messages Abraham had received through his lifetime.

Elohim, El Roi, You see me! The thrill of it almost soothed the ache in her joints and the labored effort to breathe or swallow or blink. What had happened to her? Sobering, she let the truth settle into her like a feather falls to the ground on a breezeless day. *I'm dying.* Somehow, she knew. It made sense. Without heavenly intervention, her 127-year old body would experience the universal decay of a sin-sick world—like everyone else. She and Abraham had been special among the blessed tribe of Shem, chosen and miraculously empowered to bless the nations. But they weren't immortal. Yes. She was most certainly dying.

Elohim, is this how Abraham hears from You—an inner knowing even without a voice or vision? She would die younger than any of Shem's sages. Younger than Abba's 205 years. Had she somehow displeased Elohim that He would cut her days short? Her spirit rebelled at the thought. The dream and vision He'd given felt like a kind Abba's encouragement, not an angry taskmaster's discipline.

She rang the bronze bell, calling for the daughter of her heart. Ketty would undoubtedly take the news hard, but they must quickly send a servant to tell the pilgrims Sarah wouldn't appear at the Mamre altar today.

Almost before she'd set the bell aside, Keturah ducked into the tent, chattering about the morning's plan as she carried the wooden tray laden with its usual fare. "You slept late this morning, but I kept the gruel warm." She kept the tray level, balancing two bowls and a pitcher of goat's milk as she straightened. "We'll need to hurry if—" The tray plummeted to the ground with her first glimpse of Sarah. Ketty stood frozen.

"Sit beside me, Daughter." Sarah patted the mat. "We have much to discuss, and I'm not sure how many more days Elohim will give me."

Ketty skidded to her knees at Sarah's side. "What happened? You were fine when I settled you into bed last night."

"I'm dying." It was the first time Sarah whispered the words aloud.

"You can't die!" Ketty objected. "You were given Great-Imma's beauty."

Sarah lifted both brows, letting the obvious introduce a painful silence. Her precious girl, now a woman, knew only part of the story. Sarah's ethereal beauty was indeed passed down through the blessed lineage of Shem to Sarah's imma. Abba Terah had adored his second wife, Agarin, but their marriage had caused no end of complications with the Sages—the revered ancestors who governed Semite territory. The Great Sages began as seven descendants of Noah's son Shem who had enjoyed miraculously long lifespans. Shem, Arphaxad, Shelah, Eber, Peleg, Reu, and Serug all lived well past two hundred years. Peleg was the first among them to die at the age of 239. The pagans among Semite clans deemed the Sages semi-divine because of their longevity—as they had Agarin and Sarah because of their beauty. Shem lived in a grass hut in the shadow of the tower called Babel, shepherding Elohim's truth among his Semite clans. But Elohim chose Abraham to champion His truth in Canaan, beyond the Sages' reach, where Sarah's beauty was considered more curiosity than celestial.

Ketty bowed her head on Sarah's shoulder, sniffling. "Why would Elohim take you from us, Imma?"

"Everyone returns to dust, love." With great effort, Sarah lifted a hand to stroke her hair. "Would you like to hear more about my imma?"

Ketty lifted her head, wiping her eyes. "Of course. You've seldom spoken of her."

The things she was about to tell Ketty would explain why Abraham might refuse to marry Ketty. It was better that her daughter-of-the-heart hear the story from Sarah than for Abraham to reject her and her not understand why. Sarah would likely need both Ketty's and Isaac's help to convince

Abraham he should marry again. They'd suffered for years when Sarah suggested he marry her first maid, but if she could convince them the idea wasn't hers—that it came from a personal visitation from Elohim, both a dream and vision—how could any of them refuse?

And what if they agree? The piercing realization shot through her. A memory long forgotten but as real now as it had been when she'd first contemplated giving Hagar to Abraham. Though she and Abraham hadn't been intimate for years, they were still one flesh. They *belonged* to each other as to no one else on earth. When Sarah gave Hagar to Abraham, it was for a single purpose—that she bear a son that Sarah and Abraham would raise as their own. The dream made it clear that giving Ketty to Abraham would be different. She would become his bride in every way—as Sarah had been. Could she watch her husband marry another? Could her joy at Elohim's personal touch overcome the loss of belonging she might feel? She closed her eyes for only a moment. *Elohim, help me to obey with my whole heart.*

With a deep breath, she began, "I need to tell you the story of my whole family so you'll understand what I must ask of you. Are you willing to listen?"

"I'm eager to hear, but should I first send someone to the Trees of Mamre to inform the pilgrims we won't be coming today?"

"Oh, yes." Sarah watched her walk around the spilled yogurt and goat's milk on the rug and closed her eyes. She was so sleepy. When she opened her eyes again, Ketty lay beside her, head on Sarah's sheepskin headrest, snuggled close. As a child,

Ketty had lain like this on one side with Isaac on the other while Sarah told them stories of Elohim. The bittersweet memory seemed like only yesterday, emphasizing the brevity of life on earth when the end was near. "I must have dozed," Sarah said, swallowing back her emotions. "I didn't realize you'd returned."

"It's nearly midday, Imma. Are you hungry?"

Midday? She'd slept all morning and was still more weary than she'd ever been in her life. "No, I'm not hungry."

Ketty laid her arm over Sarah like a shield, protective yet defenseless against the silent enemy stealing her strength. "I'm still eager to hear about your family."

Yes, the story before the revelation. Ketty must have context to understand. "I grew up in Ur with three older brothers borne to Abba Terah's first wife in Babylon. Abram—the master you know as Abraham—was the oldest and shepherd of all livestock. Nahor ran Abba's gemstone-cutting business. Haran was the youngest but married early and had three children by the time I was your age. When Abba's first wife died in Babylon while giving birth to Haran, he grieved deeply and found comfort in the arms of the pagan high priestess at a temple atop the abandoned Tower of Babel."

"I thought your abba followed Elohim," Ketty said. "I thought Elohim originally called Terah to Canaan."

"Abba did follow Elohim after I was born, but after we left Ur, Abram and I discovered Abba had deceived us in many ways." Sarah paused, feeling the betrayal as if it happened only yesterday. "Before I tell you of Abba's sins, I must confess my own. I remember my imma as a faithful follower of Elohim and a wonderful imma to both me and my older brothers. She had also inherited the ethereal beauty of the Great-Imma Eve and never aged a day after her thirtieth year. However, when she grew ill and death lurked, she cried out to pagan gods. I thought she was merely out of her mind with pain, but when she begged me to summon the moon god's priest from Ur's temple, I knew she was in her right mind—though wrong before the one true God." Sarah's cheeks burned even now, the confession thick on her tongue.

"It's understandable that you refused your imma's dying wish," Ketty whispered. "She placed you in an impossible—"

"I brought the pagan priest to her bedside, Ketty. Secretly. While Abba and my brothers slept. The priest spoke his incantations and burned his incense. I paid him four silver rings, and he left." The memory still haunted her, though it happened more than eighty years ago. "Imma died before dawn, and I never told anyone but Abraham. A few months later, our family discovered that my brother, Haran, and all three of his children—Iskah, Milkah, and his son, Lot—had been secretly worshiping in Ur's pagan temples under the cover of night since Haran's wife died years earlier. A few weeks later, Haran and his oldest daughter were killed in a violent attack. On that same night, Abba Terah heard Elohim's voice for the first time—and we prepared to leave Ur for the land of Canaan."

Keturah sat up, her lovely dark eyes searching Sarah's. "Why are you telling me this?"

"I want you to understand the reason I believe Elohim brought you to our camp. The reasons He chose you to become part of our family—but never to bear the children who will inherit God's covenant."

"Why would I—" Her brow furrowed. "The only covenant bearers are Master Abraham and Isaac. I would never—"

"Lie down again." Sarah opened her arms and drew Ketty closer to tell her about the dream and vision. Ketty's surprise would be like a drop in the Great Sea compared to Abraham's—and perhaps Isaac's—but they must all three obey Elohim's command. Hadn't she been equally surprised when Abba Terah told her that she and Abram must marry before leaving Ur? The difference was that she'd always adored her handsome half brother who defended her against Nahor and Haran's teasing.

"Abba said marrying me will protect you as we travel within the clans of Shem," Abram had explained. "And your beauty must remain completely covered during the entire journey." She had dissolved into tears. Nervous as a mouse in a cat-god's temple. He'd assumed she was disappointed to wed the lowly shepherd of their family.

"They're tears of joy, you silly goat!" She'd laughed through her tears, and nearly ninety years later—seeing the best and worst of him—she could never love anyone but Abraham.

"Imma?" Ketty whispered in the long silence. "Are you too tired to speak?"

"No, love. I'm only trying to decide what to say."

"You've always told me to simply say what's on your heart."

Sarah nearly burst with love for this dear girl. "All right. Tell me what you remember about Noah's three sons."

"That's what's on your heart?"

Sarah chuckled. "Humor an old woman."

"He had three sons: Shem, Ham, and Japheth."

"Which son did Noah bless?"

"Shem." Ketty knew the stories of Elohim as well as Isaac.

"And which great sages from Shem's lineage remain alive and govern the Semite tribes?"

"Shem, Arpachshad, Shelah, and Eber."

"Very good, love." Sarah mulled over the names, remembering when all seven sages held more power over the tribes of Shem because they seemed impervious to death. She imagined their wrinkled faces, recalled their raspy, wise voices. "It was Shem and his grandson, Sage Eber, who revealed Abba Terah's deceptions when Abba Terah, Abram, Lot, and I sojourned in Babylon on our way to Canaan. Abraham and I had no idea my imma, Agarin, had been with child when Abba married her, but both sages gave me Elohim's assurance that I was Terah's daughter. However, Sage Eber also declared, in the dark shadow of the unfinished Tower of Babel, that my womb was barren. He never clarified if the cause was my sin or Abba's."

"I'm so sorry, Imma." She searched for Sarah's hand and held it between hers. "Perhaps it wasn't anyone's sin. Perhaps your barrenness was simply prolonged to prove God's greatness in your latter years."

Sarah nodded. Abraham had said the same during their years of waiting, but it had done little to console her then. "I left Babylon disillusioned and broken. When Abba had taken us from Ur, he'd heard Elohim clearly say, 'Go to Canaan,' but by the time we'd traveled over a month to Harran, Abba refused to go farther."

"Was he too weary?" the young woman asked.

"Yes and no." Sarah carefully chose her next words. "Abba couldn't bear the thought of enduring more hardship. So, rather than obeying Elohim's call to enter Canaan, we remained in Harran, at the farthest reaches of Shem's tribal lands."

Ketty's intelligent eyes searched Sarah's. Even as a child, she'd never been satisfied with half-truths. "Wasn't Canaan a son of Ham—Noah's second son, the one Noah cursed to serve Shem for generations to come? Wouldn't Canaan also bear Ham's curse?" Without giving Sarah time to answer, she added, "And why would Elohim call your family to leave the blessed lands of Shem to live among the cursed tribes of Canaan?"

She'd made the explanation easier, but the truth would still be difficult to accept—for all of them. "We didn't know the full reason until after Abba Terah died. Abram, Lot, and I worked hard to honor him in Harran while we hoped for over twenty years Abba would obey Elohim. We buried him there, and that very night, Elohim spoke to Abram, promising to give my husband the whole land of Canaan. Do you remember the Covenant Promise, Ketty?" She nodded, and Sarah continued, "Elohim promised to bless any nation that blesses Abraham, so we came to Canaan as Elohim's messengers of blessing—to those willing to receive it. However, those bearing the covenant must maintain the pure lineage of Shem to convey God's blessing."

Ketty nodded, her brow slightly furrowed but not doubtful. She simply seemed contemplative. Sarah could almost hear her thoughts spinning. She was an intelligent woman, but had she fully grasped the subtle message Sarah was trying to convey?

Keturah wasn't included in Shem's blessed lineage. As part of the eastern desert tribes, she was as much a descendant of Ham as Canaanites or Egyptians—and her descendants could never become covenant bearers.

Her eyes widened with Sarah's prolonged gaze. "Are you saying I won't be welcome in Master Abraham's camp—or Isaac's—when you're gone?"

"No, my girl. I—" How could she explain that marrying Abraham was acceptable but marrying Isaac wasn't? Elohim had already deemed Abraham's descendant as the pure-blooded covenant bearer—Isaac. God had also proven willing to bless Abraham's other descendant—Ishmael. But Keturah would more likely wish to marry Isaac. Though Sarah had raised them like a brother and sister, Ketty would see no issue with such a marriage since Sarah and Abraham had the same abba but different immas. Isaac, too, would wish to protect her. Ketty would feel far more comfortable in her brother's tent than in Abraham's—a man who had barely noticed her though she'd been Sarah's maid for more than twenty years. Sarah looked away, unable to meet her sweet daughter's pleading gaze.

"Please speak plainly, *Mistress*." Use of the formal title drew Sarah's attention and broke her heart.

She reached for Ketty's hands and felt them trembling in her grasp. "Isaac must wed a Semite bride, Love. He must follow our example and produce a pure-blooded covenant bearer to bring Elohim's blessing to any tribe or nation who would receive it."

Beauty's Surrender: Sarah's Story

"Of course. Why does that trouble you so?"

"When I die, you would be unprotected when he's away from camp for days and weeks at a time with the flocks and herds. Isaac loves you like a sister, Ketty. You know it. He would marry you to protect you." Ketty's shoulders stiffened, and she tried to pull her hands away, but Sarah held tight. "Before I woke this morning and realized my beauty was fleeting and my days were few, Elohim spoke to me in a dream. He showed me whom you would marry—who will keep you safe and convey Elohim's blessing on you and your descendants." Ketty's brow furrowed, still oblivious to what seemed obvious. "Abraham," Sarah whispered, "you will marry my Abraham."

The young woman's cheeks turned the color of yogurt. "I... I... I don't know what to say."

Of course she would be surprised. "I realize you and Abraham don't know each other well."

"He's never spoken to me directly in all these years."

"Well, I'm sure you realize after watching him interact with Isaac that my husband is a man of few words. But my dream was clear. In it, you wore my golden wedding veil and held Abraham's hands during a wedding ceremony, while Isaac spoke the blessing over you." Sarah heaved a sigh, relieved that Ketty seemed to agree so quickly. "Now that we've got that settled, you should send a messenger to the fields and call Isaac back to camp. He'll be startled when he sees me, of course—as you were—but I'll explain Elohim's plan. He'll see the merit when you and I explain it to him. We'll likely need his help to convince

Abraham—considering my husband will undoubtedly think I'm reacting out of fear or unsettled emotions as I did the last time I suggested he marry my maid, Hagar."

"Are you reacting out of fear?"

Her question settled like a briar beneath Sarah's skin. "Elohim spoke in the dream and vision before I realized I was dying, Keturah, so no. The decision for you to marry Abraham is not a reaction. It's a command from Elohim." But her breathy tone betrayed rising emotions and damaged her argument. Recognizing doubt on Ketty's features, Sarah tried desperately to explain. "Ketty, you must believe me. Elohim spoke to me as surely as he appeared to Hagar at Beer Lahai Roi."

Her features softened. "Be at peace, Imma. I'll send a messenger to fetch Isaac right away." Her words sounded more pacifying than reassuring, but she hurried toward the exit and was gone before Sarah could question her.

Ketty had left the odor of doubt in her wake and a sticky mess on the goatskin rug. *Elohim, I'm awed that You finally spoke to me, and I'm grateful. But please let me live long enough to convince Keturah, Isaac, and Abraham that I've truly heard Your voice—and that they must obey Your plan.*

CHAPTER THREE

For God does speak—now one way, now another—
—Job 33:14 (NIV)

Ketty escaped Imma's tent with the truth burning in her ears. *"When I die, you would be unprotected. Isaac must wed a Semite bride."* She reached for the family's common cup near the central fire. After filling it with cool water from the spring she'd visited earlier this morning, she gulped as if it could wash away the words chasing round and round in her mind. She poured a second cupful and drank it, setting the cup down hard.

"You look troubled." Ketty jumped like a desert mouse, startled to find the seedy new shepherd, a so-called gift from Prince Ishmael, standing near her. Dirar had remained behind when Abraham's firstborn and Mistress Hagar left Kiriath Arba yesterday.

"Shouldn't you be in the fields?" she asked.

He gave her a snide grin. "I'll see snow in the desert before I take orders from a handmaid." His eyes traveled the length of her, pausing too long at certain places. "I've heard you've cozied up to Prince Abraham's son. Some of the shepherds believe you've even turned your back on the gods of our people to worship their invisible god." He leaned closer with another disapproving huff. "*Our* people, lovely Keturah. We're born to the gods we're meant to serve. Let me teach you which gods from our spice tribes remain faithful to us as slaves—because your masters and their god *will* betray you."

"I want nothing to do with you or your gods, Dirar." Ketty grabbed a wax tablet she'd left near the water jars after recording how much wool they needed for next winter's blankets. She used her thumb to clear the number and wrote the message to Isaac instead. "Take this to Master Isaac," she instructed while pressing the stylus into the wax. "He'll be in the farthest west field. It's urgent. His imma needs him immediately." She handed the tablet to Dirar.

"You've forgotten you're a slave like the rest of us." He sneered. "Someday, these pompous Hebrews will remind you—as Ishmael reminded me when he dumped me here—and then you'll look to me for mercy." He spit at her feet and turned on his heel.

Ketty held her chin high and tried to control the trembling that had worked its way from the inside out. When he disappeared over the rise, she released the breath she'd been holding, calming herself by preparing a new tray of food to share with Imma. When she returned to the tent, however, Imma was sleeping. The woman never napped. She set aside the tray and began cleaning the mess she'd made at first sight of Imma's lost beauty. Sadness rolled over her in waves while she cleaned the rug and tidied the baskets, boxes, and extra blankets. Imma slept through it all.

Truth be told, Ketty was relieved. Having never been a good liar, she would have needed to confess, if Imma were

Beauty's Surrender: Sarah's Story

awake, just how preposterous it seemed that Elohim would sanction a marriage between a daughter of Canaan and the wealthiest prince on the trade routes. She quietly slipped out of the tent to wait at the shady entrance. Settling on a soft pile of blankets, she reached for a spindle, hoping to keep her hands busier than her racing thoughts.

By the time midday arrived, she'd spun all the wool in camp into thread. Where was Isaac? She should never have trusted Dirar to give him the message. Ishmael's castoff had failed his new master at a crucial time of need. Ketty pushed to her feet and walked toward the central cook fire, watching her friends going about their duties. The other servants would mourn Imma's passing as much as she would. Sarah bat Terah was as fierce as a sirocco desert wind but as compassionate as the most tender ewe with her lamb.

Ketty waved at one of the cooks and her young daughter—a widow Imma had insisted they take into their care after the woman's husband was attacked and killed by bandits on the nearby trade route. When Imma saw a need, she filled it. When she saw a wrong, she righted it. When she saw a problem, she fixed it. But the way she intended to fix Ketty's problem after her death sent Ketty's heart racing. Unshed tears blurred her vision. She bowed her head, walking blindly forward along the camp's main path. Isaac and Imma had been the only true family she'd known, but Imma was right about one thing. When Mistress Sarah died, Ketty's place in Isaac's camp died with her. The fear of facing life alone overwhelmed her.

"Ketty?"

Startled, she looked up into Isaac's concerned features.

"I came as quickly as I could. What's wrong?" Winded and dusty, he gripped her shoulders. "The message said Imma—"

"Imma is dying, Isaac."

"What… No!"

The emotions she'd held back all morning came spilling out in words. "I took her food tray into her tent at dawn and found her lying on her mat like a withered old woman."

He stared at her, his breaths coming in short, quick gasps. "How?"

"She said Elohim appeared to her in a dream and gave her a vision before she woke this morning—before she saw her beauty had faded or realized her strength had waned." Only then did Ketty glimpse Dirar standing a few paces behind Isaac, listening to their conversation.

"Elohim spoke to her?" The wonder in Isaac's tone drew Ketty's attention to the bittersweet smile on his handsome face. "She's longed for it her whole life. What did He say?"

Again Ketty glanced at Dirar and stiffened. "I think she should tell you."

"Of course," Isaac said, placing his arm around her shoulders and starting toward Imma's tent. "I need to see her, but I also dread it. Prepare me, Ketty. Is she in pain?"

"She didn't seem to be this morning." Suddenly self-conscious about their normal sibling affection, she glanced over her shoulder and found Dirar following at a distance. His disapproving stare felt like daggers in her back. *"You've forgotten you're a slave,"* he'd told her earlier, but he was wrong. She always remembered, but it did seem Isaac and Imma sometimes forgot. Though Ketty was a few years younger than Isaac, she'd kept pace when they were children, learning side by side to read and write, and reciting the ancient stories of Elohim—the God who had captured her heart and her trust. She and her brother had become closer than two birds in a nest. They sometimes fought like jackals but, moments later, laughed like hyenas. And, today, they would weep like never before.

Ketty looked up at her brother's dirt-streaked cheeks. "You can't go into her tent looking like that. She may be weak, but she's as tenacious as a stream in the desert." They halted at the water jugs in front of Imma's tent, and she offered him the dish towel she kept tucked in her belt. Though Imma had lived in Canaan's hills for most of her life, she still embodied the meaning of "Sarah"—*Princess*—with every fiber of her being. And she'd always expected those near her to act and dress accordingly. Isaac quickly poured water into a nearby basin and washed his hands, arms, and face, then dried them with Ketty's towel.

"Better?" He straightened for inspection, but when his eyes met Ketty's his chin quivered. "I need you to come with me." She set aside the water pitcher and followed him inside.

Isaac's breath caught, and he halted three steps from Imma's mat. Ketty stood beside him and slipped her hand into his. They stared down at the shrunken, sleeping form. Ketty was astonished at the decline since earlier this morning. Even if Isaac sent word today to Master Abraham in Beersheba, would Imma live long enough to see him? The outline of her withered frame looked almost skeletal beneath the linen covering.

"She looks so fragile," Isaac whispered. "She doesn't even look like my—" He covered a sob.

Ketty squeezed his other hand. "She's still every bit our determined imma. Wake her and see."

Isaac knelt beside the mat, leaned over, and kissed her forehead. "Imma, I'm here."

Her eyes fluttered open, and a slow, sweet smile appeared. "How did you arrive so quickly?"

He shot a look of concern at Ketty before answering. "Imma, it's past midday."

She blinked at the revelation, waking more fully, and struggled to sit up. Both Isaac and Ketty rushed to help, placing pillows at her back. Breathless after the effort, she looked at Isaac with a wry grin. "If you need a victory at arm wrestling, now's the time to challenge me."

"Imma!" Her humor was lost on her son. Imma had once told Ketty that Isaac laughed a lot before the Testing—Elohim's command to Abraham that had challenged their family and ultimately split them into two camps. That event was now spoken of in whispers, as reverently as the God who shepherded them.

Imma was still chuckling at her own wit, but Ketty hid her smile while settling on the mat beside her. Isaac finally grinned, seated opposite his sister, capturing her gaze. "Ketty could probably beat us both." His playful wink filled their small circle with warmth.

The lengthening silence sobered them. Who would speak first about the awful truth?

"I'm not in pain, Isaac." Imma held his gaze. "Nor am I frightened."

"I'm grateful to Elohim for His mercy." Isaac brushed a strand of gray hair from her forehead.

"Did Ketty tell you about my dream?"

"She only told me Elohim spoke to you in both a dream and vision—as we've prayed would happen each year when we traveled to Beer Lahai Roi."

"We should have known the God who created such a variety of wildlife and plants wouldn't speak to two people in the same way or place."

Ketty exchanged a hopeful glance with Isaac. Imma's good humor was encouraging. Though she was still physically weak, she seemed more lucid and clear-minded. Perhaps the morning nap had made her reconsider the message in her dream.

"I want you to promise you'll believe me, Isaac." All humor had fled, leaving only Imma's intensity to meet her son's solemn gaze.

"I always believe you," he said. "Why wouldn't I—"

"You must help me convince your abba that Elohim has commanded him to marry Keturah."

Ketty caught only a glimpse of Isaac's shock before lowering her eyes. She couldn't bear to look up, but the silence may have been worse. She lifted her head and found Isaac and Imma locked in a stare. Five heartbeats passed. Ten. Ketty shifted. But they didn't move.

Finally, Isaac sighed. "Do you know the difference between you and Abba when Elohim's plan is revealed?" He didn't wait for Imma's reply. "On the occasions Abba hears from God, he shares nothing with anyone and leaves the *convincing* to Elohim. On the other hand, you—Imma—have one dream revealing God's plan, and you think He needs your help to bring it to pass." Isaac sprung to his feet like a desert hare and started toward the exit.

"Stop!" Imma cried. "Isaac ben Abraham, come back here!"

He halted at the tent opening and turned, having regained composure. "Forgive my outburst, Imma. I suppose that's a trait I inherited from you. I'll return to share the evening meal."

"Isaac, wait!" Imma cried. But it was too late. The tent flap closed behind him. He was gone. She turned to Ketty. "Perhaps I should have asked you to tell him about the dream. He might have received the plan better with your reassurance."

"I doubt anything I said would have changed his mind." Ketty kept her eyes averted, hoping Imma would fall asleep again so she wouldn't have to disappoint her as well.

"Look at me, Daughter." Imma's voice was quavering and weak.

Reluctantly, Ketty obeyed, lifting her eyes slowly to meet the waiting gaze of the only imma she'd ever known. Dare she speak unguarded truth to the woman who held her future? A daughter would speak without fear, but a slave would never say the words burning on her tongue. "I can't marry Master Abraham," she whispered. Then she waited to see whether Imma or Mistress Sarah answered.

CHAPTER FOUR

[Sarah] said to Abraham, "Get rid of that slave woman and her son, for that woman's son will never share in the inheritance with my son Isaac."

The matter distressed Abraham greatly because it concerned his son. But God said to him, "Do not be so distressed about the boy and your slave woman. Listen to whatever Sarah tells you, because it is through Isaac that your offspring will be reckoned."
—Genesis 21:10–12 (NIV)

Sarah inwardly flailed herself that she hadn't been gentler while sharing the news of her dream with Ketty this morning, but desperation fueled her zeal. Sarah felt her strength waning, her life ebbing away. Ketty had just said she *couldn't* marry Abraham, not that she *wouldn't*. "Tell me why you think you *can't* marry Abraham."

"He'll send me away as he did Hagar—the other maid you asked him to marry."

Sarah winced. Ketty had always possessed a hidden strength, but why show it now when Sarah had little strength to argue? "He won't send you away, Ketty. Not if he knows Elohim has commanded it." Breathless after two sentences, Sarah laid her head back and closed her eyes. "Abraham will do as I ask, Love."

"Of course he'll do as you ask. But after you're gone, he'll send me away." She'd spoken without hesitation. Arguing—like a daughter. It was both endearing and frustrating.

Sarah leaned into the silence, fighting off despair and sleep as they tugged at her in the darkness. She felt for Ketty's hand and cradled it gently to confess. "It was I who demanded Hagar's exile both times she was sent into the wilderness. The first time was early in her pregnancy, and the second was when she and Ishmael were banished permanently." She lifted her head, needing to see her daughter's reaction to the full truth. "Hagar heard from Elohim at Beer Lahai Roi that Ishmael would live in hostility toward all his brothers. When I saw Ishmael mocking my son when Isaac was barely four years old, I was terrified for Isaac's future if Ishmael was allowed to remain in camp. So, I demanded both Hagar and Ishmael leave. Abraham spent the night in prayer and received confirmation from Elohim. He sent them away, knowing it was the right thing to do."

"Right?" Ketty said with a razor's edge. "How could it ever be *right* to send a woman and her son into the wilderness to die? Don't you see how easy it would be for Master Abraham to find similar justifications to treat me the same?"

"Justifi—" Sarah scoffed with what little breath she could muster. "Abraham sent them into the wilderness to live, Keturah, not to die. When Elohim changed our names from Abram and Sarai to Abraham and Sarah, he promised I would bear a son from my ninety-year-old body and that Ishmael would be the abba of twelve kings. When Elohim assured my husband he could send Hagar and Ishmael into the wilderness, He was also assuring

Abraham that He would sustain them in that wilderness—as He'd done for Hagar at Beer Lahai Roi. So don't you dare say my husband would send a woman and her son to their deaths, girl. Don't you dare!"

Sarah's chest constricted, a sharp pain shooting through her like a spear. Suddenly unable to breathe, she felt as if a camel had lowered onto her chest.

"Imma?" Ketty grabbed her shoulders, eyes wild with fear. "Imma!" She shrieked and then ran to the tent flap and shouted, "Isaac, come! Hurry! Something's wrong!"

Isaac ran into the tent, followed by another man—a stranger. Sarah, still gasping for small breaths, felt light-headed and confused. Had she seen the man before? Darkness. Light. Ketty was beside her. Isaac helped her sit forward.

The dark-haired man held a cup to her lips. "There you are, Mistress. Drink it down."

Sarah coughed at the foul taste and turned away, but Isaac begged, "Please, Imma. Drink Dirar's tea. I can't lose you yet. Abba would never forgive me if he didn't get to say goodbye."

Abraham. The thought of dying without a farewell was unthinkable. She leaned toward the stranger and his tea, gulping down the foul concoction. *Please, Elohim, You must sustain me long enough to convince my family of Your plan.* It was her last thought before darkness soothed the pain in her chest.

When Sarah woke, only Ketty was there, eyes fixed on Sarah as if she'd kept her alive by the sheer strength of her gaze.

"Shalom, Daughter." Sarah's greeting provoked a sob from her maid.

"I'm so sorry, Imma. I should never have spoken to you that way. I'll do whatever you wish. It doesn't matter what happens to me after you're gone. It doesn't matter—"

"Shhh." Sarah opened her hand, too weak to reach out. "Who was that servant? What was in the tea?"

"His name is Dirar." Ketty looked away. "I'm not sure what he put in the tea, but it seemed to help you rest."

Indeed it had, and now Sarah felt well enough to share something she'd never told her daughter. "I followed Abraham into a distant pasture one night and watched him cut three animals in half: a heifer, a goat, and a ram. He arranged the halves across from each other with a dove and pigeon opposite each other as well. Hawks and vultures swooped down on them, but he batted them away with his staff. Night descended like a thick blanket, and he fell into a deep sleep. I watched in wonder as Adonai appeared, passing between the animal halves in the form of a smoking firepot. The sky rumbled. The ground shook. I was terrified, but Abraham slept through the whole thing."

Ketty's eyes were as large as the full moon had been that night. "What happened? What did it mean?"

"After Abraham woke, he told me the thundering was Elohim's voice. He'd promised us a son. My moon cycles had stopped years before, so I gave Hagar, my maid and dearest friend, to my husband for the purpose of bearing a child that Abraham and I could raise as our own."

Ketty's shoulders stiffened, and she sat back. "The glaring example of why I shouldn't marry Master Abraham."

"No, Ketty," Sarah said. "Your marriage would be very different. In my dream, I saw love for you in Abraham's eyes." Sarah swallowed hard when unexpected emotions threatened. "Abraham never loved Hagar. When she became pregnant, she grew desperate for his affection. She turned against me, mocking my barrenness in hopes of winning his favor. I felt betrayed and alone, but it didn't give me the right to send her away to die."

"Master Abraham should have protected her. She was his wife too."

"Abraham always protected *me*, Ketty. And in my dream, you wore my wedding garments, which I believe means he'll treat you with the same care and tenderness—"

"I'm not you," Ketty interrupted. "I would be another slave wife—like Hagar."

"I won't allow it, Imma." Isaac spoke from the shadows but walked toward them after the declaration. "We don't want to upset you again, so it's best not to discuss your dream or Ketty's future."

Isaac knelt beside Sarah, and Ketty ducked her head and hurried away. Sarah's heart rate rose with her frustration, her chest tightening with warning. She wanted to argue, to shout her demands—Elohim's plan—but her body had demands of its own. "Dying is a frustrating endeavor," she said finally.

He lifted her hand to his bearded cheek, cradling it there. "Shalom, Imma. Can't we enjoy peace during the days you have left?"

She searched his light brown eyes for the joy that had once danced there in gold flecks. He'd laughed so easily as a boy, growing as naturally into the name as the dawn rises in the east.

But since the day he returned with Abraham from the Testing, the day Abraham had proven his great faith in Elohim and a complete lack of faith in Sarah—neither of them had heard Isaac laugh again. "I would find great peace if I could see you laugh again, my son."

The lines between his brows deepened with his scowl. "Why can't you be satisfied with a simple conversation, Imma?"

She recognized her son's emotions simmering beneath the surface. Why had Elohim given the second-generation covenant bearer his imma's fierce feelings? As a woman, Sarah's emotional eruptions had been largely ignored—except by Abraham, but she refused to let him rest until he heeded her words. But as master of Prince Abraham's second camp, Isaac's emotions had ushered him into many tough corners. Were it not for the patient mentoring of their Hittite friend, Zohar—the chieftain who owned the hill country where their camp at Kiriath Arba was situated—her son might well have been ambushed by the Hittite shepherds and his own.

Sarah patted her son's cheek. "I'm satisfied to have a quiet meal with my children. Call Ketty in so we can all eat together."

His eyes narrowed, suspicion darkening his countenance. "I'll call for her, but first you must promise no more talk about your dream or plans for the future."

"My strength is waning, so I must speak while I have breath. You must know how you've misjudged your abba, Isaac."

"Why must you always defend him?"

"Because he defends me. We defend each other. It's what one flesh does because it reflects the relationship of Elohim and His faithful. We defend our God and He protects. It's the way we serve, the way we love."

Isaac pressed her hand against his chest. "With all my heart, I love you and Abba, but I will never allow him to marry Keturah. He doesn't deserve her."

"Isaac." Sarah pulled her hand away. "Your abba is Elohim's choice for Keturah's husband. I saw him look at her in the dream the same way he looked at me when he pulled aside my wedding veil. I believe your abba may someday *love* Ketty, not just protect her."

"Love? Protect?" He sneered. "The way he loved and protected you by forcing you to say you were his sister so that Pharaoh would take you into his harem?"

"I am his sister."

"You're his wife! And twice he allowed kings to take you into their harems because he feared for his own safety more than yours. It was Elohim who protected you, Imma. Not Abba."

"All right then. Can you trust Elohim to protect Keturah when she marries your abba—as he trusted Elohim to protect me in those harems?" Sarah held his gaze.

"You're asking me to do this, not Elohim." Isaac sat back on his heels. "Have I ever denied you anything, Imma? No matter what you've asked of me, have I ever said no?"

They both knew the answer. He'd been the perfect son. "This dream was a command from Elohim as surely as Abraham's command to sacrifice you on—"

"No!" Isaac shouted. "Don't ever compare the Testing on Mount Moriah to any other command. You weren't there,

Imma. You didn't look into Abba's eyes when he raised a dagger over me."

Sarah opened her arms, calling him into her comfort, but this time he refused. "You've always said those memories will fade with time, but they haven't. Nor has my confidence that I, too, proved my faith in Elohim that day—just as Abba did. I allowed Abba to bind me. I climbed onto the altar because he wasn't strong enough to lift a teenager onto the pile of stones."

"I know, Love." Sarah nodded. "And your abba knows too."

"Don't speak for him." Isaac's eyes sparked. "Abba has never spoken to me of that day. He talks only about our flocks and herds when he comes twice a year for the shearing. He's never once asked about me or cared what I think about bearing the weight of a covenant for a God who's never spoken to me."

"You heard the Voice from heaven on Mount Moriah. You heard Elohim stop your abba from sacrificing you."

"But the Voice spoke to Abba, not to me."

The longing in her son's tone shattered Sarah's heart. She'd felt that same yearning for years, and each time they'd return from Beer Lahai Roi she'd endured the same stabbing disappointment she saw on his features now. This morning's dream had fulfilled her greatest desire, to know that Adonai El Elyon, the Master Creator, had split the heavens to speak in a way she could comprehend. And then she'd declared it to the people she loved with all the wisdom of Egypt's raging hippos, never once considering Isaac's unfulfilled yearning. "Isaac, your birth was on Elohim's lips from the moment we left Harran. You have been the descendant He's promised Abraham from the very beginning, and the one to whom He assigned the covenant before you were even born."

"I'm a part of Elohim's plan, it's true, but He has no wish to know me as He knows Abba—nor does Abba have any wish to know his *second* son."

"That's not true." Her ire rose at the innuendo.

Isaac looked up, challenge in his narrowed eyes. "Which part, Imma?"

"Neither. You must cease this self-loathing, my son. Elohim brought you from a ninety-year-old womb and breathed life into your lungs. He has called you by name, and your abba loves you deeply."

A gentle huff escaped with a sad smile. "Abba loves *you*, Imma, and that is enough. I've sent our fleetest-footed messenger to Beersheba with news of your condition. I suspect Abba to arrive within two days when he hears you're dy—when he hears you're not well."

He was right. Abraham would likely race their quickest messenger into Kiriath Arba's hills when he heard of her condition, which meant Sarah had less than two days to prepare Isaac for Abraham's marriage to Keturah. Desperate circumstances called for drastic changes.

"Ketty must have my tent, Isaac. You'll move me into her tent tomorrow morning. I need nothing but my mat and a few blankets. Ketty should keep all my robes, tunics, jewelry, and cosmetics. In fact, she should begin wearing them—starting tomorrow."

He was shaking his head as she spoke. "She won't do it, Imma. She won't dress like you to impress Abba. Even if I would allow the marriage, she'll refuse. We've talked about it. She told me."

Sarah swallowed her mounting disappointment. *Elohim, help me.* "Regardless of what she decides today or tomorrow, Ketty must learn to act like a mistress if you have any hope of finding her a good husband. Remember, you must marry a Semite bride. It would be cruel to keep Ketty as a slave in your camp for the rest of her days, Isaac." He winced as if her words had pummeled him like stones. But he needed to consider the consequences of marrying anyone outside the blessed clans. On the day of Isaac's birth, she and Abraham agreed that Elohim would want their son to follow their example and marry within Shem's tribe. *Adonai, why must humans argue with what is so obviously Your will?* Suddenly exhausted, Sarah had no more strength for debate. "Tomorrow, Isaac. You move your sister into my tent and me into hers. You'll inform Ketty." Sarah closed her eyes, refusing further arguments and holding onto the hope of tomorrow.

"Ketty was right," Isaac said, mischief in his tone. "You're as tenacious as a desert stream, Imma—and still every bit as lovely."

CHAPTER FIVE

*Early the next morning Abraham got up and loaded his donkey.
He took with him two of his servants and his son Isaac.
When he had cut enough wood for the burnt offering,
he set out for the place God had told him about.*
—Genesis 22:3 (NIV)

3rd Ajaru, Sunrise

The first rooster's crow came after dawn. Sarah was startled awake after having slept peacefully most of the night. Dirar's tea had not only eased her pain but relaxed her body, mind, and soul. She felt a little groggy, entranced by the soft pink hues peeking through the narrow slit of her tent opening. The familiar sounds of the waking camp filled her with hope for a better day. Chickens clucked in protest, suggesting there would be boiled eggs for the morning meal, and nanny goats bleated in relief—proof their morning milking had begun.

Sarah waited for Ketty to hurry through the door with a new tray of food to break their fast. Surely Isaac would join them. Or had he returned to the fields? Had she angered him so thoroughly last night that he retreated to his second-most trusted confidants—his flocks and herds? She hadn't realized

Isaac's obsession with the supposed lies she'd told to keep Abraham safe. A misunderstood past created lies Isaac told himself. Perhaps giving her son healthy doses of truth about his abba would do more to convince him Ketty would be safe than all the pleading she'd tried earlier.

Ketty had been Isaac's safe place as a sister. She'd been like a clay pot, holding all of Isaac's unsightly emotions, like broken potsherds as a bottom layer. Her unconditional love provided the fertile soil that settled around his pieces, allowing something beautiful to grow as his feelings untangled and lessons took root over time. Ketty helped pull his best ideas toward the surface and discard the thoughts best left buried. Her task would change when she married Abraham. She'd need to become a plow—digging out as many words as possible from Sarah's parched-earth husband.

"You're awake!" Isaac stood over her, then lowered himself to one knee. Without another word, he slipped his hands beneath her and lifted her into his arms.

"Isaac! What are you—"

"You have a visitor, Imma, and it wouldn't be appropriate to entertain the Hittite chieftain in your tent."

Isaac ducked under the tent flap, taking her hostage into the morning sun. "No, I don't want anyone to see me like—"

"Good morning, Mistress Sarah." Zohar stood in the shade of the giant oak near her tent's entrance, his smile as forced as Sarah's while Isaac lowered her onto a set of cushions Ketty had prepared.

The girl settled a blanket over Sarah's shoulders, her lips pursed into silent apology. "Would you or Master Zohar like anything special to break your fast this morning?"

Not only did Sarah have no interest in food, but she was determined that Zohar's visit would be too short to share a meal. "I'm sure our gracious landlord hasn't come to our camp so early in the morning for mere pleasantries." She turned a penetrating gaze to the handsome, gray-haired man on the cushion beside her. "What brings you to our camp this morning, Zohar?" She'd caught only a glimpse of pity on his features before he attempted another smile.

"You're wrong, my friend. It's been too long since my last visit, and I have indeed come for mere pleasantries—and to sample some of your camp's delicious yogurt." He turned to Isaac. "Why is the milk from your sheep and goats more flavorful than our flocks'?"

Ketty had already hurried away, and only Isaac remained to prolong the facade. "The real secret"—Isaac knelt again to one knee and conspiratorially leaned closer—"is to occasionally let them graze among a garden of herbs, like Imma's." The two men laughed, their false gaiety more condescending than Isaac carrying her outside like a sack of grain.

"Are you two finished?" Sarah glared at her son and her longtime friend, then turned the full heat of her stare on Isaac. "Leave us alone to discuss what happens to this camp after my death. That's why you've summoned the chieftain on whose land we've been Bedouin squatters for nearly twenty-five years."

Isaac looked as if she'd thrust a dagger into his belly.

"Sarah…" Zohar's voice was soft but chastising. "I came because I'm concerned about you." He extended his large hand, palm up, revealing a small, triangular piece of iron attached to a delicate chain. "Another piece for your sirocco wind chime."

Her cheeks warmed. If only she were a donkey—whose beastly stubbornness wasn't compounded by careless words. She leaned back against the tree with a sigh and finally saw a genuine smile on Zohar's face. "How have you put up with me all these years?" She finally chuckled. "Abraham must endure my foolishness, but you could have simply turned me away all those years ago when I came to these hills seeking help from my old friend, Mamre, and his Amorites. So I begged you instead to help me find my husband and son after they'd disappeared from Beersheba. If you'd known intercepting Abraham on his way home from Mount Moriah with Isaac meant I'd be your permanent tenant, you might have sent me on my way."

He lifted one brow with a wry grin. "I might have let your husband pass by."

Sarah swatted his arm, but Isaac didn't seem at all amused. He issued a curt nod to Zohar and left them to speak alone. Sarah's old friend remained focused on her. "Abraham is a fool, Sarah, to have left you in these hills with me while he lived in the desert."

Suddenly uncomfortable beneath his gaze, Sarah lifted the trinket from his hand, careful not to touch the man who had always shown an interest in more than just friendship. "You shouldn't say such things, Zohar. Abraham is the best man I know, and our God has brought blessing to you and your tribe because of my husband—and the kindness you've shown our son." She draped the chain over her hand and noticed a word etched into the iron ornament. "What is the meaning of *ninda*?" He knew better than to bring her an idol or anything labeled with one of his gods' names.

He glanced down at his hands, rubbing at calluses before answering. "Ninda means many things, but in simplest form it's the Hittite word for bread."

She was dying, and he'd brought her a trinket that meant *bread*? "What are its other meanings?"

When his eyes met hers again, moisture had gathered on his lashes. "It can also mean all goodness and femininity, Sarah, that when added to the sustaining nature of bread describes the most desirable woman on earth." He looked away, chuckling as he swiped at his eyes. "I turned into a sentimental old fool when your shepherd delivered news of your condition last night. I'll miss you, Sarah. Your friendship is one of my greatest joys."

He stared into the distance while Sarah groped in the silence for an adequate response to such praise and candor. Their friendship had begun in the most vulnerable days of Sarah's life. Abraham had taken Isaac, two servants, and a donkey from their Beersheba camp before dawn without telling anyone—including Sarah—his plans. As morning wore into midday, Sarah's fear turned to panic that the Philistine Abimelek, their king, must have come in the night and somehow taken them or lured them away. It was the only explanation she could imagine. Abraham would never take their son from her without confiding in her his reasons.

So, with the aid of Eliezer—Abraham's most trusted servant—Sarah had rallied half the camp and gone to seek help from their allies in the hill country. Mamre, the Amorite, and his brothers, Aner and Eshkol, had helped Abraham rescue Lot when he'd been taken captive years before. Surely they'd help Sarah retrieve her husband and only son who'd been taken. But when she'd arrived in the lovely hilltop camp she'd once called Hebron, she'd found her Amorite allies routed and a new chieftain there. Hittites with iron weapons and stern faces met her and the defenseless shepherds with her. The sight of Zohar raising his fist in the air to halt any aggression from his tribesmen still lingered as one of her most reassuring memories.

Now she tugged at his sleeve, calling his rheumy, hazel eyes to look her way. "You could have just as easily killed me and taken my husband's livestock all those years ago. Instead, you took pity on a desperate woman. You showed mercy and kindness, Zohar, when others would have seen the opportunity to gain wealth and more power. You're a good man. A good leader. You've been a good friend and an invaluable mentor for my son. I could never repay our debt." Her heart skipped. "Yet now I must ask for one more kindness."

"Ask it," he said, his tone low and earnest.

"I had a dream that I'm sure was a message from my God. He said Abraham was to marry Keturah."

His wiry brows jumped up. "The slave Isaac protects like a sister?" He shook his head with a low chuckle. "Your son will never allow it. One of my shepherds made a coarse remark about her some weeks ago, and Isaac pummeled his face like bread dough. I made your son give the man a ewe lamb as recompense, but Isaac forced the shepherd to publicly apologize before giving over the lamb. Isaac would never give his sister to the abba he distrusts."

"Then *make* him trust." Sarah's desperate plea met Zohar's furrowed brows, and she felt his disapproval to her marrow. "Please, Zohar. Elohim spoke it in the dream. Isaac, Keturah, and Abraham must believe and obey."

"I've spent all these years playing mediator between your son and my shepherds, Sarah. It's your husband's responsibility to mediate between his god and his son—as he should have done twenty-four years ago. Neither you nor I created the gap between them, Sarah, nor can we fill it." He tilted his head with a warm smile. "But if Isaac needs help with your barley harvest, I'll send my slaves to help so he can spend more time with you."

Gratitude and regret tied Sarah's tongue too tightly to speak. She could only nod her head and answer with an equally friendly smile. Tears slid onto her cheeks, and the sight of them was like a declaration of war. Zohar had never been able to abide her tears.

"I should get back," he said, scuttling to his knees. His struggle to stand was nearly as painful to watch as it seemed to be for the eighty-year-old warrior.

Isaac hurried over from where he'd been working on wax tablets beneath an oak tree about forty paces away. "Zohar, my friend, surely you're not leaving so soon."

The old man grasped Isaac's wrist, accepting the help to stand. "I must return to camp before midday or my son will find a way to take my throne." He smiled when he said it, but there was an undeniable note of sadness in his tone. A Hittite's rule was often challenged if he could no longer fight. Though Zohar was younger than Abraham, his many battles had taken their toll.

"Think about my request." Sarah reached up to offer her hand.

He grasped her fingers and squeezed. "I've treated your son as my own since the moment he arrived on this hilltop, and I'll continue as long as I'm chieftain of my clan. You have my word, Sarah." His eyes locked on hers, full of unspoken meaning.

Would this be the last time she saw her Hittite friend? What does one say in a moment like this—the last moment after years of kindness, big and small? She felt the weight of the small, metal triangle and chain in her other hand and closed her fist around it. "Thank you, Zohar. May El Roi, the God Who Sees, watch over you and bless you, my friend."

His lips trembling, he pursed them together and bowed to kiss the back of her hand. "Goodbye, Ninda." And the Hittite chieftain strode away with the uneven gait of an old man.

CHAPTER SIX

*There are six things the L*ORD *hates,*
seven that are detestable to him:
haughty eyes,
a lying tongue,
hands that shed innocent blood,
a heart that devises wicked schemes,
feet that are quick to rush into evil,
a false witness who pours out lies
and a person who stirs up conflict in the community.
—Proverbs 6:16–19 (NIV)

Master Zohar had arrived with the sunrise, his features drawn and weary. He'd come alone—no six-man royal escort this time—saying one of their shepherds had come last night to tell him of Imma's condition. He was adamant about seeing her, fearing it might be the last time—especially if Master Abraham came. The two men had never been friendly. Though Ketty was certain there'd been no impropriety between the Hittite and Imma, their friendship had been tender, a gift to two lonely people who shared wisdom about how best to lead their camps. Zohar had respected her as an equal and taught Isaac to lead men.

But the Hittite's relationship with Isaac had cost him dearly with his own son, Ephron. A few weeks ago, Zohar confided that Ephron had begun stirring questions among their tribal council about his abba's competence. He'd always disapproved of Zohar's relationships with Isaac and the Hebrew woman who had stolen his abba's heart too soon after his own imma's death. Faced with the loss of another woman he loved, Zohar had insisted on seeing Imma right away. Isaac couldn't refuse the man he trusted more than his abba.

Ketty continued her watchful eye on quiet conversations happening under two distant oak trees and on the large iron pot of this morning's gruel. She stirred with a long-handled spoon to keep it from sticking to the bottom over the white-hot embers, while noting Imma's cheeks gaining color as she and Master Zohar talked beneath the tree nearest her tent. Isaac sat with Dirar a stone's throw away, reworking the shepherd's schedules to ensure Dirar could indefinitely remain in camp. The duplicitous newcomer had proven invaluable with the herbal potion that soothed Imma's chest pains and simultaneously secured Isaac's gratitude and favor.

Isaac reached for the steaming cup of juniper tea that Dirar had prepared, and Ketty held her breath. Was it only juniper Dirar had steeped in that boiling water? Isaac sipped from the cup and set it aside, continuing his conversation. Dirar stole a glance at Ketty. A wicked smile. A silent threat. Isaac hadn't seemed to notice Dirar's distracted look before the slave refocused on the wax tablets, but Ketty had easily deciphered Dirar's motives. After mulling several concoctions for Imma last night that had induced a sound, seemingly peaceful sleep, Dirar had asked if he might offer Isaac a special blend of spiced tea. Despite Ketty's caution, her brother accepted the potion and woke this morning with an increased appreciation for the sneaky slave's herbal talent.

Master Zohar struggled to his feet, and Ketty's hand stilled on the stirring spoon. Isaac rushed to his aid, and Dirar started toward Ketty. "Wadet, stir the gruel." She passed the spoon to the head cook. "I'll put some yogurt into jars for Master Zohar to take home."

But Dirar stepped into her path, blocking her escape. "I must speak with you, *Mistress* Keturah," he said loudly enough for other servants to hear.

"Imma Sarah is the only mistress of this camp." She spoke with equal volume and increased venom then clutched his arm. Guiding him to the shaded path behind Isaac's, Ketty's, and Imma's tents, she whispered, "The servants don't know about Imma's dream. Besides, I've refused to marry Master Abraham and will never become mistress over this camp or any other."

His condescending smile infuriated her. "So, the old man asked you to be his wife?"

Startled, she realized she'd given away too much—and then wondered what else Dirar could have meant. Had Isaac told Dirar of his plans to protect her?

Dirar's mocking laughter unsettled the birds from the tree above them. "You should see the pathetic look on your face." His smile dissolved into a glare. "You'll marry me, Keturah, and I'll be master of this camp before the week's end."

"No," she breathed, more a plea than a declaration.

"Yes." With one hand he squeezed her cheeks and drew near. "It didn't take long to discern the tension between Isaac's shepherds and the Hittites. I slipped out of camp last night and visited the Hittite camp under the guise of sharing news of Mistress Sarah's condition."

Ketty shoved him away, rubbing her aching cheeks. "It was you who told Master Zohar."

"I told Zohar, yes, but the most important conversation was with his son, Ephron, in the shadows afterward. You see, Ephron and I struck an agreement that this camp will be mine after your mistress dies."

"No! I'll tell them—"

Dirar grabbed her arm as she tried to run away. He pulled her into his arms, trapping her against him. "If you speak one word..." She struggled, but he was too strong. She thought to scream, but he whispered against her ear, "If you speak a word of it to the mistress or Isaac, I'll slip enough hemlock in their tea to end them."

Keturah stilled, chilled into silence, as the horror seeped slowly into her new reality. She swallowed hard and spoke through a dry throat. "You'll bring down Abraham's wrath on the whole camp. And the curse of his God on you and every generation after you." It was true and the only retribution she could threaten.

He released her, leering down at her with a satisfied smile. "I'll take my chances backed by a Hittite army with iron spears and swords against a Bedouin shepherd fighting with rocks and slings."

How could it be? How could Ephron, a boy who had grown up with Isaac at his abba's side, turn so quickly against him? Dirar could be bluffing just to keep her quiet. Keturah stiffened her spine, rising to full height, still barely as tall as a low branch on an oak tree. "I don't believe you," she said. "Taking such a stand against Zohar's longtime allies would place Ephron at odds with those who faithfully followed his abba all these years."

"Now you're a tribal strategist?" Dirar's lopsided grin inflicted more mocking. "I'll indulge your speculation, *Mistress* Ketty, since you will one day rule beside me. Ephron will soon take his *abu*'s throne. *Abu* is our people's word for 'abba.' I'll teach you to speak the language of our tribe, and you'll forget all the Hebrews have taught you." He waved away his own digression and continued, "Ephron said he and his abu have tried to teach Isaac to be a hunter and warrior, but he's more inclined toward study and spending time with you and his *ammatu*—his imma—in the camp. He's tense and troublesome in the fields, a nuisance at best and a threat to the Hittite's future peace at worst. Ephron was anxious to be rid of the ill-tempered, soft-handed Hebrew and deal with a more callused, savvy trader." He drew his rough hands down Ketty's arms.

Prickly skin rose with her revulsion. "Perhaps Ephron doesn't realize he's trading a fine Egyptian stallion for a viper who's hiding under a rock, waiting to strike."

His hands dropped to his sides, all geniality gone. "You can either crawl beneath the rock with me or be one of those who gets bitten." He stepped back, reached into a pouch at his belt, and drew out a powder pinched between his thumb and finger. "I can add ground hemlock to anything, anytime, lovely Keturah. Choose where your loyalty lies."

Her loyalty would never change, but how could she remain faithful to Isaac and Imma while also protecting them? A dark chasm opened inside her, a detachment she'd experienced decades ago with familiar grief. This, too, was loss, but different than the impending doom she'd felt at the first glimpse of Imma's wasting body. She'd nearly forgotten the dark pit, the yawning aloneness that came when she must turn off her emotions to survive.

Returning her focus to Dirar, she forced herself to meet his eyes. "Never forget that I'm loyal to Imma and Isaac, and I'll do whatever I must to keep them safe." She took a step closer to him, leaving barely enough space for an oak leaf to slide between them. "I will help you only if you agree to take this camp my way, Dirar."

A quiet chuckle rumbled in his throat. "Who's the viper now?"

Ketty ignored the sick feeling in her gut. "Since you've gained Isaac's trust, you must prove yourself capable of managing the camp in his absence. I'll suggest Isaac make me his concubine, not a bride, and then reassure Imma that he'll travel to the Semite clans immediately after her death to choose a true and pure bride. I'll suggest Isaac leave you in charge of the camp while he's seeking his bride in the lands of Shem. After he's safely away, you and Ephron can do whatever you like with Isaac's possessions."

"And with his concubine." Dirar circled her waist, crushing her against him.

Emotionless, she drew on her memories of the first weeks and months in the slave trader's caravan. "I'll be the least valuable possession Isaac leaves in Kiriath Arba."

A strange mix of emotions doused the fire in his eyes, and he released her as quickly as he'd grabbed her. "We've been alone long enough. It wouldn't do for gossip to taint my newfound favor with the master." He ran from her like a desert hare. She could only hope he'd seen his own depravity in her empty stare.

A shudder worked through her, and she swiped at her robe as if she could wipe his touch away. A scream clawed at her throat, but she covered her mouth with both hands and inhaled deeply through her nose. *Elohim, I need calm! I need peace to protect those I love!* What mattered most was Elohim's covenant and the family He'd chosen to bring blessing to all nations. She was only a tiny pebble on the path for His sacred family to walk on. It had been an honor to be included for even a part of their journey. She, part of the cursed tribes, had already reaped so many blessings. Now, she must be willing to set aside her desires and fears to protect those most important to Elohim's plan. *Elohim, be my Guide. Use me as their shield.*

CHAPTER SEVEN

*[Abram said to Sarai,] "When the Egyptians see you,
they will say, 'This is his wife.' Then they will kill me
but will let you live. Say you are my sister, so that
I will be treated well for your sake and my life will
be spared because of you."*
—Genesis 12:12–13 (NIV)

Move my mat to Ketty's tent, Isaac, and I'll rest there." Sarah kept her eyes downcast, hoping he wouldn't see her wipe her tears. Saying goodbye to Zohar was harder than she'd imagined.

Her son's arms slid beneath her, gently lifting and carrying her in his strong arms. "We're not moving you, Imma. Ketty will not displace you from your tent nor will she wear your robes and cosmetics to pretend she's someone she's not."

"Isaac ben Abraham," Sarah said between gritted teeth, "I'm not dead yet, and I'm still your imma, the mistress of this camp. You will—"

"And I'm the master of this camp." He stopped one step outside her tent, eyes hard as flint. "My word must be law," he said in a whisper. "The servants in our camp have always deferred to your wishes over mine, but they must learn to respect my wishes now. *You* must learn to respect my wishes. I'm no longer a child."

"But you're my child," she spoke through tears. "No matter how old you are, you're my only son." Sarah brushed his cheek with her thumb, knowing he was right. Everyone in Kiriath Arba—their servants, shepherds, all the families in their household, plus Zohar and his tribe—they must all realize that Isaac was now the sole leader of Abraham's hill country camp. However, an imma could never simply allow her son's stubbornness to rob him of Elohim's blessing. "I submit to your wisdom, my son." Sarah spoke loudly enough for those at the cook fire to hear. "You're absolutely right. Keturah should move into my tent to care for me night and day."

His eyes widened, "Imma, that's not..." He glanced over his shoulder at the maids now shouting their approval for his compassionate decision to increase the care for his imma. He ducked into Sarah's tent with a low growl. "You are a master manipulator." His cheeks were flushed, and she knew he was angry with her, yet he still lowered her to the mat as gently as he would an injured lamb. Without another word, he straightened and turned to go.

"Isaac, wait. I know you're angry." He stopped but didn't turn. "Won't you please stay? There's so much I want to tell you, and who knows how much longer I'll live—"

"Don't." He faced her, tears streaming into his curly brown beard. "Why can't our last days together be happy ones? Why do you push and push until I must go to the fields for any semblance of peace?" He bit down on his lips, looking as stricken by his confession as Sarah felt.

"You remain in the fields so long to stay away from me?"

"That's not what I meant, Imma." But she saw the truth in his guilty pallor as he slid to his knees beside her mat. Bowing his head, he let silence unravel the tension between them.

Sarah prayed—for healing from the fresh wound, for wisdom to see her son as a man, for words in the right moments and silence when her words might wound.

Isaac lifted his head but didn't meet her eyes. "You and Abba are very strong. Your beauty—a gift from Elohim—was evident to all, and Abba's fame grew from the moment he stepped into Canaan. It's difficult to be the ordinary son of extraordinary parents." He wiped both hands down his face and finally looked at her. "Sometimes I must escape the insurmountable expectations in the shadow of my parents to find solace with lowly flocks that thrill at my voice and unconditionally trust where I lead them."

"Don't you know that I thrill at your voice, and your abba trusts—"

"No, Imma. Don't do that," he said, more sad now than angry. "Please don't speak for Abba anymore. If he wishes to speak to me, he must learn to say the words himself. Because you're right. We don't know how much longer you'll be here. The time for your mediating is over. You've always tried to convince me that Abba is my protector and yours, but he must tell me—or show me—himself now."

"What else can he do?" Sarah's frustration rose. "He gave you this camp to manage when you were barely old enough to keep the records and left his most trusted servant to train you. He comes for every shearing festival to shower you with praise, Love. How else can an abba show his pride and respect for a beloved son?"

Tears gathered on Isaac's lashes, glistening in the lamplight. "He could tell me why he forced you to lie for him, Imma. He could explain why he relegated Lot to a mere undershepherd among his workers rather than making him the prince of a third camp. He could answer my questions about the past instead of saying, 'Elohim is more interested in the blessings of your future than the mistakes of my past, Son.'" Isaac's imitation of his abba's voice dripped with surprising venom.

Sarah stared at her bitter son, regret and sorrow eating away her hope. How had they fallen so far from the faith-filled family she once thought they were? How had she so utterly failed to teach her son the stellar character of his abba, the man Elohim had chosen from all other men on earth to bear His blessing to all nations? *Oh, Elohim, my time feels so short and the mountain left to climb so impossibly high.*

Isaac sighed and closed his eyes. "I'm sorry, Imma. I shouldn't burden you with all this after I've asked you to treat me like the master of this camp."

"Terah didn't force me to marry your abba," she began.

"I want him to tell me."

"And I want to live forever with Great-Imma Eve's ethereal beauty, but we no longer live in a perfect garden, do we, Son?" The tumble of words tightened Sarah's chest. Closing her eyes, she drew in a ragged breath, trying to slow her racing heart.

A hand gently rested on her arm. "We'll talk after you've rested. I see that your visit with Zohar has tired you."

"No, please." Sarah trapped his hand under her own. "Stay. I need you to understand your abba's generosity and how his faith has brought blessing to those under a curse."

He patted her hand and released a long, slow sigh. "Promise me you'll stop if you feel any pain." Sarah nodded, and Isaac lifted an eyebrow. "Should I call for Dirar to mull some spiced tea to help you relax?"

"No, I want to have a clear mind when I tell you our stories."

"All right then." Her son settled onto a cushion beside her sleeping mat, leaning forward with his elbows resting on his crossed legs. "I'm listening."

"First, your abba never forced me to lie for him. You know I'm his half sister, and we married before leaving Ur. Abba Terah thought I'd be better protected as Abraham's *wife* in the tribal lands of Shem—our ancestors. When Abba died in Harran, and Elohim called Abraham to continue into Canaan—the tribal lands of Noah's cursed son, Ham—Abraham said I could show my love for him by simply saying he was my brother."

Her son choked on a hideous laugh. "I take back what I said before about you being a master manipulator. Abba wins that prize."

"Do you question my love for your abba, Isaac?" The question sobered him. "Can you think of any time in your life that you've questioned our love for each other?" He said nothing, so Sarah pressed the one incident that he might never speak aloud. "Even when Zohar's men found you and your abba on your way back to Beersheba after the Testing and brought you here to Kiriath Arba instead, your abba and I were angry with each other, but did you question our love?"

"If you still love Abba, why have you lived in Kiriath Arba for twenty-four years while he lives in Beersheba?" It was the question he'd never had the courage to outright ask her. As much as he hated his abba's avoidance of hard discussions, Isaac struggled with the same aversion.

"We've lived apart for the same reasons you're so angry with him. When a husband is reticent to share the intimate things of his heart, a wife becomes reluctant to share anything intimate. Distance begets distance, Isaac, but love can still remain in an enduring bond of friendship and support. Your abba is still my best friend and the most admirable man I've ever known—and the cleverest. While in the lands of Shem, I was well protected as his wife because he was well known as a direct descendant of the Great Sages. However, when we left Harran, the Canaanites cared little about Shem or the Sages, and most of them knew nothing of Elohim's blessings and curses on Noah's sons.

"When we entered Canaan, they had no idea we carried a blessing from the Creator. They would see only my gift of Great-Imma Eve's beauty and the husband they must kill to acquire me as their own. On the other hand, if Abraham were my brother, the Canaanites would see the opportunity for betrothal and seek Abraham's favor with lavish gifts."

"So, Abba forced you to help him swindle the Canaanites, putting your life at risk when the plan went awry and two kings took you into their harems."

Sarah glared at her son, refusing to speak another word until he apologized. His chin jutted forward, displaying the same stubborn habit as his abba when determination outweighed sense. When had Isaac become so embittered toward the abba who loved him more than his own breath? Could their son be so completely blind to the abba who had sacrificed so much for him? Where had he heard these half-truths and twisted facts?

Isaac's features finally softened. "All right, Imma. I'm sorry. Tell me your side of the story."

My side? Though the words felt like a burr scraped against an open wound, she began the telling. "Abba Terah chose his oldest son as my husband because I was my abba's treasure, and Abraham was our family's shepherd and protector. My oldest brother had guarded our livestock in Ur and tended to me since I was a little girl. We'd always had a special bond, and Abba knew he loved me like no one else in the world. And I adored him. I still do." Her throat tightened at the thought of her husband, the only man she'd ever loved. She longed to feel his comforting arms around her. *Please, Elohim. Let him come quickly.*

"I didn't know you married Abba for love," Isaac said quietly.

She blinked once, acknowledging with less effort than a nod. "There is much you don't know. After Abba Terah died in Harran, Abraham, Lot, and I set out for Canaan, though many warned us about the severe drought. Abraham's faith took us first to Shechem and then to Bethel. He built an altar to Elohim in both places, establishing a monument to our God in the land of the cursed, believing we could bring blessing when others blessed us. And the blessings flowed—even during the drought. Your abba's wide smile and gregarious laughter won friends no matter where we wandered. But Bedouin life became harder as the ground's cracks widened and even the burned plant turned to dust in the punishing sun and heat. Our livestock was starving and thirsty—as were we—and Egypt was our only hope of survival. We made the fifteen-day journey from the Negev to Migdol in eleven days."

Isaac's mouth dropped open. "That's impossible. How did you find enough water for yourselves and the animals for eleven days of travel in a drought?"

"Many of our animals died, and we sucked on the moisture from tree roots. By the time we reached Migdol, our whole household was near death. Guards separated me from Abraham and Lot and asked each of us how we were related. I remembered what Abraham had asked me to say before we left Harran. He'd told Lot to say the same, so we all gave the same answer: Abraham was my brother, and Lot was our nephew. Only Abraham and I were allowed to proceed to the Memphis palace on a small riverboat. Lot remained at Migdol to care for our flocks and herds. Abraham had taken the last of my gold jewelry in hopes of a trade to replace our lost livestock and perhaps get permission to encamp near Migdol until Canaan's drought ended. But when we arrived in Memphis, news of my unusual beauty had already reached Pharaoh, and I was immediately taken from Abraham and placed in the palace harem."

"Abba should have told Pharaoh immediately that you were his wife."

Oh, the self-righteous clarity of an onlooker. "And what would have happened if we'd revealed our deception in that moment, Isaac?"

"Well...I...uh...I don't think—"

"No, you don't think," Sarah said harshly. "Because if you truly thought about the complexity of our situation, you'd realize a confession would have cost us both our lives—and Lot's. Someone had sent word from Migdol about my beauty, and Pharaoh had already decided he would take me into his harem. Kings take what they want and work out the details later, Isaac."

"If Abba was truly your protector—and not simply protecting himself—he would never have asked you to lie at all." Again, her son lifted his chin.

Elohim, my son is Your covenant bearer. Does he truly understand so little of the responsibility he bears? Discouragement battled despair, but Sarah pressed through the mounting exhaustion. "What is the goal of the covenant bearer's sojourn in Canaan, my son?"

He gave her a sidelong glance. "Elohim has promised to give this land to our descendants, who will be as vast as the stars in the sky and the sand on the seashore."

"And?" she coaxed, noting he'd omitted what she considered the most important parts.

"That Elohim will bless those who bless us and curse those who curse us."

"And that we'll bring blessing to all nations, Isaac."

"I'm happy to hear it," Ketty said as she ducked into the tent. "That the covenant blessing Isaac bears extends to all nations—including the eastern desert clans." Her clipped words coupled with her wobbly voice proved something was desperately wrong. Isaac stood, but Ketty was already at Sarah's mat before he could take a step toward her. Eyes wide, flitting from Isaac to Sarah like a nervous bird, she said, "I've come to make a request."

Isaac reached for her arm to calm her. She flinched and stepped back but remained focused on him. "I know you dare not leave your imma now, but if you could promise her that you'll search for a Semite bride immediately after her death, I believe you would give her a measure of peace." She turned to Sarah. "Isn't that true? Wouldn't you feel more peaceful if Isaac vowed to seek a bride from the lands of Shem after your last breath?"

Sarah looked at Isaac with a silent question, then back to Ketty. "Of course, Love. I'd be very happy if Isaac could—"

"You see?" She turned to him too quickly but smiled before taking a slow, deep breath. "I have one more request that won't please your imma, but it's important, Isaac."

Your imma? Why hadn't she said *our imma*? "Where have you been, Ketty?" Sarah asked. "While I was talking with Zohar and Isaac?"

"I helped prepare this morning's meal, as always." She stood as still as an Egyptian pillar, but she wasn't peaceful when her attention returned to Isaac. "I'd like to become your...your concubine." Her voice broke on the last word.

Isaac's mouth dropped open. He stood there like a gasping fish while Ketty's heart lay flayed before them. "Why ask tonight?" Sarah spoke softly.

"Please, Isaac." Ketty ignored her completely. "I need your protection."

He answered by holding her, wrapping her in the same strong arms that had carried his imma into the tent. The same strong arms that tended injured lambs and delivered calves and had comforted his little sister since the first time she'd skinned her knee in camp.

He looked over her shoulder at Sarah, clearly unnerved by her request.

Sarah was equally troubled. "Please don't chain your sister to a life of humiliation. We love her too much to make her anything but a wife to someone who can truly love her."

"I love her, Imma, and she loves me." He nudged Ketty behind him. "I love her the way you and Abba loved each other at first. As brother and sister."

Sarah had no words. No glib argument for the impossible situation in her own household. *Elohim, what can I do? I know this isn't Your best for them. I know You want Keturah to marry Abraham.* The words she'd nearly shouted to the camp resurfaced in her mind: *Keturah should move into my tent to care for me night and day.* How could she become Isaac's concubine while she cared for Sarah every moment of the day and night?

Clearing her throat, Sarah gained Isaac's attention, though Ketty remained partially hidden behind him. "Keturah," she said, "beloved daughter of my heart. I know you're frightened, and my rantings about marrying a man you don't know—and likely fear—haven't helped. From this moment until I breathe my last, I vow to you that I won't mention my dream again in your presence. However, Isaac and I have made a decision about our living arrangement. We've agreed that you and I need not exchange tents—as I'd proposed—but you will live with me in my tent day and night until my days on earth are ended. Then you must decide with Isaac and Abraham whether to obey or disobey the things Elohim revealed in my dream."

Ketty finally stepped out from behind the shield of Isaac's protection. "Thank you, Imma. I would be honored to remain by your side."

CHAPTER EIGHT

When Abram heard that his relative had been taken captive, he called out the 318 trained men born in his household and went in pursuit as far as Dan.... He recovered all the goods and brought back his relative Lot and his possessions, together with the women and the other people.
—Genesis 14:14, 16 (NIV)

The steaming bowl of bone broth sat at Ketty's left knee as she watched Imma sleep. She'd closed her eyes almost immediately after Ketty agreed to live in her tent and remain at her side until— The thought of Imma's last breath ravaged her inside and out. She'd barely closed her eyes last night, worried about the herbs Dirar had slipped into Imma's tea. Her stomach had pitched and rolled like a fishing boat on the Great Sea. When Dirar delivered the broth and another cup of tea this morning, Ketty sampled both in his presence.

"I told you," he hissed, "as long as you're loyal, I'm faithful." His carefully chosen words gave away little of his wicked plan.

Ketty had rushed him out of the tent, but it didn't matter. Imma continued sleeping soundly most of the morning. The aroma of the bone broth might cause Ketty to retch if she'd eaten anything since yesterday. She couldn't tear her gaze from the sleeping woman long enough to fetch a crust of bread.

How could Imma's appearance change so completely in only two days? Permanent lines now creased the once-smooth forehead as if a hundred years of worry had etched three long furrows. Feathery, translucent skin hung like draped tent flaps over her deep-set eyes. Only days ago, they'd been bright and lively. Now they were dull and cloudy. Imma's high cheekbones remained, but her cheeks were hollowed and pale. The slight smile lines that extended from her slender nose to naturally crimson lips had given way to fleshy cheeks puffed around a colorless mouth.

The beauty of the Great-Imma Eve had fled, but the imma Ketty still adored was trapped in a failing shell. Why must death steal the good and leave the bad? After Ketty's own ammatu died, Abu treated his only daughter worse than his livestock. Imma Sarah had been the only one on earth to call her *daughter*. The only one to say the words *I love you*.

"How can I say goodbye to you?" she whispered. How could she betray Isaac by helping Dirar seal his alliance with Ephron? "It's the only way to save his life, Imma." If she pretended to support Dirar, she could sway many in the camp toward a peaceful transition. Some would resist, of course, and flee to Master Abraham's Beersheba camp. There could be violence, but likely not—as long as his son wasn't harmed.

Imma's eyelids fluttered as if Ketty's traitorous thoughts had roared loudly enough to alert her to the danger. Brow furrowed, she glanced first toward the tent opening and then at Ketty. "Is it dark outside? Have I slept all day?"

"Yes, Imma, but Isaac said not to wake you." She gently brushed her arm and then reached for the bowl of broth. "Cook made this bone broth for you. We must keep up your strength so you'll be able to enjoy your time with Master Abraham." The mention of their tense subject sent a prickly feeling into Ketty's cheeks. She dipped a clean cloth into the broth and then transferred it to Imma's waiting mouth.

Imma sucked on the cloth with a hum of enjoyment. "That's delicious," she said. "I didn't realize how hungry I was." As if confirming, her stomach rumbled, making both of them laugh. Their eyes met. Held. Glistened. "Thank you for staying with me, Love. Has Isaac gone back to the fields?"

"No, Imma, I'm here." Isaac entered with a tray of three steaming cups. "I went to get some tea for us, a special blend Dirar prepared for us this evening."

Ketty's stomach felt as if it flipped in her gut. "Imma is sleeping well. She doesn't need more of Dirar's potions."

Imma's brows rose. "What has Dirar done to draw your ire, Daughter?"

She felt her cheeks flush. "Nothing. I just—"

"It's not a potion," Isaac said. "It's juniper tea with mint. Something soothing for all of us to enjoy this evening." He gave Ketty a hard stare. "Dirar is teaching the cooking maids about the herbs he's using so they can help in camp when he returns to the fields. He was a valuable gift from Ishmael. I must remember to send a yearling ram as a show of gratitude to my brother."

Ketty dipped her cloth into Imma's bone broth again and placed it near her lips, determined to fill her stomach with nourishment rather than Dirar's offering. Isaac leaned over her to place the tray of cups beside the broth and kissed the top of Ketty's head before taking his tea and settling onto his favorite cushion across from her. The innocent show of affection was nothing unusual. She'd always been short, and he'd kissed the top of her head since he'd grown tall enough to tease her about it. But after her request today and the intimacy they would someday share, she hadn't been able to look into his eyes.

"Ketty?" Imma's soft voice drew her attention to the emptied cloth still pressed to Imma's lips.

"Oh!" Ketty dipped the cloth again and concentrated more fully on her task, shoving thoughts of Isaac and their future into a dark corner with all the other raging emotions.

"I've thought a lot about what you said this morning," Isaac said to Imma. "I still have some questions I'd like answered before Abba arrives—since I'm sure he would never speak of it."

Imma pushed away the broth Ketty offered. "You're the sole master of this camp now, Son. Speak with your abba as an equal. He'll answer whatever you ask if you present your request with respect and come with an open heart."

Isaac's eyes found Ketty's in a hopeful exchange of solidarity. He'd confided in her for years, rehashing the shepherds' stories of Master Abraham's great exploits while also pointing out the corresponding neglect of family.

"And you can't rely on Ketty to help you," Imma said, drawing their attention to her scowl. "I see now that you've been grumbling about Abraham together, chewing on sour grapes until your teeth are set on edge. Well, no more!" Her voice was reedy but insistent. "Ask me whatever you're too frightened to ask your abba, Isaac, then be done with it. Accept my answer as true. Judge for yourself the man God Himself chose above all others on this earth, and then live your own life without comparison." Her stare could have bored through Isaac like Hittite iron were he not as stubborn as the woman herself.

"All right then," he said, chin jutting up. "You explained why you lied to two kings about being Abba's sister rather than his wife, but why has he relegated Lot to a mere undershepherd?"

"Did it ever occur to you that Lot might have wanted to be an undershepherd?"

Imma's tone held no venom, seeming to leave Isaac at a loss. "But I heard he was once a judge at the city gates of Sodom. How could he be satisfied with such a low station after being a leader amid a large city in the Jordan Plain?"

"May I continue my story where we left off this morning?"

Imma's calm response was met with Isaac's extended pause. Ketty hadn't heard any of this morning's discussion and was anxious to hear more about the enigmatic half-truths that had taken Imma into the harems of both Pharaoh and Abimelek, king of the Philistines. "Please continue, Imma," she said, earning a glare from her brother.

Regardless, she offered Imma another sip of broth. She swallowed it and nodded her thanks. "As I said this morning, Elohim sent His covenant bearer into Canaan to bless those who blessed us and curse those who cursed us. When Pharaoh took me into his harem, it was his magicians that divined Abraham and I were also married, and, thus, the cause of his household's illness. Rather than becoming angry about our deception, however, Pharaoh sent us away with all the wealth he'd showered on Abraham in hopes of maintaining our God's favor. Abraham acquired sheep, cattle, donkeys, camels, and more servants for our household—Hagar among them."

"Some of the shepherds said Hagar was an Egyptian princess," Ketty said. "Is that true?"

Imma grinned at her. "I'll tell you for another swallow of bone broth." Ketty gave her four sips from the cloth. She also offered a sip of Dirar's tea, having sampled some herself while Dirar watched. Though she still didn't trust him, she hoped he'd be less likely to taint supplies if he knew Ketty was testing them.

Imma's eyes seemed brighter after the nourishment. "Help me sit, will you, Isaac?" While Isaac arranged the pillows behind her back, she began her story again. "Hagar was a daughter of one of Pharaoh's concubines, so she wasn't exactly a princess, but she'd been trained to read and write in the language of trade, so we became friends very quickly. Pharaoh's men escorted us to Migdol, where Lot had fattened our livestock on Egypt's lush grasslands. Since we'd returned with more livestock than we'd left in his care, Abraham gave Lot our original flocks and herds as a gift for managing them during our absence. Pharaoh's soldiers led us to the Negev and left us to resume our wandering. However, during our month in Egypt, the latter rains had come to Canaan and begun their healing work on the soil.

"Grazing lands sprouted green, but now our flocks and herds, combined with Lot's, were devouring every sprig before it could flourish into grazing lands. Quarrels broke out between our new shepherds and the men who had grown loyal to Lot in Harran and Migdol. So Abraham suggested we divide our households, and he gave Lot his choice of land."

Isaac was already shaking his head, challenging his imma's telling. "Lot must have chosen the salty sea and the desert land of the Jordan Plain because he wanted to give Abba the terraced hills on these mountains."

Imma's expression turned stormy. "At that time, the Jordan Plain was the best land in Canaan—green and lush as the Garden of the Lord—and the Salt Sea wasn't yet salty. Your abba gave Lot the *best* land, and we took the scrub bushes, rocky heights, and hard winters. But these mountains offered us more tree cover, cooler summers, fewer enemies, and no false gods to confuse the mind and heart. Lot chose people, cities, and the constant battle against false gods."

"We've heard stories about his daughters," Ketty ventured.

"Quiet!" Isaac barked. "Those are disgusting rumors."

"The stories about his daughters are true, Son." Imma met his gaze with disquieting calm. "But Lot made many wrong choices before his daughters announced to the world their family's moral poverty. It began when he chose the best land among the highest temptation, but we saw his heart hardened completely when your abba begged him to leave Sodom, return to our camp—and to Elohim."

Isaac shared a puzzled glance with Ketty. The shepherds had never said anything about Abba inviting Lot to return before Sodom's destruction. "When was Lot invited to rejoin our camp?"

"Our nephew left us and took his flocks and herds to live in Sodom. We lived in this same camp—only a two-day journey—but didn't see him again for nine years. Our camp was called Hebron then and owned by Mamre, the Amorite, and his brothers, Aner and Eshkol. Your abba had built a strong alliance with them. We heard rumors of wars in the Jordan Valley, but no one bothered us in the hill country. One day, a man arrived in our camp after escaping the battle at Sodom. He was covered in blood and said Lot had been taken captive along with the rest of those in the city with all their goods and possessions. Abraham rallied the 318 trained fighting men born in our household. Mamre accompanied him with the Amorite fighting men. With less than four hundred men, your abba fought the army of five Semitic kings that had wreaked havoc on the whole land of Canaan. They risked everything to rescue Lot—and Elohim gave them victory.

"On the way back to Hebron, Bera, the king of Sodom, stopped Abraham and his men in the Valley of Kings outside Salem. Seeing the potential conflict, Melchizedek, the king of Salem—and priest of God Most High—came out with bread and wine to bless Abraham." She swiped at gathering moisture in her eyes and focused on Isaac. "Your abba gave Elohim's priest a tenth of all the spoils he'd taken from the Semite kings. When Sodom's king saw his offering, he came to Abraham and said, 'You keep your goods but give me the people.' Lot stood at Bera's right shoulder. That's when our nephew was made a city official. Abraham had begged him to return to camp and embrace the one true God, but Lot chose to return to Sodom and help rebuild a wicked city with its wicked king."

"But Lot didn't worship their idols or engage in their sin, Imma." Isaac's pallor proved he knew the argument was as weak as Lot's faith.

Imma didn't even acknowledge it. "Fourteen years later, Sodom was turned to ash, and Lot's wife to salt." Imma studied her hands, letting silence punctuate the sad tale. When she lifted her head, she looked at Ketty this time. "It was the one time I saw Abraham argue. As I'm sure Isaac has told you repeatedly, my husband usually runs from confrontation, but on the day those three visitors came to destroy Sodom, two of them left, and Abraham stood on an overlook and bargained with God Himself." She closed her eyes as if visualizing the memory. "It was as if he knew Lot's life depended on it."

"If Abba cares so much about Lot," Isaac said, jaw set, "why is he still an undershepherd at Beersheba?"

"You would rather accuse your abba of wrongdoing than recognize his mercy toward a broken man." Imma's scowl met Isaac's stubborn glare, locking them in silent battle.

"It seems to me Lot is hiding." Ketty's observation wrenched their attention. "After his daughters gave birth to his sons conceived after they'd made him drunk—so the story goes—he was too ashamed to live in the same town. We heard he came to Master Abraham, begging bread."

"That's not true." Imma's chin quaked. "Abraham went looking for him. Lot was begging, but within the small town of Zoar. He was alone. His daughters had abandoned him when they found husbands who would take them. Abraham brought Lot back to Beersheba and tried to make him the manager of livestock. Lot refused. He was satisfied to be an undershepherd. More than satisfied. He simply wanted to be with Elohim and away from the trappings that had ruined him in Sodom." She returned her attention to Isaac. "Your abba and I would never harm or cheat Lot. He was like our own son that we adopted when our brother Haran died in Ur. You should remember that the next time you're tempted to accuse your abba without knowing all the facts."

Isaac bowed his head, and Ketty felt the awkward weight of the silence on her shoulders too. She reached for the bone broth and offered Imma another sip, but she refused, burrowing into the pillows at her back. "I'm tired, Ketty. I need to sleep."

As Ketty reached for the nearest lamp to blow out its flame, the sound of men's whoops and ululating women filled the air. Imma's eyes opened wide. "Abraham! He's coming!" Only the Great Prince received such a welcome.

Isaac leaped to his feet at the same time Ketty stood and met his gaze. Eyes locked in silent panic, she usually calmed her brother when Master Abraham arrived, but tonight it was she who needed reassurance. Her throat closed with a devastating new humiliation. Not only did she fear the revelation of Imma's dream but now Ketty had been assigned to her tent indefinitely. Usually, her tasks as Imma's maid during the master's visits were reduced to serving meals in the tent they shared. During the days, she relied on Isaac's companionship and enjoyed spinning, weaving, and cooking with the women of camp. Now, she must face Master Abraham day and night as they cared for Imma in the same tent—until her last breath.

The thought of intruding on the couple's privacy sent heat into her cheeks. "I can't stay in the same tent when—"

"Imma promised not to speak of her dream in your presence," Isaac said, "and I don't trust Abba to care for her while she's in this condition. Please, Ketty."

"I'll keep my vow. I promise." Sarah was wide awake now. "Isaac, go and greet your abba. Ketty, I need you to quickly change my robe and braid my hair. I can't let Abraham think I've become disheveled *and* ugly."

Isaac released a sigh and kissed Imma's forehead before he marched past Ketty. She felt weighted to the earth. If only it would open up and swallow her. Pleading only with her eyes, she dared not beg but would willingly cut off an appendage to change Imma's mind.

"I'd like to wear my blue robe, Ketty. It's Abraham's favorite."

"Yes, Imma." Though her body was fading like grass in summer heat, this woman's resolve was still as mighty as the oaks outside her tent.

CHAPTER NINE

*Charm is deceptive, and beauty is fleeting;
but a woman who fears the Lord is to be praised.*
—Proverbs 31:30 (NIV)

The sound of Abraham's booming voice rose above the high-pitched sound of women's ululations and men's jovial greetings. The great Bedouin prince was a legend among both Canaanites and those in Isaac's camp—Ishmael's too, it seemed from the stories he told while he and Mistress Hagar visited. Shepherds gossiped more than women around a cook fire, and the tales were exaggerated with each retelling. The five Semite armies Master Abraham fought to rescue his nephew, Lot—with only 318 men from his household—had grown into the hundreds of thousands. He was a war hero, friend of kings, and the wealthiest Bedouin prince in Canaan. Most important to Isaac's servants, he treated them kindly and always brought gifts for their children.

But Ketty's pale face was awash with fear. Though she'd seen Abraham twice a year since she was nine years old, Isaac had made sure she remained invisible.

The crowd noise moved toward Sarah's tent, making her heart pound faster and her chest tighten. "Hurry, Ketty," she said, helping to straighten the blue robe around her torso and trying to lift her hips as Ketty pulled the long skirt of it down to cover her legs. "Don't comb my hair, just braid it." The girl gently pulled Sarah upright and away from the pillows, since she had no strength to lean forward herself, and began plaiting Sarah's long, tangled curls.

A twinge of pain caught in her shoulder, reminding her of the episode she'd endured yesterday and the quick remedy Dirar's tea had provided. "Perhaps when Abraham arrives, you could slip out and ask Dirar to brew another cup of the same tea he gave me last night."

"So you can keep the promise not to speak of your dream in my presence but still tell Master Abraham—and humiliate me?" Though Ketty was kneeling behind her, Sarah heard the tears in her voice.

"That wasn't at all my reasoning, Love." She explained the twinge of pain and heard Ketty gasp.

"Oh Imma, forgive me." The words escaped on a sob.

"There's nothing to forgive, Daughter. I know you're afraid, but ask for Elohim's help. It's what I've been doing." If only she had the strength to turn and console the girl, but Sarah was already trembling with fatigue from sitting up.

"All done," Ketty said with forced brightness, then placed Sarah's snowy-white braid over her right shoulder.

"Thank you, Love." Her daughter lowered her shoulders back against the pillows. Sarah sighed, closed her eyes, and listened to the sounds outside her tent. Abraham usually stopped at the outskirts of camp to engage the many servants and their families who met him with such devotion, but tonight he'd given little time to the usual pleasantries.

"Your kind words are a balm to my soul." His bass voice resonated just outside Sarah's tent, touching a place deep inside her. "Elohim is with us even in difficult times. He'd told me to begin my journey to Kiriath Arba before Isaac's messenger reached Beersheba, so my beloved wife and I are reunited earlier than we normally would have been. You see? El Elyon Adonai knows all. He neither slumbers nor sleeps, my friends. Shalom and good night." Abraham ducked into Sarah's tent to more sounds of approval.

The moment he straightened and glimpsed her shriveled form and wrinkled face, Sarah expected a grimace or at least the same awkward surprise Ketty and Isaac had tried—and failed—to hide. Ketty stood in the shadows at the head of Sarah's mat. Abraham straightened, his presence filling the large tent, his eyes fixed on Sarah's. "Shalom, Beloved." With shoulders as wide as two men side by side, he stood a head taller than most men, Isaac included. Abraham covered the distance between them, reclined beside his wife, and lifted her hand to his lips without ever breaking their gaze. "What's this I hear about dreaming and dying? One is acceptable. The other is not. I've heard nothing from Elohim on either matter, so let's make plans for next month's shearing festival."

Sarah grinned at the handsome shepherd she adored. *My Abraham.* He would ignore three camels in his tent and blame the odor on a servant's feet if it allowed him to avoid hard conversations. She scooted down on her pillows and turned on her side to face him, then said to Ketty, "Now is a good time to get my tea from Dirar, and Abraham will likely need a whiff of mandrake to help him sleep tonight."

Ketty was already on her way toward the exit but startled with Abraham's booming laughter. "Sarah, I've just run uphill for two days. I can assure you, I won't need the scent of mandrake to help me sleep." He swiped a single hand down his dusty face, his head still propped on the other.

Sarah grinned at Ketty. "Bring the flask of mandrake oil."

For the first time, Abraham's smile died, and he sat up, taking time to study her. Sarah's skin warmed at his intense gaze but not for the reasons she usually felt the increased emotion. She'd never before been ashamed of her appearance—or perhaps *disappointed* was a better term.

Drawing her blanket over her head, she whispered, "Stop, Abraham. I can't bear it." His was the only opinion that could truly damage her soul—*had* truly damaged her soul. "Elohim was gracious to speak to me personally, tenderly, before taking away my beauty," she said. "At least I know my aging and death isn't a punishment."

A slight tug on the blanket tightened her grip. Her husband's tender lips pressed against her right fist, then her left, as his hands worked gently to unshackle the makeshift veil covering her completely. She released the blanket. He pulled it down slowly. She lay on her back, eyes tightly shut, arms at her sides, clothed in her favorite blue robe but feeling more exposed than she had on their wedding night.

His hand slid gently down her arm. "You are as beautiful in this moment as the first time I held you in my arms. As beautiful as you were with double braids and sackcloth, running after my sheep in the pastures of Ur. As beautiful as you were on the day you became my wife. As beautiful as you were on the day—" His voice broke, and Sarah opened her eyes to see tears rolling into his grey beard. "As beautiful as you were on the day Elohim gave us a son. I've been old since the day we married, Sarah bat Terah." He chuckled through his tears. "You're just now catching up."

She opened her arms, and he draped himself over her, careful to bear most of his weight at her side. His right arm slid beneath her waist and the left under her shoulders. He enveloped her. All of her. Like a cocoon. Her safe place. At least, what had once been her safest place on earth. They must talk about what must happen before the end, but first... "Did the messenger or Isaac tell you what the dream was about?"

A pregnant pause. "No," he whispered but didn't move. "Isaac said only that you'd promised not to speak of it in your maid's presence."

"I must tell you what Elohim commanded in my dream, Abraham, before Keturah returns."

He jerked away, dropping her to the mat as if she'd become a fire that burned. "There's no need, Sarah." He sat now with his back toward her.

Stunned, offended, she snapped, "But you need to know!"

Turning his head slowly, he met her eyes. "Elohim tells me what I need to know."

Angry tears burned her eyes. "What if my faith had been so stubborn all these years, and I'd required equal information from the God we serve?"

"I think it's clear that in the beginning, I trusted Elohim and you trusted me." He paused, his lips quaking. "I suppose it was part of Elohim's plan that you stopped trusting me—because your faith now matches your resolve." He blinked once, sending more tears over his bottom lashes. "Elohim revealed that I must marry your maid, but for the first time—I'm struggling to obey."

A soft gasp escaped before Sarah could restrain it. "Abraham."

"I will obey my God," he said flatly, jutting out his chin as his son had done earlier. "It's just harder when I know the consequences. I willingly took Isaac to sacrifice him on Mount Moriah—fully believing he'd be restored so I could return him to you—but that obedience cost me. I obeyed immediately without a word to anyone. Perhaps this time, I'll give the command more thought, more time to evolve."

She held her tongue, considering her conundrum. On one hand, she wished to hurry the sun and moon along their courses, speeding the change of hearts Elohim would surely bring. Yet every day that passed was one less of her remaining life. Which was more important, treasuring the *now* or preparing those she loved for the future? Could Sarah trust that eternity held greater glory than this life's sacrifices required? Must she be willing to obey Elohim no matter the cost—as Abraham had done—and entrust the future to those left behind?

CHAPTER TEN

*Then the angel of the L*ORD *told [Hagar],*
"Go back to your mistress and submit to her."
*...She gave this name to the L*ORD *who spoke to her:*
"You are the God who sees me," for she said,
"I have now seen the One who sees me."
...So Hagar bore Abram a son, and Abram gave
the name Ishmael to the son she had borne.
—Genesis 16:9, 13, 15 (NIV)

She stared into her husband's glistening eyes, fear rising. Was now the time to lance the boil that had festered for twenty-four years? Abraham had been more forthcoming in his last four sentences than in the past four decades. How could she offer any less? *Elohim, give me wisdom.*

Reaching for his hand, she hoped to reassure him before the hard words came. "It wasn't your obedience that drove the wedge between us. It was your mistrust of me. When Elohim appeared to Hagar, and she returned to camp and submitted as my slave, I always felt you trusted her more and me less because Elohim spoke to her personally and not to me." He started to protest, but Sarah lifted her hand. "Please, let me finish. I'm not blaming you or saying you were wrong to share that special bond with Hagar. I'm simply explaining what I witnessed happen between you two and the wedge it placed between you and me. My slave proved her trust in the God Who Sees, while I'd trusted you *first* all my life. It was the way I'd shown you my love since we were children—by trusting and obeying you. The same way you trusted and obeyed Elohim."

Sarah stroked his gray beard, trying to soften the hard words. "Before Hagar showed her faith and obedience to Elohim—and rattled the very foundations of my existence—you and I shared everything. You had always opened your heart to me but kept others at a distance. Then Hagar gave you a son. She'd told you the name El Roi had spoken in the desert, but I didn't know it until the day Ishmael was born."

"Sarah, I—"

"We loved Ishmael together," she continued, "raised him as our own. Even though I assigned Hagar duties away from my tent, you and I still grew apart because we focused more on the child than each other. We became even more distant after Isaac was born and after I insisted on Hagar and Ishmael's exile. But on the morning I woke to find you'd taken Isaac from me—"

"Why must we speak of this?" Abraham pushed to his feet. "I want our last days together to be peaceful and filled with happy memories, Sarah. I refuse to—"

"Elohim will decide my last days!" Her outburst, though emotional, ebbed with a wave of peace. "Sit down, Abraham. Please. We have much to discuss, and you must discuss even more with our son. It's time, my love." Her quiet tone was a different approach, and her husband couldn't have looked more surprised if she'd turned into a six-humped camel.

He reached for a nearby cushion and settled beside her mat. "More than your appearance has changed, Sarah bat Terah. It frightens me."

"I'm frightened too, but talking will help us both. I promise."

With an irritated snort, he waved one hand—dismissive yet indulgent.

Not knowing how long he'd endure the conversation, she began with the hardest question first—the Testing. "When Elohim told you to sacrifice our son, why did you take Isaac from Beersheba camp without confiding in me?"

His right eye twitched. "I didn't tell anyone where we were going, Sarah. Not even the servants or Isaac, who went with me."

"Why not?"

"Because I knew God had promised Isaac was the son that would bear the covenant to generations more numerous than the stars in the sky. Isaac couldn't die on a mountain—or if he did, God would raise him up. I even told the servants, when Isaac and I left them with the donkeys at the foot of Mount Moriah, that my son and I would return after we worshiped." He leaned close, his voice raised, face crimson. "*We*, Sarah. I told them *we* would return!"

She remained calm. "There were other things to consider, Abraham."

"No. Nothing else mattered," he growled, massaging his temples. "You see? Talking is useless. Why dredge up the past? We can't change it. I obeyed Elohim, and the covenant is secure. All nations will be blessed through Isaac." He lowered his hands and sighed. "Preserving the covenant is our calling, Sarah, the reason we live and breathe."

"I thought we lived and breathed to know God and share Him with all nations—together."

"It's the same thing."

"No, Abraham. It isn't." She reached for his hand before exposing her darkest thought, the root of what had separated them for twenty-four years. "You believed you had to choose between obedience to Elohim and trusting me."

His head moved back and forth in silent rebuttal, his lips trembling as if straining to hold back the torrent of answers that could heal them. If only...

"Say it," Sarah begged. "Speak the words you're thinking."

He looked down and she followed his gaze. Their hands had piled on each other, like a tower of strength, without even realizing it. Could they rely on each other again to walk through her last days? Could they rebuild the trust that had been lost and its absence ignored for so long?

"It wasn't you I didn't trust." Abraham's words came in a whisper. He pulled his hands away, straightened his spine, and locked eyes with his wife. "I didn't trust *myself*, Sarah. If I'd spoken aloud what Elohim had asked of me—to sacrifice the son I loved more than anything—I feared I wouldn't obey God's command. So I said nothing. For three days' travel, I said nothing to anyone, because every moment of every day, I thought of nothing else but where I could hide from Elohim with you and our son. Where I could go and escape the awful responsibility laid on my shoulders." A barely perceivable scowl lifted his upper lip. "Now you see the detestable man you trusted all those years."

"Perhaps you're human after all," she offered. "To know you had doubts doesn't make you detestable, Husband. It helps me understand, and it will wipe away so much of your son's insecurity."

"Insecurity? Our son is the bravest man I know. He knew what Elohim required, though I said nothing. He allowed me to bind him and lay perfectly still on that altar, prepared to die without a single complaint or question."

"Yet he, like me, believes you kept the reason for the journey a secret because you didn't trust him to obey Elohim—as Ishmael did when he chose circumcision."

Abraham's forehead creased. "The two situations were completely unrelated."

"Not in Isaac's mind. We've repeatedly told him the story of Elohim's covenant of circumcision because it's when El Shaddai confirmed his birth, changed our names from Abram to Abraham and Sarai to Sarah. Isaac knows his brother—your firstborn son, the one we raised and loved as our own—was thirteen when you presented him with God's command. You've always spoken of Ishmael's faith and bravery in submitting to the flint knife as a man of thirteen. But you never gave Isaac credit for his choice when he was even older. In his mind, you believed his faith weaker than Ishmael's, that if you had told him your destination and that God had demanded his life, he would have refused."

"That wasn't it at all." Abraham leaned back, dragging fingers through his white hair, exhaling his frustration. "Have I been such a wicked man that my family thinks so little of me?"

She let his preposterous question hang in the silence before shining truth on the lie. "Just the opposite. I nearly worshiped you as a perfect man, which intensified your unreasonable expectations of yourself that then isolated you from your family, who needed to see your flaws." She waited until his wandering eyes came back to hers then held his gaze. "We must see Elohim forgive your flaws to rest assured that He'll also forgive ours."

"How can you trust me as you did before if you see how broken I am?"

"I hope to never trust you as I did before."

His eyes widened at her declaration, but she continued. "I trust in Elohim more than I'll ever trust any man. My faith could never have grown in the shadow of yours, Abraham. Elohim gave us these years apart."

"He *gave* us these years?" He choked out the words. "It has not been a gift to wake up alone in my bed, Sarah. Isaac's faith was growing under my care until Zohar's men intercepted us on our way home to Beersheba after the miracle on Mount Moriah. They brought us to Kiriath Arba as if we were fugitives, and when I tried to explain, you were completely irrational. So I left."

"You tried to explain?" Fire raced into her cheeks. "There was no explanation, Abraham. You saw Zohar standing beside me and accused me of running to another man for 'comfort.' We both said things we shouldn't have in front of our son, and you left before we could resolve it. A week later, your chief servant arrived. Eliezer taught our son to manage your second camp at Kiriath Arba, but we didn't see you for six months—not until the spring shearing. We've seen you twice a year since then and never once have you been willing to speak of the Testing. Not once!" A sudden, searing pain shot through her chest. She cried out.

"Sarah!" Abraham grabbed her. "Isaac, get in here!" He lay beside her, cradling her in his arms. "Shhh, my love. Shhh."

Sarah pressed her head to his chest, gritting her teeth against the pain.

"Abba, what's—"

"She's in pain, Son. Get the healer."

Sarah didn't even look up but concentrated on her husband's heartbeat, pounding beneath her cheek.

"You're right. I wasted twenty-four years by refusing to face our conflict, but Elohim has been good to us in spite of me. I see how strong your faith has become, and Isaac has not only grown into a skilled shepherd but also a man of strong faith under your tutelage."

"He wants to be like his abba," she whispered through clenched teeth. "He adores you." She inhaled sharply as another pain grabbed her. When it ebbed, she added, "He'll need you more than ever when…when I'm gone."

"I know, my love." A sob escaped.

Sarah cried out again with another pain.

"Isaac!" he shouted again. "Shhh. They're coming. Think of paradise. Think of what's on the other side, waiting for you."

"I don't know what's on the other side. You never spoke of it."

He released a groan of both humor and dread. "I really must talk more."

Sarah grinned in spite of the pain. Perhaps her point had been made.

Abraham pressed a kiss to her forehead and tilted her chin up. "Elohim assured me we'll spend eternity together, but I'm not quite ready to let you go. Please, don't leave me yet."

CHAPTER ELEVEN

The wisdom of the prudent is to give thought to their ways,
but the folly of fools is deception.
—Proverbs 14:8 (NIV)

"Imma, Dirar is here with your tea." Isaac's voice sounded far away.

Abraham sat up, cradling her into his chest, his arms tight around her. "Who is that? I've never seen this servant in camp."

"His name is Dirar, Abba. He was a gift from Ishmael. He saved Imma's life yesterday." Isaac nodded permission for Ketty to take the cup from the tray.

Sarah's chest felt like a vise had tightened around it, making breathing nearly impossible. Limp as a rag, she let Abraham support her head to drink from the cup Ketty held to her lips. Dirar and Isaac stood behind the girl, watching the warm liquid trickle down her chin.

"Slower!" Dirar nudged Ketty aside and took the cup, then gently held it to Sarah's lips, barely tipping it. The tea flowed steadily into her mouth and warmed her belly. "Well done, Mistress. Keep swallowing. Keep going. As much as you can." His patience was commendable, and he was relentless, holding it to her lips, coaxing, until the cup was empty.

He sat back, and Sarah's whole body shuddered. The aftertaste of onion, garlic, and mint nearly made her gag. "Ohhh!" She shuddered again. "That's awful!"

Isaac and Abraham chuckled, as did Dirar. "I know, Mistress. I'm sorry for the taste, but you drank it more bravely than some soldiers I've treated."

"She's always been brave." Abraham kissed her temple. "Are you still in pain?"

"It doesn't work that fast!" She rolled her eyes, teasing, though the pain in her chest had subsided even before the tea. Winning another chuckle from the men, Sarah felt more than physical relief—but then noticed Ketty standing in the shadows.

Her daughter had removed herself from the conversation and the men. Dirar had been unkind, but he'd reacted to the urgency of the moment. He was a skilled healer. It was obvious. He could teach Ketty so much, and the camp would need a healer when Sarah was gone. Dirar was gifted, of course, but Isaac would need him in the fields.

When she looked around the tent, Sarah realized all eyes were on her, waiting. "Well, toads and lizards!" she huffed. "How can you expect one cup of tea to—" She started to chastise them for thinking the tea could help so quickly. But it had! Sarah turned her wonder on Dirar. "What is in that tea?"

He grinned. "You're feeling better then?"

"The pain is gone. My chest is still a bit tight, but I can breathe." She tried to sit up but couldn't. "I'm still weaker than a newborn lamb."

"I'm afraid I have no herbal remedy to restore the gods' ageless gift."

The gods? Abraham's arms tightened around her. Both he and Isaac had purchased slaves who worshiped other gods, but they were never allowed to remain unless they proved their commitment to Elohim and His covenant by circumcision.

"Dirar has only been in our camp for a few days," Isaac added quickly, standing over the servant's left shoulder. "We haven't yet spoken about his commitment to Elohim's covenant, but we will, Abba."

"Perhaps now is a good time for you and your abba to talk about many things." Sarah glanced at Ketty as she spoke. "I'd like Dirar to teach Ketty and me some of the herbal recipes he's learned, and I'll share my knowledge with him as well. Ketty will then have the knowledge of two skilled healers to serve this camp when I'm gone." Her daughter's head remained bowed. No response.

Sarah patted Abraham's arm that still rested around her waist. "Help me lie down, Love, and go talk to our son."

Isaac immediately turned to leave, but Abraham's pause proved his reluctance. "What are we to talk about, Sarah?" he whispered against her ear.

Flummoxed, she almost quipped, *Your toenails,* but decided on a more productive response. "Why not start with, 'I love you, and I'm proud of you, Isaac.' That should open a door you haven't yet walked through."

"Humph." He laid her on the mat, elevated slightly with pillows Ketty arranged behind her back. Sarah couldn't see her daughter's face but recognized near panic on Abraham's expression. She watched his quick retreat with no small disappointment. Why did even strong men become insecure boys when facing possible rejection?

Dirar stood and bowed as Abraham left and then resumed his place on Isaac's favorite cushion at Sarah's right side. Ketty sat on her left, silent, head still bowed. It wasn't like her to pout.

"Ketty," Sarah said, "is there something between you and Dirar that I should know?"

Her head shot up, eyes wide, looking first at Sarah, then Dirar, and back at her imma. "No. He's a servant like any other. Truthfully, I don't care to be in his presence any longer than necessary."

Surprised at her daughter's rudeness, Sarah turned to Dirar and noted his casual smile. "I see her attitude toward you comes as no shock."

"I believe your maid is jealous, Mistress."

"Jealous?" Ketty's tone was rancid. "Of you?"

Dirar's brows rose over lazy eyelids. "Master Isaac has spent most of his time with me during the past two days. It's my understanding that he usually spends his time with your maid. I can only assume she's jealous of the favor your son has shown me."

Ketty's lips were pressed into a thin line, her arms crossed, but no argument. Unusual. Her daughter could debate Isaac into a corner. Why would she let a servant—a man she'd met less than a week ago—cow her into silence? Sarah had thought Ketty had withdrawn because she'd been embarrassed in front of

Abraham, but he was gone. What kept her from putting Dirar in his place now?

Sarah returned her attention to the slave that Ishmael had given them as he and Hagar left a few days ago. "How long did you serve Abraham's firstborn son, Dirar?" She kept her tone light but intentionally included the suspicion inherent when the second-born was chosen as heir.

"I served Master Ishmael for five years," Dirar said, seeming unperturbed, "with the same skill I've shown in my short time with you. I suspect that skill is the reason Master Ishmael chose me as his treasured gift to this camp." He leaned closer to Sarah, casting a conspiratorial glance at Ketty. "The servants in Master Ishmael's camp weren't especially fond of me either. My skills tend to overshadow others, but I believe Mistress Keturah has great potential to learn the healing arts."

Ketty scoffed at his teasing but still said nothing. Dirar chuckled, his eyes focused on her far too long. Something had most certainly passed between them before this encounter, and Sarah didn't like his games. "That's enough," she said, snagging Dirar's attention with her sharp tone. "You're here to teach, so teach. My abba died with similar symptoms to what I've experienced. I heard him cry out in the middle of the night. Abraham and I rushed into his room and found him clutching his chest— but also his left arm. I immediately gave him a tincture of mandrake to sooth the pain and steeped a tea for pain in the chest similar to the one you gave me—onion, garlic, and mint."

"I'm sorry, Mistress," Dirar said before she finished. "Your abba's condition was more serious than yours. His symptoms began while sleeping, without an external trigger of emotion or extreme heat or cold. The mandrake would have eased his suffering but couldn't address the real issue."

"How do you know the real issue without seeing the man in person?" Sarah's unsettledness grew as Dirar's face began to blur. "We don't allow divination in this camp, Dirar. And I want to know what you put in my tea."

"Be at peace, Mistress." He placed his hand on her forehead. "I'll willingly divulge the contents with you and Ketty—except the secret ingredient passed down to my family from ancient pharaohs." He lifted his gaze to Ketty. "You should get a wax tablet to take notes. Or do you plan to remember everything I say?"

"I've remembered your every word since the first day you arrived."

"Hmm, yes." Dirar's tone sounded like a purr, and she could barely make out his features. He turned toward her, but she couldn't focus. "As I said, Mistress, your maid is very bright. The contents of your miracle tea are: garlic, onion, mint, and dried meadowsweet. I also added a bit of poppy tonight so you'd sleep soundly after such an emotional day."

"But the secret..." Sarah's tongue felt thick. "The in... greed...ingrediennnt passed down frrrrom pharaooohs." Her eyelids were too heavy.

"Sleep now, Mistress. I'll teach Ketty everything she must know to care for this camp after you're gone." A gentle hand covered her eyes, and she fell into inescapable oblivion.

CHAPTER TWELVE

Then God said to Abraham, "As for you, you must keep my covenant, you and your descendants after you for the generations to come. This is my covenant with you and your descendants after you, the covenant you are to keep: Every male among you shall be circumcised.... For the generations to come every male among you who is eight days old must be circumcised, including those born in your household or bought with money from a foreigner."
—Genesis 17:9–10, 12 (NIV)

"What have you done?" Ketty cried, laying her ear against Imma's chest to listen to her heartbeat.

"I'm giving us time to talk alone." He grabbed her arm and stood in one fluid motion, forcing Ketty to hop over Imma's sleeping form. Dirar caught her in his arms, forcing her against him in a grip as hard as Hittite iron. "You feel as soft and pleasing as I'd imagined."

She fought him quietly, but he captured her waist with one arm and trapped her head with his hand and whispered against her ear. "Go ahead and fight, my little she-jackal. Even if you alert the masters outside this tent, you'll never know which supplies I've laced with poisons. Your masters could be dead by morning."

She tried to calm herself and kept her voice at barely a whisper. "Master Abraham is a prophet, and Elohim's covenant promises a curse on anyone who attempts harm against him or his descendants."

"Humph." Dirar loosened his grip to show her a scowl. "Yet you're willing to help Ephron and me take Isaac's camp."

"I'll help *only* if it keeps them safe and avoids violence for the people of this camp."

He released her with a little shove. "Which is why we need to talk. After witnessing the way this camp received Master Abraham, Ephron may have overestimated the ease with which Isaac's servants will accept me as their new master."

Perhaps Dirar wasn't a complete fool after all. "I'm glad you see the folly of such a plan. If you're loyal, Isaac will treat you fairly. He might even make you his chief steward as Master Abraham did Eliezer. He's treated more like family—as I am."

"Why must beautiful women be so stupid?" He sneered and raised his hand to massage his neck. Ketty flinched, preparing for a blow. The gleam in his eye mocked her. "Fear not, lovely Keturah. I would never mark you—not when our masters would surely know it was I who was responsible. And we will find a way to win the servants' loyalty, you and I, before the mistress dies and Isaac leaves to find his bride." He touched one finger to her cheek, traced her jawline, slid down her neck, over her shoulder, and then roughly turned her to face him. "You will be mine, Keturah, and we will build an alliance with the Hittites, making this camp powerful enough to someday repay Abraham and his sons for maiming every male slave in their households." He cast her aside, suddenly in a hurry to leave.

Maiming every male in their households? Dirar's anger toward Ishmael and Isaac finally made sense. Ishmael must have ordered Dirar to be circumcised without his consent, or at least without his commitment, to honor Elohim and His ways. Isaac also required his male slaves to be circumcised, but only after explaining the meaning of Elohim's covenant and that by joining this camp, they would help bless all nations. It was the way Master Abraham had managed his household, a kind but firm stance that built a camp of strangers into a family of willing servants. In those rare cases when a slave chose not to embrace Elohim and His covenant, Isaac always worked to find an honorable master that would purchase him. Had Ishmael sent Dirar to Isaac's camp knowing he'd cause trouble? Or had Dirar himself hoped to wreak havoc on the covenant bearer?

"Ketty?" Isaac touched her arm, and she jumped as if he'd shouted.

"Oh, Isaac." She pressed a hand over her racing heart and then realized she'd spoken too informally while Master Abraham stood behind him. She dropped her head and bowed slightly. "Forgive me, Master Isaac. I didn't hear you come in."

"You need not call your brother 'Master' because I'm here, Keturah." Master Abraham spoke as he approached Imma. "She's sleeping too soundly. What did Ishmael's slave put in her tea?"

Ketty stared wide-eyed at Isaac. Was Master Abraham actually asking her? Isaac nodded, coaxing her to speak. "He…uh, Dirar…he added poppy. It's a seed that's crushed and then—"

"I know what poppy is and what it can do." The master looked at Isaac. "I don't like it. That slave was too assertive."

"He's confident, Abba. A healer must be confident."

"He was *controlling*. There's a difference, Isaac." The master turned to Ketty. "What do you think of this Dirar? How did Sarah react to him? Did she approve the tea's contents?"

"I don't...she...well..." Ketty looked at Isaac, pleading. She couldn't think, let alone speak, with Master Abraham's intense dark eyes staring at her. The great man had never even spoken her name, let alone asked her opinion. How could she answer and still ensure their safety from Dirar's threats?

Isaac stepped between her and his abba. "You're frightening her. Can't you see Ketty is upset about Imma?" He turned, grasping Ketty's hands. "Abba isn't angry with you, but you're receiving his ire. He's angry that I allowed Dirar to treat Imma—a new slave who hasn't yet committed to worship Elohim. His harshness is one reason I won't allow—"

"Stop!" Ketty said before he mentioned Imma's dream.

Master Abraham sighed, now standing near Imma's mat. "I haven't slept in two days and would like to rest while my wife sleeps and wake when she wakes. Would you two please leave us?"

Ketty turned a withering gaze at her brother. Had he not told his abba that she was to remain in Imma's tent day *and night*?

He released a short huff and squeezed the bridge of his nose. "Abba, before you arrived, Imma asked Ketty to tend her personal needs and stay in her tent at all times. If you'd like to sleep in Ketty's tent next door—"

"I'll sleep at my wife's side tonight and every night," he said. "Her maid may stay or go. It matters not to me. But I will tend to Sarah's needs—personal, emotional, spiritual, and eternal. If you two wish to stay, please be silent." He lay beside Imma, snuggling close on his side and pulling her into the bend of his large form.

Ketty turned away, feeling like an intruder. Isaac stood beside her, shoulder to shoulder, facing a stack of extra blankets and baskets of supplies. Isaac reached for her hand, and she squeezed.

"I'll bring your sleeping mat over," he whispered. "Stay right here. Abba won't leave Imma. He'll sleep, and you'll be safe." He left her there, and she felt his absence like a ripping of flesh. Tears stung her eyes. The stillness magnified every sound. Imma's heavy breaths, slow and steady. A slight rustling close behind her. Isaac must have forgotten something.

"Keturah?" Master Abraham's breath smelled of cloves.

What could he want? "Yes, my lord?"

"Forgive me if I sounded cross. I don't trust Dirar, and neither should you. You must be my eyes and ears, watching every ingredient he adds to her food and drink." He snapped his fingers. "Oh! And thank you for ignoring my wife's command to bring me a flask of mandrake oil to sniff. I don't want anything to dull my wits if she needs assistance in the night."

"Of course, my lord." Ketty offered a slight bow as he returned to the mat. She hadn't ignored Imma's command but simply forgotten to bring the flask.

Isaac rushed in with her rolled mat and sheepskin headrest tucked under his arm and carrying the headscarf she wrapped around her braids when she slept. Without a word, they worked together to prepare the back corner of Imma's large, square tent as Ketty's private space, arranging a few baskets like a waist-high wall to give her some measure of privacy. When they finished, both Imma and Master Abraham breathed deep and steady, Imma lying like a lentil inside the master's protective shell.

Isaac nudged Ketty's arm and offered her headscarf, his eyes lingering on hers in the lamp light. *Are you all right?* He mouthed the words without a sound.

She nodded. Even smiled a little. Glancing at the two gray-haired lovers on the sleeping mat, she felt an ache in her heart. Imma had lived her whole life in Master Abraham's love. Though the master was a hard man in many ways, Isaac had been blind to some of his tenderness. He adored his wife, and Imma was a woman most blessed to have known such security.

Isaac's hand touched her cheek, wiping away moisture she hadn't realized was there. He frowned, took her hand, and led her out of the tent. Once outside, they stepped around the corner, hiding from prying eyes.

"Did Abba say something else to upset you?" Isaac asked. "Are you frightened to sleep in the same tent with him? My abba is many things, but he would never harm you, Ketty."

"*My abba is many things.*" "What sort of *things* is your abba, Isaac?" His brows drew together in silent question. "I've watched him visit this camp since I was nine harvests old. He's exacting and difficult at times, it's true, but I see how loving and tender he is with Imma. Do you appreciate that? Not many men love their wives with such devotion—or longevity."

Even in the shadows of moonlight, the change in Isaac's features was notable. Eyes narrowed, he said, "So, you've changed your mind? Now you wish to marry him?"

"No!" Ketty cupped both hands over her mouth as Isaac shushed the booming reply. His suggestion was too ridiculous to justify an explanation. She wished to marry no one, but she must give herself to Dirar to save both Isaac's and Master Abraham's lives. "I wish to be safe, Isaac, and to protect those I love."

She kissed his cheek and bade him good night, stemming tears until she entered Imma's tent and crumpled into the dark corner of her sleeping space. *Elohim, I don't ask this for myself—since I'm merely a woman from the cursed tribes—but I ask You to keep Imma alive long enough for Isaac and Master Abraham to find peace in their relationship.* They would need it to endure the conflict and grief when Ephron and Dirar stole their camp at Kiriath Arba.

CHAPTER THIRTEEN

So Abram went to live near the great trees of Mamre at Hebron, where he pitched his tents. There he built an altar to the LORD.
—Genesis 13:18 (NIV)

Next Day - 4th Ajaru (April)

"Sarah, my love." The quiet voice accompanied a gentle but persistent jostling of her arm. "Sarah, you must wake. I can't bear to be so close and not spend time with you. Wake up, Love. Wak—"

Her eyelids flew open as a gasp filled her chest. "Abraham."

"Shh, I didn't mean to frighten you."

"No, no! I just forgot you were here." She looked around her sun-brightened tent and heard the clamor of camp noise. "Have I slept the whole day?"

He grinned, the deep dimples in his cheeks disappearing into his thick white beard. "No, my love, but it's midmorning, and I couldn't wait any longer to talk with my best friend." He brushed her cheek with a callused thumb. "Isaac and your maid are waiting to share a meal with us and speak of important things."

"Important things? What things?"

He laughed, big and booming as always. "Whatever important things you force me to speak of." He winked, and her heart flipped.

His flirting still thrilled her. "You'd better be careful, Abraham ben Terah, or you'll send me into another spell."

"Don't say such a thing." Immediately sober, he said, "I was more afraid last night than ever in my life, and I don't trust the slave Ishmael left here with you. Whatever he added to your tea made you sleep too soundly and too long."

Though Sarah agreed, she dared not rouse her husband's fear, or Dirar would find himself in the next slave train to Egypt. She lifted a hand to his handsome face. "I'm ready to break my fast. Invite the children in."

"Oh, no," he said, pushing to his feet. "You've been lying on this mat far too long." Without further explanation, he scooped her up and carried her outside.

"Your son did the same thing yesterday." The moment she said it, regret prickled her cheeks.

Abraham looked down at her, halting the distance of an arrow's flight from the central cook fire. "Where did Isaac take you yesterday? Surely you didn't meet with pilgrims at the Mamre altar in your weakened state."

"I haven't been to the altar since the beauty left me." Hoping to avoid telling him with *whom* she met, she pointed to the oak near her tent. "Isaac carried me to the shade over there. It was such a nice day…" Her voice trailed off. She was terrible at secrets and even worse at lying. The two times she was taken into a king's harem, she'd sequestered herself from the other women because she knew she would likely have told them the whole truth within a half day's time.

"Zohar came, didn't he?" The harsh lines etched around Abraham's frown left no doubt about his disapproval.

"Of course he came, Abraham. He's our ally, and he's proven his loyalty for nearly twenty-five years."

"Humph." He began a determined march without another word, his neck and cheeks growing more crimson with each step toward the cook fire.

Sarah waited for more discussion. None came. He obviously had something to say, something that burned all the way up his neck and into his cheeks. Something that had changed his flirting and laughing to the sullen conveyance that jostled her senseless. "Could you at least carry me with the care you would give one of your sheep?"

"At least my sheep recognize a jackal when he enters the sheepfold."

"Oooh! How can you say Zohar is a jack—" He walked past the central fire, nodding at the servants. "Wait! What—" Sarah lifted her head to look behind them. "Where are Isaac and Ketty? I thought they were joining us to break our fast?"

"They are joining us."

"Where?"

Again, no words.

Sarah fumed in silence until she could stand his silence no longer. "Abraham!"

He stopped at the edge of camp, sheltered in a copse of trees just before they reached the first pasture. Her husband plopped down beside a giant oak and situated Sarah in his lap. "You've never recognized the danger of Zohar's feelings for you. Or perhaps you enjoy his attention. Is that the reason you've never returned to me in Beersheba? Isaac is skilled enough to manage this camp alone, yet still you remain here—choosing your son over your husband."

"I remain because pilgrims come to the great trees of Mamre to gain my wisdom."

"And they come to Beer Lahai Roi when Isaac moves the second camp for winter. Tell me the real reason you refuse to return to Beersheba, Sarah."

Heart pounding furiously, Sarah felt more than physical pain at the choice before her. Dare she give voice to what had drained the lifeblood from their marriage all these years? She'd challenged Abraham to be open and honest. Could she do the same? "Zohar has been the support and encouragement Isaac and I need when we feel abandoned."

Her husband's breath hitched, but his features remained hard as stone. "That was more than twenty years ago, Sarah. Will you never—"

"Zohar gave shelter to me when I feared my husband and son were dead. When his scouts returned with you and Isaac, you lauded Elohim's miracle. But when I asked why you hadn't confided in me *before* taking Isaac, you were furious and left without explaining. For months—years even—Isaac battled confusion and fear, asking why Elohim required his life as a sacrifice. I attempted to answer. Me, Abraham. Because you stayed in Beersheba. When Isaac's temper boiled over toward Hittite shepherds trespassing on the land Zohar allotted to us, it was the Hittite chieftain—not you—who taught our son diplomacy."

The pain in his eyes stole her breath. "And now my son looks to Zohar as his mentor. You've let Zohar replace me, Sarah."

Her anger flared. She'd invited Abraham to Hebron many times in the early years, but he'd always found an excuse to avoid hard conversations. "By choosing to visit so seldom, *you* let Zohar become an important voice as Isaac formed opinions about himself, life, and the world around him. Zohar believed—still believes—you treated both Isaac and me unfairly. I have taught Isaac all I know, but only you can train him to be the *man* Elohim wants him to be. No one can replace you, Abraham. You are Elohim's covenant bearer, and Isaac is your heir. You will always be the only one whose approval Isaac truly yearns for, but you must settle the past with him while I'm here to mediate—or Zohar will influence Isaac's decisions after I'm gone."

Abraham glared at her, his lips curled in disdain. "Do you agree with Zohar, that I've treated you and my son unfairly? Have you helped Zohar steal my son's allegiance?"

Had he no idea how hard she'd worked to keep her son's heart from completely hardening toward his abba? Such an accusation deserved no defense. "Say my name," she whispered.

Confusion pinched his features. "What?"

"You heard me. Say *Sarah* or even *Sarai*. Because surely you've forgotten to whom you're speaking. I'm the little sister who toddled behind you in Abba's fields. I'm the frightened girl you saved in Ur's city market when I ventured there alone and men fought over who would take me. Say my name, Abraham, to remember the delighted bride who has loved you her whole life. Say *Sarai* to remember the half sister who mourned Abba's death in Harran before we obeyed Elohim together and entering Canaan though we knew the drought was severe." She held his cheeks between her hands. "But I'm no longer Sarai because God renamed Sarah the same day He called you Abraham and gave us a son who would *never* plot against you. Say. My. Name."

He leaned his forehead against hers and released a long breath. "Sarah," he whispered and again, "Sarah. Please. Try to understand how terrifying it was to feel like I'd lost my family. I didn't know what to say to either of you or how to say it, and Elohim has been silent. He hasn't given me any guidance on the matter."

"I know you've been frightened, but I want you to imagine the morning I woke to find you and Isaac gone. I thought Abimelek had captured you. My only hope was Mamre and his Amorite tribe, our allies in this camp—what we'd known as Hebron until the smoke of Sodom's destruction drove us to the coastal plain." She lifted her head, hoping to lighten the air between them. "Eliezer has surely told you the details since he's more loyal to you than your flea-bitten donkey."

Abraham's eyes remained downcast, but she continued with words too long left unsaid. "Eliezer brought me and half our household guard—as well as half our flocks and herds—to plead for help from Mamre and his household. Instead, we met Zohar's Hittites that had ousted the Amorites months before. He had divided Hebron into four plots, calling it 'Four Cities'—*Kiriath Arba*. He could have killed us and taken your livestock. But he was kind to me. Fed our shepherds and our servants. Sent out search parties to find my husband and son. Then let us remain on one of his plots when you returned to Beersheba."

Abraham looked at her then. "And has hoped to have you for a wife ever since."

"Never has Zohar made an improper advance toward me. Besides…" She lifted a single brow. "He's forty years too young."

"You looked fifty years younger than him until now."

Meant as jest, his words felt more like a blade in her belly. Sarah hid her flushed cheeks against his chest. For the first time since he'd arrived, she was embarrassed by her appearance. "We should go. Isaac and Ketty are waiting." They'd talked enough.

"You see why I don't speak?" He draped his arms around her with a pained sigh. "I always say the wrong thing."

"Perhaps if we practiced more, we'd get better at it."

His low chuckle made her feel a little better. He braced his back against a tree and pushed himself to his feet.

When he set out toward the pasture, she suspected where he might be taking her. It wasn't long until she saw Isaac and Ketty in the distance.

"The altar," she whispered.

"I thought it the best place to speak of important things."

CHAPTER FOURTEEN

Abram traveled through the land as far as the site of the great tree of Moreh at Shechem.... The LORD appeared to Abram and said, "To your offspring I will give this land." So he built an altar there to the LORD, who had appeared to him.

From there he went on toward the hills east of Bethel and pitched his tent, with Bethel on the west and Ai on the east. There he built an altar to the LORD and called on the name of the LORD.
—Genesis 12:6–8 (NIV)

Sarah laid her head against Abraham's chest, focusing on the steady beat of his faithful heart. Even during the months of silence between his visits, she never doubted Abraham's love or his faith in Elohim. These were the things their son needed to remember, the vital character qualities Ketty needed to recognize in the man God had chosen to be the abba of her children.

"You must tell Isaac that Elohim also told you to marry Keturah." She spoke quietly as they neared the altar. "He doubts my dream, but he won't doubt your word."

Abraham answered with silence as he crested the familiar hilltop where pilgrims had come seeking Sarah's wisdom for years. Ketty stood to greet them, having prepared a veritable feast on the blanket where they normally spent their days. Isaac stood five paces away beside the stacked-stone altar Abraham had built. After one of their greatest heartaches, they'd returned to this hilltop, offered a burnt sacrifice, and made Hebron their first real home in Canaan.

Their separation from Lot had nearly gutted both Abraham and Sarah—for different reasons. When their nephew chose the Jordan Valley—the best, most fertile land in all of Canaan, Sarah mourned because he'd chosen to leave rather than settle the differences between their herdsmen with Elohim's guidance. But Abraham was most disappointed in Lot's failed character. He'd chosen to live among the sinful cities of the plain. Chosen to ignore Abba Terah's teaching to take the lesser and give others more, leaving room for Elohim to turn sacrifice into abundance.

"Imma, you're crying!" Isaac hurried over, leading the lamb he must have chosen for a sacrifice. He glared at Abraham. "What happened? Did you two argue on the way?"

"No," she answered before Abraham could voice the frustration plain on his face. "I was just reminiscing about the day your abba built this altar. Have I told you—"

"Yes, Imma. I know the story."

"I haven't heard it." Ketty spoke up. "But it must be a sad story if it's made you cry."

"It's not sad," Abraham grumbled, setting Sarah on the blanket and striding toward Isaac and the lamb. "We should make our offering before we eat." Ketty bowed her head and knelt beside Sarah, cowed by the finality of Abraham's declaration.

"Abba, Ketty wants to hear the story." Isaac's voice was strained. "The offering can wait."

"I—" Abraham extended a hand toward his son and turned to Sarah as if presenting some sort of evidence. Sarah lifted her brows, waiting for him to choose. Would Abraham run from Isaac's oversensitivity—created by years of misunderstanding and pain—or would he use this moment to prove he was willing to change? Her husband expelled a long, slow breath, placed the accusing hand on the back of his neck, and inhaled calm. When he looked up, his gaze fell on Ketty, and his expression revealed the gentle husband-brother Sarah had always adored. "Forgive my rush to the task," he said, drawing Ketty's attention. "I'm often too quick to act and slow to explain my actions—if I explain them at all—which makes my focus on Elohim appear as disregard to those on earth."

Her husband's suddenly eloquent words left them all spellbound. He began speaking as he knelt to inspect the lamb Isaac had chosen since they would never offer less than their best. "We'd just lost our nephew, who at the time was our only hope of an heir. God told me to stand on an outcropping and look north and south, east and west. Then He said, 'Go, walk through the length and breadth of the land that I will give to you and your offspring forever.' After we'd walked and walked, finding most of the land harsh and dusty, Elohim spoke to me again. 'Your offspring will be like the dust,' He said, 'too numerous to be counted.'"

Sarah added, "So Isaac is the first speck of dust in the fulfilled promise."

They all laughed—even Isaac—and Abraham placed a hand on his son's shoulder. "You've chosen a fine yearling lamb, Son. Well done."

"Thank you, Abba." The happy moment suspended in silence, lengthening, searing into their memories.

From their vantage on Canaan's central ridge, Sarah scanned the craggy hills and rugged pastures and broke the reverent silence. "Canaan's dust is as endless as the descendants Elohim has promised us."

The lamb bleated, infringing on the holy moment—or perhaps initiating the next. Abraham offered his knife to Isaac, and Ketty turned away. "The sacrifices are the one thing I dread about the shearing festivals each year. I love the celebration of harvests in spring and fall, but I can't watch Master Abraham cut the yearling ram in quarters and arrange it on the altar."

"I don't enjoy watching it either," Sarah admitted, "but when I remember it's a sacrifice of worship, I can bear it." She leaned against the giant oak behind her, strength beginning to fade.

"Worship?" Ketty's forehead creased. "I know it shows our gratitude for the harvest, but I've never equated it with *worship*. Worship seems more like dancing and celebration."

Sarah pointed to her two men, their heads now leaned together in private whispers. Isaac hadn't yet taken Abraham's knife. Their son still held the yearling ram between his legs, calming it with whispers as his abba spoke.

"Worship means we assign *worth* to whatever we've offered as our sacrifice. That's why an offering must always cost us something. The more it costs, the more worth we've assigned to the thing—or the One—we've come to worship. A yearling ram is quite valuable but the God to whom we offer it, infinitely more."

"No, you do it!" Isaac's raised voice snagged Sarah's attention and Ketty's too. Abraham bobbed the hand still holding the proffered knife and continued speaking quietly, calmly. Their son stared at the blade as if it were a viper that might strike him at any moment but finally took it from his abba's hand.

Still holding the lamb between his knees, Isaac straightened and looked toward his imma and Ketty, hands slightly trembling at his sides. Abraham addressed Ketty once more. "It occurs to me that I should also tell you about the first two altars I built in Canaan so you understand why this altar in Hebron is so special—and why Isaac will present today's offering."

Sarah reached for Ketty's hand. So that's what all the secrets were about. Abraham was building up their son and encouraging his leadership. Pride and adoration welled up, overflowing in happy tears as she listened to Abraham's quick recounting.

"The first altar was in Shechem, only days after Abba Terah died and Sarah, Lot, and I left Harran. The altar built at the tree of Moreh commemorated our first treaty with Canaanites, the first time Elohim promised to give the land to us *and* our offspring, and the first time Adonai appeared to me."

Ketty's breath caught, and she bent toward Sarah to whisper, "How did Elohim appear to—"

"If you have a question, Keturah, ask me." Abraham's booming voice sounded angry, though Sarah knew he wasn't.

"You need not shout at her, Abba." Isaac's defenses flared again. "You've never spoken to Ketty in all the years you've visited Kiriath Arba. But she'll soon be a permanent part of my family, so perhaps she'll trust you—eventually."

Sarah's heart jumped to her throat. She hadn't yet told Abraham that Ketty had requested to become Isaac's concubine. The confusion on Abraham's features rushed Sarah to speak. "Ketty was simply curious about how Elohim appeared to you, my love."

Abraham avoided Ketty's eyes and spoke almost too softly to be heard. "When Elohim appeared to me at Shechem, it was late at night. I heard the Voice and saw only a shimmer in the moonlight. There was no real form as He manifested in later years. Is that helpful?"

"Yes. Thank you."

He inclined his head but didn't look at her as he continued, "After leaving Shechem, our caravan wandered for weeks. When the drought became so severe that we knew not where to go or how to survive, I built a second altar in the hills between Bethel and Ai and cried out to Elohim. That's when Adonai—our Lord and Master—directed us south to Egypt, where our blessings really began."

He then turned to Isaac. "After the bounty of Pharaoh's gifts, we separated from Lot and he went his own way. When you remained here with your imma in Kiriath Arba, we didn't separate, my son. You are still a part of me. You are still the heir of Elohim's covenant—the covenant bearer. Kiriath Arba is *your* camp, Son. When your imma leaves this earth, you must make your decisions with El Elyon's help alone." He nodded toward the knife in Isaac's hand. "Worship is the best path to wisdom, Isaac. Learn to sacrifice, and Elohim will meet you in the discomfort."

Isaac stood as still as a pillar, with the knife in one hand and the lamb bleating between his knees. Staring at Abraham, his eyes filled with tears. "I don't think I can do it. I've only protected animals from my own flock. Never killed them. I've healed them, guided them, broken a leg and carried them on my shoulders when they refuse to stay with the others." He blinked tears down his cheeks. "If I do this wrong, he'll suffer, Abba."

"You are a good shepherd, my son. It's supposed to be painful. A sacrifice that costs us nothing isn't worthy of the Creator who gave us all we have." Abraham stepped closer to whisper something to their son, too quietly for Sarah to hear. Isaac listened and nodded as Abraham stepped back.

He bent, gently stroking the lamb's jaw, and pointed to the kill zone on its neck. "Ready?" he asked Isaac, tilting the animal's head up. Isaac leaned down and made a single, merciful slice.

Ketty didn't look away this time. She squeezed Sarah's hand as the two men gently laid the lamb on its side, stroking its fleece and murmuring words of blessing.

When the lifeblood had drained into the soil, Abraham lifted his voice to Elohim. "Now, we place our offering on this altar, O God, and light the fire. May its incense be a pleasing aroma of our worship, acknowledging that we are merely pilgrims on the earth, reliant on You to supply every need. We recommit ourselves, as Your covenant family, to continue our journey and fulfill the purpose for which we have been called—to bless all nations in Your name—until the day we join You in paradise. Now, El Shaddai, bring my son, Isaac, into the fulness of this covenant as he leads Your people at Kiriath Arba."

Isaac looked up with tear-stained cheeks. "Thank you, Abba." Just as he started to embrace Abraham, Ketty sprang to her feet.

"Forgive me, I'm not feeling well." Before anyone could question, she raced toward camp.

"Imma, was she ill?"

Sarah had no answers for her daughter's sudden departure. "She seemed fine before the sacrifice." *Before Abraham's prayer.*

Isaac watched Ketty's retreat, then looked down at the lamb, obviously torn between his concern and his commitment. Abraham laid a hand on their son's forearm, garnering his attention. "It will always be this way, Son. A man who deeply loves his family will often feel torn between what his family needs and what Elohim requires in the moment. You must decide in each of those moments which is your priority and then bear the consequences—trusting Elohim to increase your family's grace in equal measure with your faith."

CHAPTER FIFTEEN

Then Sarai said to Abram, "...I put my slave in your arms, and now that she knows she is pregnant, she despises me...."

"Your slave is in your hands," Abram said.... Then Sarai mistreated Hagar; so she fled from her. The angel of the LORD found Hagar near a spring in the desert.
—Genesis 16:5–7 (NIV)

Tears blurred Keturah's vision as she ran through the rutted pasture toward the forest surrounding the camp. She couldn't return to the tents. She must be alone to think. To plan. To escape. *Escape.* It was the only answer. How had she imagined Isaac and Master Abraham would ever give up Kiriath Arba—no matter how many servants shifted loyalty to Ephron the Hittite? Imma's decision to separate from her husband after the Testing and relocate to Hebron hadn't been based on fond memories. She hadn't remained here simply to find respite. Kiriath Arba was sacred, its altar built as a declaration of the covenant bearer's first Canaanite home.

Lungs burning, legs trembling, she hid behind the largest tree at the edge of the forest. Finally alone. Gasping for breath. Grasping for answers. *Elohim, what should I do?* Imma's dream came to mind, but the thought of marrying the wealthiest Bedouin prince in Canaan—in the known world—was too fantastical. Seeing both the master's frustration with her today and Isaac's continued protectiveness made that possibility no more than a strange prelude to Imma's swift decline. Imma slept so much now, she could have a dozen more dreams before—

Ketty's thoughts stopped cold with the realization of Imma's imminent passing. A shiver shook her from head to toes. Master Abraham had seemed surprised that Isaac planned to take Ketty as his concubine. Would he object? *I don't even want to become my brother's concubine.* She loved him more than anything and would give her life for him. But she didn't feel passion for him—nor a sense of peace when she considered it. *How do I know Your will, Elohim?*

Her mind circled back to escape. If she left before Imma's death, perhaps she could drain at least some of Dirar's hubris. Without a partner to win the other servants' favor, he'd be no benefit to Ephron. But could Ketty escape the camp and find somewhere safe to serve? She remembered Mistress Hagar's terrible stories about wandering alone in the wilderness. The Angel of the Lord had appeared to her and asked, "Where have you come from, and where are you going?"

Hagar had come from serving Sarah, but her roots had been planted in Egypt. She was the daughter of Pharaoh, though borne of a concubine and easily cast off as one of the slaves given to Abraham when he and Sarah were hurried out of the country with great wealth. Ketty had come from an equally heartless abba, but she was fleeing to protect Imma and Isaac—and their home in Kiriath Arba.

The image of Master Abraham standing beside the altar came to mind, tall and strong as he encouraged Isaac to be brave. *"A sacrifice that costs us nothing isn't worthy of the Creator who gave us all we have."* Could Ketty sacrifice all Elohim had given her—family, security, comfort—to strip away the only power Dirar brought to his alliance with Ephron? Dirar's power over Ketty was the threat of harm against the family she loved, but Imma and Master Abraham already suspected Dirar. They'd be cautious of his potions, and Ketty could watch him closely today, playing along as if she was still part of his plan until darkness made her escape more feasible. Tonight then? The thought made her heart gallop.

"Where have you come from, and where are you going?" The two questions of Hagar's angel replayed in her mind again, and she realized the second was still unsolved. Where would Ketty go? Not only was it dangerous for a woman to travel alone, but the terrain between Hebron and—well, anywhere—would be difficult on foot. Master Abraham had made the journey from Beersheba in less than two days, but he was accustomed to herding sheep and climbing rocky crags. Ketty had nearly fainted running across a single pasture. She buried her face in her hands. *Elohim, where do I go?* She knew in the very marrow of her bones that she must leave to stop Dirar and Ephron, but such a decision without a destination seemed reckless.

"Here you are." Dirar's sudden appearance startled a yelp from Ketty. His leering chuckle made her skin crawl. "Why aren't you with the others at the altar?"

"I was. I—" If she was going to make her part in his plan believable, she must begin now. "I told them I wasn't feeling well so I could return early and talk with you, but I needed a moment alone to gather my thoughts and questions."

He stepped closer, slipping his hands around her waist. "A moment alone. That sounds nice."

She broke from his grasp, stepping into view of servants in camp a stone's throw away. "But we're not alone yet, Dirar, and we won't be until Isaac leaves to find his Semite bride."

He grinned, sucking air between his front teeth, while studying her closely. "It almost seems like you're happy to wait, but I've never been a patient man, Keturah. I met with Ephron last night. He sent a messenger to me after hearing Abraham had arrived. He sees it as a chance to kill both Abraham and his weak-kneed son, gaining the wealth of Kiriath Arba and Beersheba with one strike."

"No!" she hissed. "You promised the takeover would be peaceful, that I could help you win the servants' loyalty while Isaac was away, and no one would be harmed."

He shrugged. "Plans change."

"They do indeed." Her implied threat registered in his surprise. Her anger boiled into rage as she stepped close enough to whisper the rest. "What makes you think I won't reveal your plan and bring Zohar's full wrath down on his son Ephron's head and yours?"

Dirar's hand was around her throat before she could scream, cutting off her breath and nearly lifting her feet off the ground. "Because if you dare speak a word of this to anyone, I'll make you watch while Ephron kills every person in this camp.

Then I'll make you beg to join them—but keep you for my own amusement."

"Keetttyyy!" Isaac's desperate howl distracted Dirar, and Ketty stomped the top of his foot, breaking his stranglehold.

Without looking back, she ran toward Isaac's continued shouts. "I'm coming!" Both her brother and Master Abraham huddled over Imma's body. Flames rose from the altar. Terror pushed her quicker than her legs could move. She stumbled and cried out as Dirar passed her.

He reached the blanket before Ketty and fell to his knees beside Isaac. "What happ—Oh, I see." Dirar stared down at Imma, whose face drooped severely on the left side.

Her eyes darted from Dirar to Ketty. "Cun...jit dejide... neee." The slurred plea of *come sit beside me* broke Ketty's heart but even more when she saw the fear in Imma's eyes. When she tried to raise her arms to Ketty, and only her right arm lifted from her lap, Imma cried, "Hat ij haffening to neee?" Fear turned to a desperate whine, but her body refused to move, denying her even the ability to express the terror obvious in her eyes.

"Do something!" Ketty shouted at Dirar.

Master Abraham used no words but locked his large hand around Dirar's throat instead. "No more of your tricks, healer. Can you help my wife or not?"

"Maybe," he croaked.

"We'll never know," Isaac shouted, "if you don't let him try, Abba."

The master released Dirar, eyes narrowed as he said, "Ketty will watch every ingredient you place in the remedy."

"Fine, but we must hurry." Dirar was on his feet and started toward camp. "Hurry, Ketty! You and I will prepare the tea while they bring Mistress Sarah," he shouted over his shoulder, running at a full sprint.

Ketty followed him, blinded by tears and torn by this morning's uncertainties. *Elohim, please don't take Imma yet. I'm not ready. Our world isn't ready to live without her.*

CHAPTER SIXTEEN

> *By the sweat of your brow*
> *you will eat your food*
> *until you return to the ground,*
> *since from it you were taken;*
> *for dust you are*
> *and to dust you will return.*
> —Genesis 3:19 (NIV)

Abraham cradled Sarah in his lap while Dirar held a warm cup of foul-tasting liquid to her lips. "Keep drinking, Mistress," Dirar said, holding a cloth against her chin. She felt the softness only on her right side and the hot liquid pouring only on the right side of her tongue. "More. More. Keep swallowing if you can, Mistress."

If she could? Of course she could swallow…or could she? The cloth he held to her chin now felt damp. Was only the right side of her throat working? Was she now only half a woman? Had the whole left side of her body died? A sob escaped. Tea choked her. Abraham sat up and placed her against his broad shoulder, patting her back like an infant.

Her daughter knelt beside them and whispered, "I see you, Imma."

Her neck wasn't strong enough to lift her head, so she lay there, coughing, staring into Ketty's eyes. *I'm still here, Love. Don't give up on me.*

"Imma, listen to me." Ketty wiped her cheeks and straightened her shoulders. "Dirar used a different herb than the one for your chest pains. He said Master Ishmael purchased this new herb from a merchant who traveled to the Far East, to lands even beyond the Zakros Mountains. It's very powerful, so he added only a pinch. We'll try more if it renders good results. It seems to have stopped the progression of paralysis." She stroked Sarah's right cheek and forced a smile. "I made sure Dirar left out the poppy so you could stay awake."

Sarah's coughing had ebbed, so she tried to speak. It came out like a moan. Frustrated, she squeezed her eyes shut and opened them, hoping the girl would realize she approved of the poppy-less tea.

Ketty's breath caught. "You're communicating, aren't you Imma? Are you pleased he left out the poppy?"

Again, Sarah blinked her eyes tightly.

"Master Abraham, look!" Ketty said. "Imma winked her right eye to say yes!"

Winked? Only then did Sarah realize her paralysis had made her intended blink merely a wink.

Abraham gently lowered her into the bend of his arm. She tried to smile, but when her brawny shepherd saw the attempt, his features crumbled. "I'm not ready to lose you, my love." He bowed his head, weeping.

She tried to lift her right hand to hold his cheek, but she hadn't the strength. *Elohim, please! There's so much left unsaid. Undone!*

"I'm not sure how much of the herb she actually swallowed," Dirar said. "I'll go out and prepare another half cup."

Abraham's head snapped up. "Ketty, go—"

"I'm going." She rushed away, leaving Sarah to gaze at her husband. Though fear and grief clouded her mind, she still had the wits to blink a yes or perhaps leave her eyes closed for a prolonged stretch to signal a no. Maybe—

The sound of sniffling startled her. *Isaac.* With what little strength she had, Sarah pressed her right hand against Abraham's chest and tried to point in the direction of the sniffling. Would Abraham understand what she wanted?

"What does she want, Abba?" Isaac's voice trembled.

"I believe your imma wants to see you." Abraham's lips quaked as he shifted so Sarah could see their son.

Isaac sat three paces away, but distance couldn't lessen the pain on his creased brow. His back was stiff as a measuring rod, cheeks pale as goat's milk. Leaning closer, he fairly shouted, "Imma, can you hear me?"

Too weak to nod, she squeezed her eyes closed and then opened them again.

"You do understand!" He lunged forward, pressing a kiss to her forehead. "Dirar will bring you back, Imma. Another dose of his secret herb, and..." He looked at Abraham and back into her eyes, stumbling over the words. "I mean...you'll...feel better, Imma. We want you to…to feel better." It was as if her dying had only then settled into his reality. As if he'd just realized no secret herb would heal her. Dirar could only make her dying less abhorrent.

"For dust you are and to dust you will return." Abba Terah's last words rushed over her like a wave from the Great Sea—the same words originally spoken by the Creator to define the consequences of sin. One choice doomed all flesh. Had they been allowed to eat from the Tree of Life, they would have lived forever in sinfulness. So God banished them from His garden, and with one promise—the coming Serpent Crusher—gave all humankind the hope of redemption. Death became the door to Life.

Will death be a relief, Elohim? The thought had never occurred to Sarah. She would certainly never hasten its coming, but if El Elyon made death the portal of escape from this broken world, perhaps she could look forward to what waited on the other side. Would it be more like the Garden? Would she meet the Great-Abba and Great-Imma there? The thought captivated her, finally seeing the beautiful woman whose appearance she'd inherited. Would Sarah's lifelong health and beauty be restored when she arrived or—?

"Since she isn't responding—" Isaac's words drew her back to the moment. "I'll assume she would want me to tell you the whole truth, Abba." He sat beside Abraham, lips pursed into a tight, nervous line. "After an appropriate mourning period for Imma, I plan to make Ketty my concubine. I'll then leave Kiriath Arba in her capable hands and travel north to the Semite clans, where I'll choose a bride from our relatives."

Sarah groaned and kept her eyes closed, but her negative signal meant she couldn't see Abraham's reaction. When she opened her eyes, his neck and face had flushed the color of ripened grapes.

His arms tightened around her, but to his credit, he didn't respond right away. Abraham sniffed. Wet his lips. Sniffed again. Then calmly said, "I have several questions for you, my son. May I ask them now? Or would you rather discuss them when we're alone?"

Isaac looked down at Sarah, seeming rather surprised by his abba's consideration. "I think it would be good for Imma to hear our discussion even if she can't fully participate."

Sarah wished she could scream at the top of her lungs. Instead, she lay there like a half-dead fish.

Abraham nodded and inhaled deeply before speaking. "Are you or are you not aware of the message Elohim spoke to your imma in both a dream and a vision?"

Isaac glanced at Sarah before raising his chin. "Of course I'm aware."

"Has she told you yet that Elohim also confirmed the same message to me—before I arrived at Kiriath Arba?" Isaac's eyes widened, and a soft gasp behind Sarah proved Ketty had entered in time to hear Abraham's revelation. He turned toward the sound and added, "You should join this conversation, Keturah, since it involves your future."

"Keturah will not marry you." Isaac's tone was as sharp as a blade.

Ketty settled on a cushion beside him. Dirar followed her, intruding on their discussion by placing a cushion in the shadows behind Isaac. He neither asked permission to stay nor offered to leave.

Abraham's eyes lingered on the slave only a moment before returning to their son. "How long have your imma and I been in Canaan?"

Isaac's brows tented, seeming surprised by the change of subject. "I don't…why…I suppose over sixty years."

"In all that time, have either your imma or I traveled back into Semite territory?"

Isaac studied his abba before answering. "I assumed, though you trust Eliezer completely, you chose not to leave the full responsibility of your Beersheba camp in a servant's hands."

"Your assumptions are shortsighted and incorrect. We have remained in Canaan because your imma and I wouldn't be safe in Semite territory. Elohim's original calling was to Abba Terah, but he stopped in Harran, which lies at the farthest border of Shem's tribes. Entering Canaan meant cutting all ties with family and tradition. Abba couldn't do that—not completely. When he died, your imma and I left Harran and obeyed Elohim's calling. It was a declaration of independence from the Great Sages who govern our Semite clans. We left our land, our family, and our heritage to bring Elohim's blessing to *all* clans, Isaac. And when our nephew, Lot, was taken captive nine years later with the Canaanite residents of Sodom, I took 318 men from my household to fight a union of five *Semite* armies—and Elohim gave us victory over them. In doing so, many from our homeland consider me an enemy. So, as I said, you may not be welcome on Semite land."

"But I've done nothing wrong."

Abraham lifted his hand to silence him. "If, by chance, you find favor among the Sages—the Great Sage Shem and his grandson, Eber, who will undoubtedly hear of your return to their clans the moment you step foot across the border—they will wish to gain your favor. You are my sole heir, Isaac. We've built great wealth. However, you've inherited something far more precious than wealth, something the Sages don't understand. You are the covenant bearer of Elohim's *blessing* to all nations. They don't comprehend the eternal treasure of this covenant, Isaac, nor the authority we hold to bless those who bless us and curse those who mistreat us." He held their son's gaze, pausing with the weight of his words. "But this covenant is conditioned on our obedience. If you ignore Elohim's authority—choosing to obey only the commands you understand or agree with—you've broken His covenant."

Silence filled the space between abba and son as Isaac's breathing grew ragged. His nostrils flared and lips trembled as Sarah watched his fury mounting. Oh, how she ached to speak, to sooth the tension crackling in the air like heat lightning in a desert sky. *Why must I be mute when my words could help, Elohim? Heal me, I beg You!* But healing didn't come. She lay in Abraham's arms, helpless, while her men locked eyes like angry bulls preparing to charge.

Finally, Isaac shifted his gaze to Ketty. "I will not dishonor you by making you a concubine." Turning back to his abba, he said, "But neither will I allow my sister to marry a man who would neither honor nor protect her. If Elohim truly considers me His covenant bearer, why hasn't He told *me* whom Ketty must marry? Why does He speak to you and Imma—even to an Egyptian handmaid—but never to your sole heir?"

"Isaac, you are Elohim's covenant bear—"

"Then let Him speak to *me*!" he shouted and bolted to his feet. "As you said, I'm the master of Kiriath Arba. If Elohim plans to take Imma and Ketty from me, I demand He tell me so Himself. If He refuses to speak, then I'll marry Ketty myself." Without awaiting further discussion, he whirled and strode away.

"Isaac!" Abraham called—to no avail.

Sarah moaned like a wounded animal. Abraham looked down, his desperation mirrored in her continued wailing.

"What, Sarah?" he asked. "What else would you have me do?"

With all her strength, she lifted her right hand and pointed toward the tent flap. "Gggggooo." She forced the single word from her throat.

"All right!" Abraham turned to Dirar. "Elohim hasn't yet revealed what you're about, but I don't trust you. You will give Keturah instructions to administer what's in that cup and then come outside with me." He gently laid Sarah on her mat while Dirar whispered to Ketty.

Releasing a deep sigh, Abraham stood, making a visible effort to soften his manner when he turned to the woman Elohim had chosen to be his next wife. "I realize I can be harsh, Keturah, but when Elohim commands, I obey with all my heart. I will marry you, protect you, and care for you—but only if you come willingly into this marriage Elohim has commanded." He, too, turned and left the tent without awaiting her answer, looking over his shoulder only once to see Dirar following.

Ketty stood motionless, staring at the tent flap even after it closed. The cup Dirar had given her remained in her hand until trembling overtook her. She turned to Sarah with tears streaming down her cheeks. "I must leave tonight," she whispered. Kneeling beside Sarah, she tipped the cup, gently administering healing while breaking Sarah's heart. "I don't yet know where I'll go, but I'll make it appear as though it's been well planned and I'm safe. They'll be less likely to look for me if they agree that I've made a reasonable choice. They seem to be talking more freely together. Maybe they can even speak of the lingering scars from the Testing if I'm not here to complicate their relationship. I refuse to be the blade that completely severs their relationship, Imma."

Trying to protest, Sarah choked on the last swallow of tea. Ketty set the cup aside and pulled Sarah forward, embracing her as she patted her back. Sarah laid her head on the girl's shoulder. "Nnnooo." The word came out slurred but the meaning clear.

Ketty held her more tightly, and they sobbed together quietly as dusk stole the day. Wrung out like a rag, Sarah had no strength left when Ketty lowered her back to her pillows and wiped tears from both their faces.

She offered Sarah a wan smile. Without the words to coax her daughter, how could Sarah discover the thoughts brewing behind Ketty's dark eyes? The girl looked away, fiddling with her hands. A sign she was gathering courage.

"I didn't know Elohim had also confirmed to Master Abraham that...well, you know." Ketty covered her cheeks but was unable to hide the deep blush. "I can't even speak the words, Imma. How could Elohim choose a slave woman for the Great Bedouin Prince? His blessed covenant bearer? I could never be worthy. It makes no sense. Master Abraham would despise me because I'm not you. He loves you too much to accept any other woman or to—" She shook her head and whispered, "Or to give me children."

Sarah groaned, snagging her attention, then closed her eyes—lingering there, hoping Ketty realized her complete opposition to everything she'd just said.

When Sarah opened her eyes again, a timid smile played at the corners of Ketty's mouth. "How can you fuss at me without any words at all?" When she bent to kiss Sarah's cheek, her sadness had returned. "I must leave Kiriath Arba, Imma. Tonight. Before—"

Sarah moaned and flailed her right arm, frantic.

"Shh, Imma," Ketty whispered, settling her arm with a gentle but firm touch. "Please. It's the only way to keep Isaac safe."

Sarah's breath hitched. Ketty's eyes communicated more than she was saying.

"You must trust me in this. I would never leave you or this family if there were any other way. And I must believe that if your dream is truly from Elohim, He'll find a way to make it happen."

She pecked another kiss on Sarah's cheek and hurried toward her sleeping area, where she filled a shoulder bag with a few necessities. Returning to Sarah's mat, she wrapped some hard cheese and bread in a cloth and added them to her bag. Then, with a final kiss, she whispered against Sarah's forehead, "Because you gave me a life and love and Elohim, you made me the wealthiest woman on earth. Goodbye, Imma." She raced away and was gone.

Alone, Sarah peered down at her dead hand and leg. Perhaps Dirar's potion had forestalled more damage, but it didn't seem to be reviving her left side or her ability to speak. If only she could shout for help. Shout for Abraham or Isaac to chase Ketty and bring her back. Bring her to her senses. *Elohim, please! Why reveal Your plan for my family if You won't help me bring it to pass?*

A cold chill ran through her. Had she just demanded that God help *her* complete His plan? Isaac's jesting replayed in her mind: "*On the occasions Abba hears from God, he shares nothing with anyone and leaves the* convincing *to Elohim. On the other hand, you—Imma—have one dream revealing God's plan, and you think He needs your help to bring it to pass.*" Had Elohim taken her speech and mobility so she couldn't interfere with His work? No. She didn't believe Elohim would harm one child to help another. But her body's decline had forced her to accept all the limitations that heralded death's approach. Death would become her ultimate surrender, and she'd face many skirmishes along the way. Would she grapple with every new limitation and make her final days miserable for her and everyone around her?

Her iron will—refined like a Hittite sword—had served her well through life's impossible moments. But it was time to lay it down in this first act of conscious submission: *Elohim, I will trust You to keep Ketty safe in the foolish quest she's undertaken. I can't bring her back to this camp—to Abraham and the good future You've promised her—but You can.* Her next thought was of Isaac. How could he question his role as Elohim's covenant bearer? *Elohim...* Well, surely she could help resolve that issue.

CHAPTER SEVENTEEN

*Trust in the Lord with all your heart
and lean not on your own understanding;
in all your ways submit to him,
and he will make your paths straight.*
—Proverbs 3:5–6 (NIV)

The sun had already disappeared behind the hills and a full moon rose over the camp, lighting Ketty's escape. She slipped around the corner of Imma's tent, remaining unseen while listening to evening sounds, hoping to assess the locations of those who might spot her departure. Only one large oak tree stood near the tent. Then she must cover twenty paces of grassy clearing before reaching the forest. Most of the servants would be busy preparing the evening meal, but what about Isaac and his abba? Where had they—?

"I refuse to answer your questions," Isaac shouted, "about a woman who means nothing to you!"

"A woman who obviously means very much to you. Do you really want Elohim to speak, Isaac, or is your will firmly set on having Keturah as your wife?"

No! Ketty peeked around Imma's tent but saw no one. Where could they be? Their shouts sounded so close, but…

The dim glow through Isaac's tent opening revealed their location.

"I care for her as my sister—only. But unless Elohim tells me otherwise, I'll marry Ketty and honor her with children to save her from a life of your disregard."

Master Abraham let out a terrifying growl. "You're as stubborn as your imma, boy! I do not take Elohim's commands lightly, nor would I disregard Keturah as my wife. I was seventy-five before Elohim spoke to me! You've not even seen forty harvests. Why can't you trust God to—"

"Trust?" Isaac shrieked. "I let you tie my hands and feet, then lay as still as a stone on an altar while you raised a dagger to kill me, Abba. Don't talk to me about trust!" Isaac's last word came out on a sob, and Ketty could bear it no longer.

As she raced across the clearing in the moonlight, their voices faded, but a flicker of hope fanned into flame. At least they were talking about the Testing. Perhaps Isaac could finally address the wounds that had eaten away the trust in his abba all these years. Reaching the forest, Ketty ducked under branches and leaped over fallen trees, finding the well-worn path Isaac and Master Zohar used often. The full moon provided enough light through springtime's budding trees to light her only path to refuge.

When Master Zohar had renamed this hilltop Kiriath Arba, he'd divided it into four camps, giving one of them to Abraham's wife and son and keeping the other three to rule as chieftain of the Hittites. When his oldest son, Ephron, chafed at his leadership, Master Zohar had made Ephron manager of one camp until he inherited leadership of all three upon his abba's death. Ketty's only hope to protect Isaac—and Imma, while she still lived—was to warn Zohar of Dirar's scheming. She could never speak ill of Ephron or reveal his involvement. Master Zohar would undoubtedly kill her for such an accusation. But if she could alert him to a scoundrel in Imma's camp, the Hittite chieftain would almost certainly send troops to protect her and Isaac, which would also foil Ephron's plot to overtake the camp. *Lord, let it be so.*

Ketty hoped Master Zohar would be willing to repay her loyalty to Imma by hiding her as a slave in one of his camps. She'd make up a reason, some story that would save Isaac's pride—maybe even seeming to protect him—and convince the chieftain she must leave Isaac's camp. If he refused to keep her, she would beg him to provide her safe passage to the coastal trade route where she could travel with a caravan to Egypt. The plan seemed plausible. Almost God-directed.

Now deep in the forest between their camps, she felt satisfied with the plan and reached into her shoulder bag for a piece of hard cheese and bread. She'd visited Master Zohar's camp only once with Imma and Isaac, when he'd invited them to celebrate the barley harvest—last year, before Master Abraham arrived for the spring shearing. Every strange sound grew louder. She stumbled over a protruding tree root. Her stomach roiled. No longer hungry, she rewrapped the cheese and bread and tucked it back into her bag.

Would the Hittite chieftain believe her tale about conspiracy and takeover? The deeper into the forest she walked, the darker the path and the more doubts assailed her. Would Master Zohar risk his friendship with Isaac to hide or help an escaped slave? The Hittite chieftain was an intelligent man. Would he demand to know more about her reasons for leaving?

A twig snapped behind her. Ketty whirled, peering through gathering darkness. Heart thudding, she thought to call out, *Who's there?* But she stepped behind a tree instead. Had Dirar followed her? Or was it a different kind of predator? She hadn't thought to bring a weapon. Scanning every tree, leaf, and shadow, she saw nothing and no one following her.

If she stopped at every sound she heard, she'd never make it to Master Zohar's camp. Forging her will, she took to the path again and marched farther up the tree-covered hills. Legs churning, she felt her thighs burn. She stopped to pick up a long stick beside the path and used it as a staff for the challenging trek. How many times had the Hittite chieftain hiked this path to bring gifts of forged blades and cooking pots to Imma and Isaac? Ketty had always attended Imma during his visits, but she couldn't remember a single time Master Zohar had ever spoken to her directly. Would he recognize her? Or would he ask for some proof of her identity as Imma's personal maid?

A stick cracked behind her, closer this time. She spun in the darkness, holding her staff like a spear. Again, she saw nothing. No one. Angst drove her past exhaustion. Legs numb, she felt as if they might buckle beneath her. Ahead in the distance, she heard the braying of donkeys. *Master Zohar's first camp!* She crouched low behind a row of prickly shrubs. Having lost their colorful blossoms during the latter rains, they were now green and leafy and would provide adequate cover from camp guards until dawn. She didn't want to be mistaken as a threat—or easy prey. Ketty reached again into her shoulder bag and removed the heavy cloak she'd brought from Imma's tent then placed it on the ground. She curled on her side, pillowed her arm beneath her head, and pulled the cloak over her. When dawn came, she'd present herself to the guards with the genuine urgency of Mistress Sarah's imminent danger.

CHAPTER EIGHTEEN

Surely, Lord, you bless the righteous;
you surround them with your favor as with a shield.
—Psalm 5:12 (NIV)

Next Morning - 5th Ajaru (April)

Ketty bolted upright at the sound of nearby footsteps then ducked low behind the shrubs. On the other side, two Hittite guards walked the perimeter of their camp. Having passed her hiding place, they were now walking away. The sky's gradient glow proved she'd risen before sunrise. Good. She must appear desperate, as if she'd escaped from Isaac's camp and tromped through the night with urgent news. Scurrying to her feet, she shoved the cloak into her bag, mussed her hair, and inhaled a sustaining breath. *Be brave, Keturah, for Imma and Isaac—and Master Abraham.* After watching them together for the past two days, she now believed Master Abraham could be as tender as Imma had described him.

Finding a break in the shrub line, she hurried toward the Hittite guards—not too quickly, for fear they'd see her as a threat. One of them turned, his eyes widening when he saw her approach. He slapped his partner's arm and pointed. Both men's jaws went slack. Why so unnerved by an unarmed handmaid in a field? Hittites were supposed to be ferocious warriors.

Still thirty paces away, she shouted, "I must see Master Zohar right away. I'm Keturah, sister of—"

"We're here to see your chieftain." A large hand grasped her arm and stole her breath. Master Abraham added, "Immediately." Master Abraham pulled Ketty to a halt twenty paces from the guards, holding her arm like a vise, his eyes focused on the soldiers.

The Hittites' hands rested on their swords. "What is this about, Prince Abraham?" one of them asked.

"Zohar will wish to hear the news we bring about my wife."

The other guard backhanded his friend, mumbled something, and then turned back to the visitors. "Of course, my lord. Follow us to the chieftain's camp."

Ketty wrenched her arm from his grasp as they stepped toward the waiting guards. "You followed me," she whispered.

"Why did you come here?"

But they'd reached their escort before she could contrive a suitable lie. One walked ahead of them and one behind. Marching in silence, they passed through several pastures and then the first camp, drawing stares from early-rising servants. Tromping through another livestock pasture, they saw flocks similar to Isaac's—likely the chieftain's own. Isaac had taught Zohar's shepherds all they knew of raising animals in Canaan, but Elohim's blessing on Isaac's flocks and herds was undeniable, their size and quality unattainable by mere human skill.

When they passed through a small copse of trees, a heavily guarded, enormous tent came into view. "Wait here," the first guard said. He approached the tent's entrance, speaking quietly to the fierce-looking men Ketty assumed were Master Zohar's personal guards.

One of the men disappeared inside the tent. Ketty had barely exchanged a worried glance with Master Abraham when the guard returned and shouted to them, "Master Zohar will see you immediately in his audience chamber."

Master Abraham placed his hand at the small of Ketty's back. An inconsequential, or perhaps even unconscious gesture for him, it sent indescribable warmth through Ketty. One gentle touch had said she belonged to him. She looked up into his intense brown eyes. They promised protection. Not with words but with silent knowing and a subtle nod.

"You will tell Zohar why we're here, Keturah."

He would trust her to speak for them?

"Elohim brought you here safely. He has a plan for you."

So different than Imma's need to understand the plan. "I'll explain to Master Zohar." Breathless, she followed the guard inside. The chieftain's tent was like another world, filled with all things Hittite iron. Weapons of every size and shape. Images of every beast in the field and forest. Mounds of jewelry in baskets stacked in the corner.

Master Abraham stood behind her and leaned close to whisper, "Tell me, now, anything I should know before Zohar hears it." It wasn't a threat but rather a plea.

She looked over her shoulder, their faces close. "I…" She could barely breathe. "You must take Imma and Isaac to Beersheba. They're not safe."

"What—"

"Prince Abraham." Master Zohar's deep voice stole her attention. He slipped between a divided curtain and bade them to be seated on the only soft surfaces in the tent. Eight embroidered cushions sat in a neat square, two per side, with the iron tables at each corner. The skin above and beneath the chieftain's eyes was puffy as if just awoken, but his dark eyes were sharp, assessing his guests like a blade skinning a fresh kill. "When my guard first told me you'd come, I was concerned for Sarah's health. Now that I see no grief on either of your features, I'm more intrigued by your visit than fearful for my friend." He glared down his beaked nose at Master Abraham. "Or should I remain concerned—since her husband has never shown much interest in his wife or his son?"

"You have no—"

"Please, Master Zohar." Ketty interrupted Master Abraham's fury with an urgency of her own. "I've come to beg your favor and ask you to make me a servant in one of your Hittite camps."

The chieftain studied her, glanced at Abraham, and back at Ketty. "Is this some sort of trickery?"

"Sarah has not released you," Abraham said in barely a whisper. "You'll break her heart, Keturah."

"Please, Master Zohar," Ketty repeated, ignoring Abraham's plea, "when I reveal the danger in our camp, I'll no longer be safe there." Again the two men glared silent accusations while Ketty considered how much truth to reveal. Her first priority was to save lives, but she must also preserve the relationship of Elohim's covenant bearers. "Prince Ishmael gave Master Isaac many gifts when he and Mistress Hagar left a few days ago," she said. "One of the gifts was a servant, Dirar, whose herbal skills have kept my mistress alive—so far. However, Dirar plans to use his herbs for harm."

"I knew it." Master Abraham's eyes narrowed.

Ketty continued before her courage failed. "Master Abraham has wisely set watchful eyes on Dirar while he prepares the herbal treatments. Dirar had planned to take the camp by force after Mistress Sarah died and Master Isaac left to find a bride."

"Isaac isn't leaving to find a bride." Master Abraham studied her as he spoke.

"But he must!" Ketty answered too quickly.

Zohar's wiry brows lifted. "I'll send a troop of my men to Isaac's camp, seize this healer, Dirar, and everyone will be safe." He brushed his hands together. "Done."

Ketty glanced at Abraham, who lifted equally wiry eyebrows, challenging her to find issue with the chieftain's solution.

Ephron won't wait! She ached to tell Master Abraham but couldn't—at least, not while in the presence of Ephron's abba.

Master Abraham leaned forward, pinning her with a stare. "Before Zohar joined us in this audience chamber you said to me, 'Take Imma and Isaac to Beersheba. They're not safe.' How are they in danger?"

His betrayal was like a blow to Ketty's chest. Where was the protection she'd sensed? Isaac had been right about his abba. Why had she trusted him?

Master Abraham turned his fury on Zohar. "My wife's maid traveled alone through the forest to beg you for refuge and gave you the name of a known traitor. Why would she see you as an ally?"

Zohar met his subtle accusation with a smirk. "You came with her."

"I followed her and had no idea why she'd come. I was as surprised as you when she asked to serve in your camp before Sarah died. And equally surprised when she told me to take Isaac and Sarah away to keep them safe. Two things are clear, Zohar. One, the traitor, Dirar, is the real threat. Two, Keturah believes my wife, son, and I are still in danger even after Dirar is dealt with." He turned to Ketty, his features softening. "And Keturah is willing to sacrifice her future, giving herself to serve in this camp, in order to ensure our escape from the Hittites. Who among the Hittites is threatening our camp, Keturah?"

"What?" Master Zohar sneered. "My people are loyal to me and would never—"

"Our animals are twice as valuable as Hittite livestock," Abraham shot back.

"Livestock is all you care about!" Zohar shouted. "Take your flocks to Beersheba, and leave Sarah and Isaac with me!"

"And stealing my wife and son is all you care about!" Master Abraham shook with rage. "I will—"

"Wait!" Ketty lunged to her knees in the middle of the square. "Master Zohar and his people are innocent." She glanced at the two powerful men and settled on Master Abraham first. "Master Zohar has been a true and honorable friend to both the mistress and Isaac." Then she turned to the smug chieftain. "But your son, Ephron, has made an alliance with the traitorous healer, Dirar. Ephron wishes to take Isaac's camp and intends to use Dirar's threats to gain my influence with those currently serving Isaac in hopes they'd remain as Ephron's slaves."

She looked down at her hands, unable to meet either man's eyes as she explained her role. "I agreed because when Dirar first told me, he promised there would be no bloodshed if I helped them. But yesterday, Dirar met with Ephron, who now refuses to wait. He ordered Dirar to speed Imma's decline while his Hittite soldiers prepare to invade the camp and kill both Isaac and Master Abraham. Dirar will maintain Isaac's camp in Kiriath Arba, and Ephron intends to seize the wealth in Beersheba as well."

Ketty released a deep sigh, her dignity and worth leaving with it. At least the truth was out. All of it. Though she'd been trying to protect those she loved, the truth sounded so horrible when spoken aloud. The lengthening silence raised prickly flesh on her arms. She didn't dare look up. She'd kept the terrible secret from Master Abraham and accused a Hittite prince of treason in his abba's tent. Which of the two powerful men would punish her first? Would it be torture? Death?

"Ephron is in Damascus."

"What?" Ketty gasped and met Master Zohar's gaze. "But how..."

"He's been gone for two weeks and won't return for another month. At least forty guards accompanied him." He turned to Abraham, frustration evident by his half-hooded eyelids. "I can have their wives and children paraded into my tent to testify to their husbands' departure if you don't believe me. My son isn't the culprit nor am I, Abraham. It would seem Ishmael's gift brought more harm than good." He gave a derisive snort. "Would you like to dispose of this vermin, Dirar, or shall I?"

Master Abraham trembled with barely controlled fury. "I will handle Dirar."

"And you." Zohar's tone was mocking. Ketty turned to see his eyes fixed on her, his smile like a hyena before it howls. "Sarah told me the dream she had about you and Abraham."

Ketty shook her head, too humiliated to speak.

"Sarah would never forgive me if I took you into my camp knowing that her God has ordained your marriage to Abraham."

Master Abraham leaned forward, capturing the Hittite's attention. "You were wrong, Zohar, when you said I cared only about livestock. I'm fully focused on obeying my God, and that includes blessing those who have blessed my family—as you have blessed Sarah and Isaac. Though I don't trust you, I can't deny the generosity you've shown my wife and son. When we leave here to dispose of the traitorous healer, I'll make sure my son sends you ample gifts to show our gratitude for the many years you've protected my family in Kiriath Arba. The gifts are but trinkets compared to the blessing my God will give you." Abraham pushed to his feet and grasped Ketty's arm, helping her to stand. He then released Ketty and offered his hand to the Hittite. "My wife and son are the greatest gifts my God has given me, and we all live to please Elohim. It is the way of His covenant bearers."

The Hittite looked as if he'd swallowed his sword sideways. He struggled to his feet, grasped Master Abraham's wrist, and nodded a wordless truce. Master Zohar ushered them out of his tent and assigned two guards to escort them back to Isaac's camp. The sun had risen high enough to peek through the forest by the time they reached the highest hills. Imma and Isaac would be worried about them by now. What would they think when they realized both Master Abraham and Ketty were gone?

"Did you tell anyone you were following me?" she asked.

"I didn't know I was following you." He glanced at her and back at the path without giving away any emotion. "I knew only that I was to walk toward the Hittite camps before dawn. Isaac and I talked until after the moon's zenith, so Sarah's tent was dark when I entered. I didn't realize you weren't on your mat when I went inside to get my staff. The moonlight guided my way on the path. And then you were there, curled on that cloak like a desert fox."

Her throat tightened. "I'm sorry for keeping Dirar's secret, Master Abraham. I thought I could keep everyone safe." She suddenly realized that Dirar had been alone with Imma all morning—when Isaac still trusted him. "I pray Isaac has been watchful and kept Dirar from harming her."

"Humph." His stern features remained. "Though we can try our best to protect those we love, I learned decades ago that Elohim is a far better Protector than I could ever be."

CHAPTER NINETEEN

Now Abraham moved on from there into the region of the Negev and lived between Kadesh and Shur. For a while he stayed in Gerar, and there Abraham said of his wife Sarah, "She is my sister." Then Abimelek king of Gerar sent for Sarah and took her.
—Genesis 20:1–2 (NIV)

"Ketty?" Isaac's hoarse whisper roused Sarah from a fitful sleep. "Ketty, are you ill? Since you were still sleeping, I watched Dirar prepare Imma's tea, but—" His breath caught. Even in the dim light of two small lamps, Sarah recognized his panic. He whirled on Dirar. "Where is she?"

Dirar, carrying a cup of steaming liquid, stepped around him to peer at Ketty's empty mat. "When was the last time you saw her?" His voice was menacing and low.

"She's gone." The words from Sarah's lips were clearer than she'd expected.

"Imma, you're better!" Isaac rushed to her side. Kneeling, he demanded, "What do you mean, Ketty's gone?"

Sarah glanced over his shoulder at Dirar and remembered Ketty's strange comment. *"I must leave Kiriath Arba.... It's the only way to keep Isaac safe."*

"I've brought you more of my special herb." Dirar seemed anxious in the silence, and he hurried to her other side. Kneeling opposite Isaac, he motioned for his master to lift Sarah's shoulders while Dirar supported her head. "Your left side still seems impaired, Mistress, but your speech is intelligible. The herb is working."

"It could be your tea," she said, trying out more words like a new pair of sandals. "Or Elohim Himself has healed me."

He offered a condescending smile while tipping the cup to her lips. Sarah swallowed only a sip before turning her head away. The man cursed when liquid spilled down her chin.

She glowered at him, and he apologized. But her suspicions grew under Dirar's intense gaze.

"Imma, you must drink the tea," Isaac said. "It's obviously helping."

"Please," she said to her son, "I want to speak with you alone."

He sighed and dismissed Dirar with a nod. Before the servant had left the tent, Isaac began chiding her. "You were rude, Imma, to the man who saved your life—more than once. We've never treated our servants that way."

When the tent flap fell closed behind Dirar, she whispered, "Ketty left because you were in danger, and I think Dirar had something to do with it."

Isaac stared at her, his expression blank. "Did he say or do anything inappropriate? Try to harm Ketty in any way?" He glanced around the tent. "Where's Abba?" He'd only then realized Abraham was also gone.

Sarah shook her head, praying silently before she spoke. *Elohim, please soften my son's heart and keep him from doing anything rash.* "Ketty packed a bag right after you and your abba left my tent last night to have your private discussion. I fell asleep to the sound of your arguing and woke late to the sound of silence. Abraham's shoulder bag was also gone by then."

"If Abba has gone to find her, she'll be terrified. She'll fear being punished as an escaped slave, and she'll hide the moment she sees him coming."

Sarah was already shaking her head. "Ketty knows we don't consider her a slav—"

"Ketty knows I can't protect her unless she's in my camp, Imma! If she sees Abba coming after her alone, she'll panic!"

But it was Isaac's voice that betrayed true panic, and Sarah realized that no amount of reassurance would calm him. Isaac could hear only the fear screaming horrible possibilities in his imagination. *Elohim, only Your whisper can speak louder than the lies his tortured thoughts are shouting.*

"Could you sit on my right side," Sarah asked, "and hold my hand?" Grateful for renewed strength—whether from the herb or from the God who created its seed—she lifted her right hand.

Reluctantly, Isaac moved to grasp it, lips pursed into a thin, white line. "I must find them, Imma. I don't want to leave you, but—"

"Then don't leave me." She held his gaze. "You've accused me too often of thinking I must help God when I see His plan unfolding. I challenge you now, Isaac, to let Elohim bring Ketty and your abba home in His time and in His way." Seeing the same indecision on her son's features that she'd often fought, she added, "I've told you many stories about how well Abraham trusted God, but there were times he tried to mask his fear with what appeared to be faith—and I was angry with him as you've been."

"I knew you were angry when we stayed in Kiriath Arba," Isaac said, "but you've never admitted it to me."

"Parents don't speak of their deepest wounds to their children, my son. At least, not until it becomes evident that the experience can bring healing instead of more pain." Isaac kissed her hand and pressed it to his chest, bolstering her courage to release the words she'd held inside for so long. "I've never doubted your abba's great love for me nor his faith in Elohim, but there have been many times I've doubted both Abraham and Elohim. Abraham is human, flawed, so I can question his decisions without questioning his character. But Elohim is God, perfect in both love and justice, so if I question His commands, I also question His character."

Isaac grimaced. "That's not necessarily…" He released a slight sigh. "I'd never considered that Elohim's perfection meant any doubt of His command also cast doubt on His character."

At least he was listening. "In the early years of our marriage, I applied the same principle to both Abraham and Elohim, trusting commands and character equally, my obedience never questioning. Your abba and I shared every secret thought, every revelation from Elohim—until Hagar heard from El Roi in the wilderness. Regardless of whether I changed due to insecurities or your abba's opinion of me declined, we no longer shared our hearts as transparently. Misunderstandings became more prevalent. Suspicion grew between us, and even my suspicion of Elohim's perfection increased. Then the three visitors came to Hebron and promised I'd bear a son from my own body by that exact day the following year. Two of them left, while God remained to tell Abraham of His planned destruction for Sodom and Gomorrah. I listened to your abba negotiate for the pagan city's rescue. *'For the sake of ten, I will not destroy it,'* God said. Yet the next day, fire and sulfur rained down on the plain. The smoke was so intense that we had to leave Hebron and move our whole camp to the coastal plain."

Isaac nodded. "That was the second time Abba told you to say you were his sister, and the Philistine king, Abimelek, took you into his harem."

Sarah's stomach knotted. She'd left out the details of this story when smoothing over her son's anger. Dare she reopen his wound that finally seemed to be healing? "This time it was your abba who told those in Gerar I was his sister—not me. I didn't contradict him, but neither did I affirm the half-truth because..."

Sarah's cheeks warmed. She'd never spoken of womanly things with her son. It was completely inappropriate, but she must tell him in order for him to understand the full weight of the wrong Abraham committed against her—and against Elohim. "On the day the three visitors came and prophesied that a son would come from my body, I laughed because I hadn't bled with the moon courses since we'd lived in Harran. But while Abraham negotiated for Sodom's survival, my womb was revived, Issac. Your abba knew I was fertile when he allowed me to be taken into Abimelek's harem. And I was angry—so very angry—while I waited over two months for Elohim's rescue."

"Over two months?" Isaac's features hardened. "Did Abba just leave you there?"

She gave her son's hand a reassuring squeeze. "No. Both he and Elohim remained very close during those days. On the day I was taken into the harem, all in Abimelek's household were struck with infertility. His wives and concubines miscarried, and the king himself couldn't—well, couldn't couple with his women. When Elohim finally appeared to him in a dream, explaining that Abraham was a prophet and could heal Abimelek and his whole household by praying for them—if the king released me unharmed—Abimelek conferred with his whole household. He even told his servants what had happened, testifying to the great power of Elohim, before chastising Abraham for his duplicity."

Isaac released her hand with a cynical huff. "So that's why Abba has always had a love-hate relationship with the Philistine king and the shepherds surrounding the Beersheba camp. Abimelek gave him that land because he feared Elohim and honored Abba as a prophet, but he still bears ill will because of the deception and pain it brought to his household."

Sarah nodded, hoping her son was seeing her flaws as well as his abba's, and perhaps would even acknowledge his own, exposed by the concept. "Do you see that fear motivates rash decisions that can produce long-lasting consequences? If Elohim hadn't closed all the wombs in Abimelek's household, and the king had taken me to his bed, your lineage might have been in question as Abraham's sole heir." She reached for his hand again, this time pulling it to her chest. "But Elohim intervened. He protected His covenant bearer, both Abraham and the son I would bear nine months later. The experience taught me I must trust Elohim more than your abba. Unfortunately, it also intensified my need to fix situations I thought I could control. In trying to protect you, I insisted your abba send Hagar and Ishmael away. In order to ensure your faith was built on Elohim alone—not on your abba, as mine had been—I insisted we remain in Kiriath Arba after Abraham's Testing."

"*That* was the reason we stayed in Kiriath Arba?" His eyes were as round as the camp's cooking pot. "I thought you feared Abba would try to sacrifice me again."

Perhaps she, too, had been guilty of avoiding difficult conversations. "I was angry when your abba took you to Mount Moriah, Isaac, but it wasn't because he obeyed Elohim's command. It was because he didn't trust me enough to confide in me before he left. I've been angry at Abraham *and* God many times, mostly when I'm forced to do nothing but trust. Like last night—when I couldn't move or speak—and could only watch Ketty walk out of my tent." She forced a one-sided smile. "I was angry when Abraham circumcised you at eight days old. What kind of God mutilates a perfect little boy like mine?"

He rolled his eyes and grinned. "Well, at least now you know I'm not perfect."

They both sobered. "Now, we both know it's best to trust God's goodness *especially* when our fear questions it, for that's the time when faith roots deeper, Son. We must let Elohim bring Ketty and Abraham back to camp. And He will. I know it as surely as your Abba knew he would bring you down from Mount Moriah—alive and well—because I have seen your abba marry Keturah in both a dream and vision."

Surprisingly, he didn't protest but rather bent and kissed her cheek. "I've learned things today I'd never heard before. Thank you, Imma."

Overwhelmed by the love in his eyes, she suddenly felt the weight of exhaustion. "Thank you for listening," she whispered, her eyelids drooping. "Will you stay with me while I sleep?" She sounded like a frightened child, but something about Dirar's presence in camp made her uneasy.

Isaac lay beside her. "I'll be right here, Imma."

CHAPTER TWENTY

*If you, L*ORD*, kept a record of sins,*
*L*ORD*, who could stand?*
But with you there is forgiveness,
so that we can, with reverence, serve you.
—Psalm 130:3–4 (NIV)

Low whispers surrounded Sarah, beckoning her from a sound sleep. Her eyelids felt too heavy to open, so she lay in the land between wakefulness and dreams. Listening to familiar voices. Deep and rumbling. Abraham and Isaac were upset, anxious. One more voice, Ketty's, shrill and trembly.

"Stay with Imma." Isaac was angry. "I'll deal with you after we find Dirar."

"Isaac, I—"

"No, Ketty. I don't want to hear anything else from you."

Isaac's angry words stirred Sarah to wakefulness, but her eyes remained closed, waiting for Ketty to enter. She heard the shuffling footsteps. Then silence. Sniffling. After a deep sigh, soft footsteps approached her mat. The scent of cloves proved Ketty's presence. She often chewed a dried leaf to keep her breath fresh when talking in close proximity with anyone. Further proof of her lingering insecurities. The musky smell of sweat, wet earth, and leaves settled around her. She must have hiked through the forest. Where had she—

"I'd rather confess while you're still asleep," Ketty whispered. "I'm not sure I could endure seeing the same disapproval in your eyes that I saw in Isaac's." Her voice cracked.

Sarah wanted to sit up and pull the girl into her arms but knew she hadn't the strength. If she opened her eyes, would Ketty stop talking? Would Sarah only discover the truth if she continued her ruse?

"Dirar threatened to kill Isaac, you, and Master Abraham if I didn't help him steal this camp," she whispered. "He told me Ephron was behind the plan. I escaped to tell Master Zohar—if not about his son's involvement, at least about Dirar. Master Abraham found me, forced the whole truth, and we discovered Ephron was in Damascus. Dirar had deceived me into betraying those I loved. Master Abraham and Isaac have gone to find him and mete out his punishment. I hope they skin him and roast him over the fire," she hissed.

Sarah's chest constricted, and she struggled to maintain her sleeping facade. It all made sense now. *"I must leave Kiriath Arba.... "It's the only way I can keep Isaac safe."* Ketty would have given up everything familiar to gain Zohar's help. But how had Abraham known where to find her? *Elohim, You guided him, didn't You?*

"Isaac is angry, Imma. Will he forgive me, or have I lost the only brother I've ever had?" More sniffing. "Could any man truly love me? Not as Master Abraham loves you, of course—no man loves like that. Dirar wished to have me but only because I belonged to Isaac. I don't think Elohim made any other man like Isaac or Master Abraham—certainly, none like your husband, who brings a fresh breeze wherever he goes. It's as if the grass stands taller when he arrives and the livestock flex their muscles for his approval. How can he be older than you, Imma, and still ruggedly handsome? Master Abraham has spoken to me directly for only two days, and now I'm questioning everything Isaac has said about him. Master Abraham doesn't seem unfair or unkind. It appears to me that he simply feels no compulsion to justify himself to anyone but Elohim. What freedom that would be."

She released a low groan, and Sarah finally opened her eyes. Ketty had buried her face in her hands. "Even if I believed your dream was from Elohim," she continued, "and I yearned to marry Master Abraham, Isaac would never allow it. Especially now. After what I've done. Maybe I deserve a man like Dirar."

"You will marry Abraham." Sarah's voice brought her daughter's head up, her face a mask of horror.

"Imma! How much did you hear?"

Sarah grinned. "All of it."

"You were awake?"

"If I'd opened my eyes, I would never have heard your heart."

"But..." Ketty's eyes filled with tears, and she started fiddling with her hands. "You heard Dirar's plan and the secret I kept from you?"

"Yes, and that you went to Zohar to offer yourself as his slave in hopes of saving our lives." Sarah stilled Ketty's fidgeting with her right hand. "Isaac is angry because Dirar deceived him, and he's frightened for our safety. When he and Abraham have meted out the traitor's punishment, Isaac will forgive you. You haven't lost his love. He'll always be your brother—and he will allow you to marry Abraham because Elohim has commanded it."

Ketty looked up. "Isaac will never allow me to marry his abba."

For the first time, Sarah heard a measure of grief in the statement rather than triumph. "Their relationship is complicated, I know. Isaac sees only his abba's flaws, but he respects Abraham's faith, and is developing his own strong faith. My husband will obey Elohim, and Isaac will also eventually be convinced. The real question is, Will *you* obey Elohim and choose to marry Abraham?"

Her daughter looked as if Sarah had tossed cold water in her face. "I…it's not…I can't…" She shook her head and pursed her lips, while tears glistened in her eyes.

"Will you refuse to obey then?"

"No, but—"

"But what?"

"But Isaac—"

"I already told you," Sarah said calmly. "Elohim will convince my son, and He already prepared Abraham to obey before my husband arrived in camp. You can't use either of them as an excuse for your reticence. You must take responsibility for your choice. Will you obey or disobey Elohim's command to marry Abraham spoken clearly through my dream?"

Ketty blinked, sending a stream of tears down her cheeks, then wiped them away. Quiet and pensive, she paused before answering, which was good. Sarah didn't want—nor did she expect—a glib answer from the daughter she'd taught to make her word a vow.

When Ketty finally looked up, she straightened her shoulders and lifted her chin. "I—"

Isaac burst into the tent. "Dirar is gone!"

Abraham followed close on his heels. "We've sent messengers into the pastures to see if he's hiding among the livestock, but it's doubtful he's there."

"Since he avoided any real work since the day he arrived." Isaac laced his fingers behind his head. "How could I have been so blind?" With a roar, he lunged for a clay cup and threw it against a tent post.

"You have good aim," his abba commented, lifting a single brow in their son's direction. "You'll throw the first stone when we bring him back for judgment."

Sarah's two men nodded a silent pact, sending a shiver down her spine. Her husband seldom showed his anger, but when he did, it was as frightening as the righteous wrath of God. However, even in vengeance, Elohim would be honored, and their son would learn his role as covenant bearer.

"When do we leave?" Isaac asked.

Abraham glanced at Sarah before answering. "I don't wish to leave you, my love. I couldn't bear it if we were gone when you—" His lips quaked, and he sniffled before turning back to

Isaac. "I don't know. I must seek Elohim's guidance." He hurried from the tent as if chased by a pack of jackals.

Sarah's throat closed around a knot of uncertainty. What if Abraham and Isaac were gone when she died? Her family would have considered it a tragedy if Dirar had killed her with his potions, but what greater agony for her if Dirar stole them away when she needed their reassuring goodbyes.

"Please, Isaac, don't leave me." The words barely squeezed past her surging fear. Her son rushed toward her but hesitated to kneel, glowering at Ketty until she moved to the opposite side. His pettiness cleared Sarah's thoughts and sharpened her tone. "You will treat your sister with respect!" she said. "You have no idea how helpless a woman feels when a man's threats seem insurmountable. Ketty did what she could to protect us."

"She deceived us, Imma." He glared at his sister. "You deceived *me*."

"That's not true." Sarah said before the girl could answer. She used her only working hand to clutch Isaac's forearm. "You listen to me. Ketty didn't deceive anyone. She was *secretive*, and there's a difference. She never lied to us but rather hid the truth in hopes of protecting us. I don't like it any more than you do, but I'm beginning to realize there's a subtle difference in the motivation between the two. Your abba has been secretive in the past, but he's never been deceptive with me or with you, Isaac."

He stared at Sarah, his right eye twitching while it seemed he processed her explanation. "What about Ishmael?" he asked, surprising her. "Was my brother being secretive or deceptive when he gave us Dirar as a gift? Did he keep the slave's herbal skills a secret, or did he place Dirar in Kiriath Arba to steal my camp through his servant's deceptions?"

Ishmael's dark motives hadn't occurred to Sarah. Hagar and Ishmael had seemed so sincere when they'd come to reconcile. Sarah didn't want to believe it, but it would be foolish to ignore Elohim's prophecy about Abraham's firstborn. "As master of Kiriath Arba," she said to Isaac, "you must ask your brother those hard questions—but only after you've calmed down. Ishmael and Hagar came under the banner of peace, so we dare not make sinister assumptions. Though Elohim told Hagar that Ishmael's hand would be against everyone and that he would live in hostility against his brothers, you must gather more facts before you accuse."

She released his forearm and softened her tone. "You've lived most of your life with false conclusions about your abba. I'd hate to see our newly established peace with Hagar and Ishmael shattered by more assumptions that prove untrue. Dirar's herbs were helpful when used correctly. Perhaps he was meant as a true gift—neither secretive nor deceptive."

Isaac brushed Sarah's cheek with a feather-light touch and then looked at his sister. "I still don't approve of what you did, Ketty. You should have come to me right away."

She nodded. "I'm sorry, Isaac."

His features softened. "We'll find Dirar and be done with it." He'd phrased it as a promise, but with both eyebrows raised, it was also a pact awaiting her agreement.

Ketty nodded again. "Yes, brother. Your kindness is beyond what I deserve."

"No, Ketty. It's not. You're my sister, and I would die to protect you."

Ketty peered down at Sarah and forced a smile. "You see, Imma? I need not make a decision." After pushing to her feet, she grabbed the large water jug on her way out. "I'll draw today's water for Imma."

Isaac watched her go and then returned a puzzled gaze to Sarah. "What did she mean about not needing to make a decision?"

"Just something I'd asked her before you came into the tent." She patted his cheek, knowing now wasn't the time to press him further. "Will you find your abba? I need to speak with him—alone."

CHAPTER TWENTY-ONE

When Abram was ninety-nine years old, the Lord appeared to him and said, "I am God Almighty; walk before me faithfully and be blameless."
—Genesis 17:1 (NIV)

Abraham's large frame curled around Sarah, waking her again. Dying certainly required a lot of sleep. "How long have I been sleeping this time?"

"Only the afternoon. It's just past sunset." He nuzzled his soft beard against her cheek and pulled her closer.

"Are you going to tell me what happened between you and Zohar?" She'd begin with what would likely be a confession. Abraham had seldom met with the Hittite chieftain without saying something for which he later needed to apologize.

"Keturah told him her concern about Dirar. He offered Hittite guards to help. We got to the root of the deception and then left."

Sarah pulled away slightly so she could look into his eyes. "It's never that simple between you and Zohar. What are you keeping from me?"

"Why can't it be that simple?" Abraham laughed and snuggled close again. "All right. I also thanked your old friend—and have already sent a significant amount of gold, silver, and livestock—for his many years of kindness to you and Isaac."

Sarah lay in the stillness. "Thank you, Abraham. Zohar has been a good friend but nothing more. Tell me you know that."

"I know." His arms tightened around her. "Do you remember the first time I held you like this? You were so frightened."

"I was frightened? You were just as nervous."

"It's true." She giggled, while his laughter filled the tent and warmed her to the core.

"Milkah couldn't believe Nahor wanted to make her his wife." Sarah turned to face him. "She bore our brother eight sons, Abraham. Eight. It was good for Nahor and Milkah to marry after Haran and Iskah died so tragic—" She shook her head, unable to find the words. Their brother Haran's death—as well as his daughter Iskah's—had been so senseless. Abba's youngest son had hidden his decline into idolatry and bitterness toward Elohim after his wife's death. Worst of all, he'd made all three of his children—Iskah, Milkah, and Lot—complicit in his deception, raising them amid midnight ceremonies of the moon god, Sin. Both he and Iskah had paid for the deception with their lives at the hands of Iskah's bitter lover, and Abba Terah had witnessed it.

"Our family seems prone to deception." Abraham's tone was as flat as the desert plain. "Nahor gave Milkah eight sons, but how many other women's beds had he visited before she discovered his roaming?"

Sensing his mood darkening, Sarah tried to brighten the conversation. "I've heard Milkah's youngest son, Bethuel, is a fine man. He's stepped up to help her manage their estate in Harran."

Abraham offered a grunt. "While Nahor weakens his household by taking a concubine and giving her four sons to fight his heirs for their inheritance."

She turned his face toward hers, demanding he meet her eyes. "Nahor and Milkah have established a life in Harran with children and grandchildren. Bethuel likely has at least one daughter by now who would make a fine wife for Isaac, Abraham. You must set aside your disapproval and bring a wife into our camp for Isaac. He can teach her the ways of Elohim. He's helped me teach Keturah, and his faith is strong, Love. We're not responsible for what has happened in our brother's household since we left Haran, but we did agree to match our son with a wife of Semite blood. Elohim could never intend a Canaanite wife for the covenant bearer."

Abraham pulled her into his arms, resting his chin atop her head. "I'll make sure our son marries a woman from our relatives, I vow it." She felt the muscles in his neck tighten and then heard a quiet gasp. "But I can't imagine my life without you in it."

She nodded against him, feeling the overwhelming finality of death's approach. "I'm frightened," she whispered. "I never thought I'd be frightened."

Her husband sniffed and wiped his face on his shoulder. "We need not fear death, my love. Elohim told me you'd be with Him when you close your eyes in this world, and I'll join you someday."

"It's not the destination I fear, it's the 'getting dead' that's rather daunting." She tipped her head back and grinned. "Don't you think?"

"Getting dead?" Abraham chuckled. "That's a strange way to phrase it, but, yes, I suppose that uncertainty is the most frightening part."

"I love your laughter," she said, laying her head against his chest again. "It's one of the reasons I love you so."

"You've always been able to make me laugh."

"I wish we could hear more laughter from the son who bears that name. I've barely seen him smile since the Testing, you know."

Abraham remained silent.

"It's not your fault. It's something he and Elohim must work out together, Love."

Sarah heard his heartbeat race, and he shifted but didn't loosen his arms around her. "I love you, Sarah. I haven't said it enough—but I've loved you all my life, and I'll love you till I join you in paradise."

"I know—"

"No, let me finish," he said. "You say I stopped trusting you after Elohim visited Hagar, but that isn't true. I've always trusted your love for me, but I needed to guard my growing faith when you began questioning yours. After God spoke to Hagar, your fear that Elohim had blessed your maid over you turned into a bludgeon against my heart. Your disappointment, acted out against me, could easily have weakened my faith, so I stopped sharing my own deep struggles and lessons. Though you continued to rely on me as your safe place—and I still am—I needed to make Elohim my only safe place. It was my only hope of leading the blameless life of faith God required. At the same time, I entrusted you to Elohim, certain He would prove Himself faithful to you—as He repeatedly has done." Abraham paused, but Sarah sensed he had more to say. "After seeing your painful episode," he whispered, "I fear sharing hard things because it could take you away from me."

Sarah lay quietly, listening to Abraham's pounding heart, realizing how much courage it had required for him to say those words. With his heart splayed open before her, she must phrase her response carefully. If she'd had more strength, she would have shown him her repentance in the way only one-flesh lovers could. But words would have to suffice.

"You were my safe place, Husband. It's true. And I'm sorry to have overburdened you with that sole responsibility. No human should bear such a duty alone. Though our years apart have been difficult—" She used all her might to sit up and meet his gaze. "I couldn't have come to know Elohim as I do today in the shadow of your faith in Him. I needed to trust Him for myself—as did our son—learning daily that only He could provide for our physical and emotional needs here in Kiriath Arba. Your faith is so big, my love, so strong. Isaac and I never needed to find faith for ourselves until we lived apart from you." Tears burned her eyes. "It was a sacrifice, yes, as surely as the one you were willing to make on Mount Moriah, but I believe it has been just as pleasing to Elohim."

His tender smile came with a nod of approval. "And the hundreds of people who visited the altar on this hilltop to hear your wisdom would certainly agree." He cupped her cheek with a callused hand, searching her eyes for several heartbeats. A shadow crossed his features before he spoke. "I can't imagine ever loving another, Sarah bat Terah, but I will obey Elohim and marry Keturah if she's willing. It's Isaac I'm most worried about, however. He watches over her like a hen guarding its only chick."

Exhaustion weighed on Sarah at the thought. "Why would Elohim add more thistles and weeds to your relationship when there's already a wall of briars between you two?"

Isaac ducked into the tent, his features drawn in concern. "The messengers returned from pastures. As expected, there have been no sightings of Dirar. The longer we wait to begin the search, the farther he'll get, Abba."

"I don't yet have clear direction from Elohim." Abraham glanced at Sarah and back at their son. "We need to stay with your imma until Elohim gives us liberty to leave her."

Isaac paled and rushed toward her. "Imma, are you weaker? Are you—" His face twisted with emotion. "I can't bear it. I can't lose you."

Sarah leaned over him, resting her arm over his back and her head against his. To comfort, yes, but also because her strength had left her. "Everyone returns to dust," she whispered. "Besides, you'll still have your sheep and Elohim to confide in about your problems." She'd hoped to lighten the mood.

Isaac lifted his head and helped her lie back on her pillows. "That's not funny, Imma."

Would he ever return to the carefree boy he'd once been? "Isaac, your abba and I must discuss something with you before the two of you leave to hunt Dirar. I believe Ketty would be agreeable to marry Abraham if you would allow—"

"No!" He glanced at his abba and back at her. "How can you talk about this now?"

"When else will we speak of it?" she asked. "Please give me the joy of seeing my dream fulfilled before I leave this earth."

The tent flap suddenly opened, and a servant appeared without request or permission. "Masters, Mistress—Keturah has been taken."

Isaac and Abraham bolted to their feet, and Isaac met him in two strides. "What do you mean 'taken'?"

"Some women came running back to camp from the well and said Dirar shot out of the woods, grabbed Ketty, and led her away, both riding donkeys."

"Donkeys?" Abraham turned an accusing glare on Isaac. "Where did he get donkeys? Has Keturah been helping him this whole time?"

"No!" Isaac and Sarah responded together.

The servant added, "Ketty dropped her water jug, my lord. It shattered, and all the water spilled into the dirt. We—servants, my lord—we would never waste a full jug of water."

"She's not a servant," Isaac ranted, then looked at his abba. "But he's right. Ketty would never betray us, Abba. She was secretive about Dirar's plan, but she would never *deceive*. I'm sure he stole the donkeys from our herd or Zohar's."

Fear nearly strangled Sarah. "Both of you, go," she said. "Find Ketty. Take every guard in camp to help."

"Imma, no! We can't leave you—"

Abraham grabbed his son's collar. "We leave now, find Keturah, and bring her home. Elohim will sustain your imma until we return."

"How do you know Imma will be alive when we return?"

Abraham turned to his wife, eyes full of promise. "Because Elohim will allow her to witness my wedding to Keturah."

CHAPTER TWENTY-TWO

*She gave this name to the L*ORD *who spoke to her: "You are the God who sees me," for she said, "I have now seen the One who sees me." That is why the well was called Beer Lahai Roi.*
—Genesis 16:13–14 (NIV)

Dirar had avoided the Central Ridge Road and taken a narrow path that wound farther into the rocky hills, his beast behind Ketty's. He'd prodded both donkeys into a trot with tamarisk branches he'd stripped and bound to use as a whip whenever either animal lagged. Ketty's whole body felt like cream shaken into butter, every muscle taut, head throbbing. But hope soared when she glimpsed several shepherds with a large herd of camels in a valley below.

She drew breath to cry out, but Dirar spoke first. "Those shepherds would pay me plenty of silver for you. They won't be nearly as picky as the slave traders in Egypt, but they'll likely leave you in the desert when they finish with you."

Ketty glanced behind her at Dirar's smug expression but quickly faced forward so she didn't lose her balance and plummet over the edge of the rocky hillside. Dirar's laughter echoed off the rocks at their left, making her cheeks burn.

"Isaac will come for me," she shouted over her shoulder. "He'll kill you."

"You're a fool if you think Isaac or Abraham will leave Mistress Sarah to look for you when the old woman is clearly dying. But—in case I've misjudged their heroics—we'll stay hidden two days. They'll return to Hebron by then."

He was right, and what little hope had surged through Ketty when she'd spotted the shepherds evaporated like morning mist. "How did you know your plot had been discovered?"

"I've made a friend in Zohar's camp who heard everything you said to the chieftain."

"A friend or a paid spy?" Ketty scoffed. "He's not a *friend* if you're paying him to report what he sees."

"*She* will undoubtedly say I promised more than friendship, and her abba will find it more difficult to get a bride price since she's no longer pure. But who knows, Ketty? Maybe I left her with a child. What better payment for keeping me apprised of news from her abba's tent?"

Ketty gasped, turning to glare at him. "You lay with one of Zohar's daughters?"

He shrugged. "I have many skills."

Repulsed, she faced forward. How could any human being be so vile? A slave market suddenly seemed the better option.

"Tomorrow, we'll descend into the eastern valley and begin our trek through the wilderness," Dirar said. "We'll fill the waterskin if we find a spring on our way to the Desert of Paran. I've herded Ishmael's sheep around every slope and cave of that mountainous wasteland. No one will find us there."

A wave of nausea overtook her, and Ketty leaned to the side, heaving only air since she hadn't eaten since yesterday. She wiped her mouth and held fast to the donkey's mane while it maintained the incessant trotting. "We must stop to eat something," she said, suddenly dizzy. "Please, Dirar. I can't keep going at this pace."

"Fine," he growled. "Rein your donkey toward the tamarisk."

She obeyed, tugging gently on the reins toward the spotty shade of a scraggly old tree. The hot sun beat down through sparse branches but gave at least some shelter. Dirar stopped his beast beside hers, opened the flap of one saddlebag, and unwrapped some hard cheese and bread. He broke off a tiny piece of each and handed them to Ketty. "When this is gone, I'll teach you to prepare meals in the desert. Roots, leaves, seeds—they're all good for water and food to sustain us." The wilderness would be Ketty's prison, no need for chains when they both knew she'd die without water and his wits. Dirar's eyes roamed her like a hungry wolf. "You'll grow accustomed to life with me, Ketty."

Life with me? Hard cheese poised at her lips, Ketty realized then—he had no intention of selling her. She stepped back. "Please, Dirar. If you defile me, you'll hate me for it. I'll be nothing but another callus added to your heart."

His features hardened, his brows together. "I already hate you—and everyone else who has everything while I have nothing."

Ketty tried to swallow, but her tongue stuck to roof of her mouth. "If only you would give instead of take."

"Because that worked so well for you?" His cynical laugh was wild with hate. "You gave and gave, but Isaac would have made you his concubine—or worse, left you a slave in his new wife's tent."

"Isaac and Imma gave me love and knowledge," she said. "They gave me Elohim, the only true God."

"They fed you lies!" he shouted. "Where was your Elohim when I took you from the well? You're mine now, Ketty, and I'll either sell you or make you my wife. If I sell you, I'll get enough silver to begin a new life without you. If you try to escape, I'll slit your throat and leave you for the jackals. Do you understand what you're worth to me, woman?" He scoffed. "Very little—but at least Isaac won't have you. Now, be silent and eat!"

He stomped back to the donkeys to retrieve the only waterskin he'd brought, drank deeply, and then handed it to Ketty. There were barely two swallows left. Tipping the waterskin to her lips, she savored the last drops and sniffed back tears to conserve her body's moisture. Their water was gone. They'd ridden more than half the day, but Dirar would no doubt push them until dusk. What would they drink then? Or tomorrow?

Dirar ate half the cheese and bread then rewrapped it and placed it in the saddlebag. He reattached the empty waterskin and mounted his donkey. "We'll reach the Desert of Sin by dark." Ketty mounted her gray donkey with no help from Dirar. At least now he rode ahead of her at a gentler pace, and merciful silence accompanied them till dusk.

Ketty could barely hold her head up. Her legs were numb yet throbbing by the time Dirar led them off the narrow, rocky trail to a cave. Both animals halted, seeming as grateful as their riders for a respite. Ketty leaned forward, relieving pressure off her backside in hopes of regaining feeling in her legs. Her donkey tossed its head, unnerved by Ketty's forward posture.

"Shh, now." Dirar calmed the beast and took its reins from Ketty. She laid her head against the animal's strong neck and, from the corner of her eye, saw Dirar tying both donkeys to a nearby tamarisk tree. He came toward her and gently pulled her off her mount and set her feet on the ground, supporting her waist. "Can you stand?"

"I'm not sure." She tried to step forward, but her legs buckled.

Without warning, he swept her into his arms. "Don't worry," he said, grinning. "You won't have to ride that donkey much longer. We only needed them to speed our initial escape. They'll likely die quickly in the wilderness."

Ketty turned away to hide her revulsion. They would spend tonight on this rocky escarpment, overlooking an endless sea of brown and gray. Rocks and scrub bushes. Hopelessness and death. The Desert of Sin, the first testing ground within the Wilderness of Paran. It was a wasteland few people dared cross and even fewer survived. Dirar kicked a few rocks into the cave to stir any animals that might have claimed it before them. No sounds from inside increased the likelihood of its safety.

He walked a few paces into the dark interior and propped her against the cool rock wall. He turned to go and called over his shoulder, "I'll return with roots and leaves, which will likely be the only moisture we get tonight. That is, unless your God leads me to a spring."

He walked away chuckling, and Ketty's hand clenched an egg-sized rock. If only she could be certain her aim could deliver a lethal blow. She released the rock, letting her head fall back against the cave wall. Despair threatened to swallow her as darkness closed in, and Dirar's words replayed in her mind. *Unless your God leads me to a spring.*

Hadn't Elohim showed Hagar a spring in the wilderness? He was certainly able. Of course, Hagar wasn't completely devoid of human compassion as Dirar was, but she was rebellious against Sarah at the time. *Go back to your mistress and submit to her,* the angel of the Lord had commanded. Surely not the message Hagar had wished to hear. But she'd obeyed, and Elohim had fulfilled every promise He'd made to her in that wilderness—to both her and to Prince Ishmael.

"El Roi," Ketty whispered into the darkness, "You saw a slave woman in the wilderness years ago and showed her mercy. Will You be El Roi to me? Do You see me now?" She wiped a single tear from her cheek, too dehydrated for a proper cry. A rush of gratitude rose within her, pushing aside her fear. With unexplainable certainty, she was confident El Elyon—the God of Heaven and Earth—saw her, even if Isaac, Imma, and Master Abraham didn't know where she was. "You have blessed my life, Elohim, placed me with an imma and brother who loved and protected me. They gave me greater treasure than the spice kings or Egypt's pharaohs possessed. They gave me You, and no matter what happens next, no one can take You from me. Not Dirar. Not slavers. Not even death. You are mine, Elohim, and I am Yours—forever."

With peace settling deep into her bones, she curled onto her side and pillowed her head on her arm. Last night's fitful sleep at the edge of Zohar's camp had caught up with her, and the blackness of the cave encircled her like a lullaby.

Jolted awake by a horrendous shriek, Ketty shot upright. Shouts followed, distant yet close enough to build terror. She stood on aching legs and placed a hand on the cave wall to guide her toward the entrance. A half-moon and brilliant stars lit the night sky and cast eerie shadows through the sparse tamarisk outside the cave. The two donkeys were still tied to the tree, prancing and ears twitching at the disturbance in the wilderness below.

Peering left and right, Ketty whispered, "Dirar?" Could he be hiding somewhere close, keeping watch to protect them? "Dirar, are you there?"

No one answered.

The shouts below gave way to hushed conversation and a low moan. She had to see who was in the wilderness below. Rousing her courage, she crawled from the cave to the edge of the rocky perch. To her left was a gentle slope. About halfway down, she saw a group of men gathered around a heap on the ground. The heap was still moaning when the largest man kicked him. "Where is she?" he shouted.

The moaning ceased. The big man nudged him again. Silence.

A second man pulled an arrow from the dead man, held it up in the moonlight, and studied the fletching. "That's my arrow," he said. "Looks like I'll get the bounty Zohar's offering."

Another man bent, producing another arrow. "This was the kill shot. Look! The fletching bears my mark."

When the two men started shouting, the largest man stepped between them. The moon lit his face, revealing a long, silver-gray beard and intense, dark eyes.

Master Abraham? Before she could cry out, another group of at least ten men joined them. Ketty recognized several of them as Isaac's shepherds. Her throat tightened with emotion. *They came for me.*

"Master!" She croaked as she hobbled to her feet. "Master Abraham, I'm here!"

Every head turned toward the rocky ledge where she stood, but she focused on only one man's features. "Keturah!" Master Abraham shouted and laughed at the same time. "I'm coming, little one!" He rushed up the slope like a mountain goat, leaping from one rocky foothold to the next.

She collapsed to the ground, sobbing, before he reached her.

He knelt, bracing her shoulders. "Are you injured? Did he harm you?"

"No. No, I'm all right."

"Praise be to El Shaddai." He tucked his finger under her chin, gently coaxing her to look up.

She saw her relief mirrored in his glistening eyes. "How did you find us?" she asked. "And travel so quickly? We were on donkeys."

"The donkeys made you easier to track." He brushed hair from her face and tucked it behind her shoulder. "When Zohar discovered what Dirar had done to his youngest daughter, he sent his best shepherds with ours. We're better than donkeys at climbing hills." His low chuckle warmed her. "But our success was entirely due to Elohim. He gave us strength—to rescue my bride."

Ketty's breath caught. "But Isaac won't allow—" She suddenly wondered where he was. "Did he remain in camp with Imma?"

"No, he insisted on searching the main ridge road and led his other trained men in that direction." A sad smile drained his joy. "It's your permission I need, Keturah. Your decision—not Isaac's. Will you be my wife?"

Ketty could almost believe she saw hope in his eyes. "I will, *Abraham*." He smiled at the first time she'd used only his familiar name. "I would be honored to become your wife."

He lifted her hand to his lips and then helped her stand. "Come. We will water the donkeys and travel through the night and reach camp by morning. We'll trust Elohim to deal with my son and bring him home at the proper time." He turned toward the wilderness below, released an ear-piercing whistle, and then shouted to the men below. "Send our fastest messenger to tell Isaac that Dirar is dead and we've found Ketty. There's no time for rest. We must leave now if we're to reach Kiriath Arba before midday."

CHAPTER TWENTY-THREE

*If thieves came to you,
if robbers in the night—
oh, what a disaster awaits you!*
—Obadiah 5 (NIV)

The night had stretched long since Abraham and Isaac left just after midday with all the trained men of their household and Zohar's best guards. Every shepherd from Isaac's camp had taken to the fields to guard the livestock, leaving only women and children in camp—and Sarah alone. After sunset, the cook's young daughter brought her a plate of stew and a small loaf of bread. The girl stared at Sarah, wide-eyed and horrified, from the moment she stepped into the tent. She stumbled over her words and took only three steps toward Sarah's mat before bowing her head in awkward silence.

Hadn't she seen Sarah's decline when she and Zohar sat beneath the oak tree? Or when Abraham carried her back from the altar? Or was her appearance so much worse today than yesterday? Sarah had asked the girl to light one lamp and leave. She'd been too embarrassed to admit she couldn't scoop stew with one hand and too proud to ask a beautiful young girl for help.

Groggy and weak, Sarah slept but fitfully. Never fully asleep or alert, she was uncertain how long she'd lain in silence alone. The rustling of footsteps outside her tent jostled her awake. Had someone found Ketty and returned? The tent flap opened revealing the dark night and a man's form. Unfamiliar. Who—?

The stranger straightened to full height and glanced around her tent. Sarah closed her eyes, pretending to sleep. Peering through slits, she watched the intruder. He rushed directly toward her baskets of clothing and riffled through each one until he found her wooden jewelry box. His low chuckle made her bristle. Some of her gemstones were irreplaceable, cut in Abba Terah's glyptic shop in Ur. "Take all the silver and gold you want," she said, "but leave my abba's gems."

Startled, the man shot to his feet and whirled to face her. Her wedding veil was draped over his hand, its gold chains and gemstones sparkling even in dim light. "I'll take whatever I want, old woman."

"Please." Sarah swallowed the lump in her throat. "Take anything but that. Take all of it—except my wedding veil." How could Elohim's dream be fulfilled if a thief stole the veil she'd seen Ketty wearing for the ceremony?

"You're obviously in no condition to stop me." The man stared down at her with a menacing grin.

"Who do you think you are—to steal from Elohim's covenant bearers?" Sarah tried to sound brave, but her voice trembled.

The man barked out a laugh. "I'm a man who heard Master Zohar ranting that you'd been left alone while your son took all his guards to find a servant girl."

Master Zohar. He was one of Zohar's men. "If you leave now, there will be no curse on your head."

He sobered, which made his approach more frightening. "They say you're a sorceress."

"I'm no sorceress, young man. I serve only Elohim."

"Too bad. I might have left the gemstones for your promise to curse my wife." He scoffed, scanning the length of her. "Unfortunate for you, too, I suppose. The gossips say you were a real beauty. Now, your face is twisted, and you drool like a camel."

Mortified, Sarah turned away. "Get out."

He laughed. "I'll leave after I fill my bag with—" A shofar blast sent him to the tent opening. "It's Zohar!" he said, turning to scan the room. "I must travel quick and light."

"You're a dead man."

"Shut up, old hag." He raced toward Sarah's dagger—a gift from Zohar—that lay on her cosmetics table. Its gem-studded hilt and Hittite blade made it both a fine and valuable weapon. He stuffed her bridal veil into his waist pack, grabbed the dagger, raced to the back of her tent, and cut a slit large enough to climb through. Sarah cried out as her greatest treasure was stolen and Ketty's future with it. She then turned helpless sobs toward the mayhem erupting through her tent's entrance. Men shouted. Women screamed. If it was Zohar, why did her servants sound afraid?

"Everyone stay calm!" a man called out. "We're here to protect, not to harm!"

Finally, footsteps drew near her tent. "Mistress Sarah? Are you safe?"

"Help, Zohar!" she wailed. He rushed inside, and she pointed toward the slit in her back wall. Zohar's eyes widened. He immediately stepped outside, shouted orders to his waiting soldiers. Sarah, near hysteria, feared he would leave her—yet feared he might return and stay with her. What would Abraham think if she and Zohar were alone in her tent?

Her chest tightened, pain stabbing as if the stolen dagger had plunged into her. She tried to calm herself, to breathe deeply, but her right arm began to tingle. Her vision blurred. Her right hand curled into a claw. She tried to look down but couldn't, no longer able to lift a hand or turn her head. What was happening? *Elohim, please don't let me die alone!* The thought sent more pain through her chest. A bestial moan escaped. Then a gurgle. *Elohim, please don't take me yet! I need to see Abraham again!*

"Shh, my friend." Zohar's voice. He leaned into view, his brows drawn together. "I'm here."

Sarah tried to speak again, but only more gurgling came. She closed her eyes, unable to bear Zohar's pity.

"I'm so sorry, Sarah." His words were broken by sobs. She opened her eyes and saw his face in his hands, shoulders shaking. "I should have come sooner, or at least sent my own guards. Why did Isaac and Abraham leave you without protection? I would have expected it of Abraham. He's never protected you. But Isaac. He should have known better." He looked up then and held Sarah's gaze. "Can you understand anything I'm saying?"

She blinked twice—or at least she tried.

"Yes, you can!" His relieved sigh came with a kiss on her forehead.

Sarah inhaled sharply and closed her eyes, startled by his inappropriate gesture.

When she opened her eyes, he was grinning at her. "Forgive me, Mistress Sarah, for that small indiscretion. I was overcome with joy that we could still communicate."

Was she blushing? Perhaps she could at least smile. She tried to curve her lips but wasn't sure if they obeyed. Instead, she blinked twice, hoping he understood she appreciated his friendship—and his presence. Calmer now, the pain in her chest was subsiding even without Dirar's tea. *Thank You, Elohim.*

"I'll make Dirar pay for what he's done to us."

To us? What had Dirar done to Zohar?

Her friend had sobered with his vow, then released a long sigh and grabbed a cushion to settle more comfortably beside her. "Remember my youngest daughter, Timnah, who I'd saved for a treaty marriage with the Amorites? She's a little older—nearly twenty harvests—but she's splendid. She and your Ketty are much alike. Strong and lovely, our daughters know their minds but are judicious with opinions." His features hardened. "Also like Ketty, Timnah was deceived by Dirar. He promised her adventure in faraway lands, and my daughter gave herself to him. That's why I placed the bounty on Dirar's head. My men will find him—and Ketty. They'll kill Dirar and bring your daughter home." He lifted a single bristly brow. "I suppose it's up to you whether you allow Ketty to marry your irresponsible husband."

If Sarah could have ordered him out of the tent, she would have. A weak snort was the best she could manage.

Zohar leaned on one arm and gave her a snide grin. "You always defend him. I suppose he did send me many nice gifts. Lavish, really."

She held his gaze. *Why can't you try to understand Abraham's side of things?* Even if she could speak, would it have been a fair question? Hadn't even she and Isaac neglected the hard work of understanding Abraham? During Sarah's years in Kiriath Arba, she'd spent more time sitting at the hilltop altar helping others with their problems than cleaning out the cobwebs in her own family tent. What efforts had she made to clarify the misperceptions—intentionally or unintentionally—she'd passed along to Zohar and others about her complicated husband? *Oh, Elohim, forgive me.*

"Oh no! Sarah, please don't cry!" Zohar reached for a linen cloth in his belt. "May the gods forgive me, I've made you cry!" He dabbed at the corners of her eyes.

"Old habits are hard to break, and I'm accustomed to criticizing your husband," he said. "I should have also told you that Abraham and I had a very civil conversation when he and Ketty came yesterday morning with word of Dirar's scheming. It was after our positive exchange that he sent the gifts. I believe our relationship is improving, Sarah." He stroked her hair. "You don't have to worry about us when you're gone. I'll watch over Isaac, and I won't antagonize Abraham." He cleared his throat and turned away, patting the linen cloth against his own eyes before tucking it away in his belt.

"Enough of that." He leaned over her. "I'm sure my men will find the wretch who damaged your tent and bring him back here for judgment. I'll take care of all that."

Don't leave me! Panic shot through her. Another gurgle erupted.

"Shh, all right." Zohar cupped her cheek. "Something I said riled you. Are you frightened of the man who came into your tent?"

Sarah closed her eyes. She knew Zohar and his men would deal with the intruder. When she opened them, he was still studying her.

"Do you fear I'll judge him too harshly?"

Again, she closed her eyes, assuring her friend that she trusted him.

"Hmm, what then?" She looked up, and he was combing his beard with his fingers, pondering. Slowly, he turned back to meet her eyes. "You're afraid when I go judge him, I'll leave you alone."

Two blinks affirmed his guess. Before the latest weakening, she feared Abraham's wrath more than she needed Zohar's presence. Not anymore. Surely Abraham would understand. She didn't want to face dying alone. The pain. The uncertainty. Though she knew Elohim was near, she still needed someone with flesh and blood to hold her hand in this life while she met whatever waited beyond.

"Master Zohar!" A shout sounded from outside her tent.

He released her hand and shot to his feet before inviting his guard inside. "Come!"

The short, stout man ducked inside, his eyes only glancing at Sarah before he saluted his master with a fist to his chest. "We've apprehended the culprit and recovered Mistress Sarah's belongings." He untied a pouch at his waist and dropped it into Zohar's hand, then slipped the decorated dagger from his belt and surrendered the second treasure as well. "The scoundrel fought when we tried to bind him. His death was unavoidable, my lord. Please accept our deepest apologies for robbing you of that privilege."

"You're forgiven," Zohar inclined his head. "Well done, Malchus. I want you and the men responsible for finding him to ride back to my encampment. Each one of you may choose one piece of jewelry for your wives and a new dagger for yourselves from my own collection."

Malchus's lips parted, clearly stunned. "You're too generous, my lord. I'm sure the men—and our wives—will be grateful."

Zohar placed his hand on the man's shoulder. "Tell the other guards they're to remain on watch in Isaac's camp until either Abraham or Isaac returns with Mistress Ketty. I'm staying with Mistress Sarah to tend her needs."

"You're tending—" The guard glanced at Sarah again, then lowered his voice so she couldn't hear. But his concern was obvious. Why would the Hittite chieftain demean himself to care for a lowly Hebrew woman? What would their men think? And what if she died while in his care? Would Abraham blame Zohar?

At least, those were the questions raging in Sarah's mind.

Zohar released the man with a pat on his back. "Thank you, Malchus. You're a good man." The guard left, and Zohar returned to Sarah, sitting beside her on the cushion he'd chosen earlier. He set aside the dagger and opened the waist pouch. He reached inside and lifted out her wedding veil by its gold-corded headband. The delicate gold chains hung down, dripping with dozens of gemstones. Each stone etched by Abba's own hand with a Sumerian letter that, when read in order, surrounded the bride with Great-Abba Adam's first words to the Great-Imma: *"You are now bone of my bones and flesh of my flesh."*

"This is exquisite," Zohar said, stretching it between both hands in the dim lamplight. "I can almost picture what you must have looked like wearing this." He looked down at her and tilted his head. "You're crying again, my friend, but this time I'm sure they're happy tears. Was this a necklace or a headband?" He studied it again in the lamplight and then leaned over her, laying the veil across her neck. "How long has it been since you've worn this lovely piece of jewelry? I think you should celebrate its return, but know that you're worth far more than any treasure."

He reached for her withered hand, kissed it, and placed it back at her side. "It's nearly dawn. Let's sleep a little. No one will harm you while my men and I keep watch over Isaac's camp." Though Sarah couldn't turn her head, she glimpsed Zohar busily gathering more pillows to lay between them. He finally settled on the other side of the cushion barrier and snuffed out the single lamp. "Be at peace, my friend. You are safe. Sleep well."

Zohar was a good friend. A good man. She could only hope Abraham would appreciate his help, not feel threatened by a man sleeping beside his wife—no matter how close to death she was.

CHAPTER TWENTY-FOUR

You have made my days a mere handbreadth;
the span of my years is as nothing before you....
But now, Lord, what do I look for? My hope is in you.
—Psalm 39:5, 7 (NIV)

Next Morning - 6th Ajaru (April)

Thankfully, Zohar had left Sarah's humiliating private needs to one of the women in camp. Her complete dependence on others meant a long night of fitful sleep. Not only did her neck seem to be fused, making her head immobile, but she'd also discovered her eyes only moved vertically. Thankfully, she could still blink, so Zohar had instructed the maids that every question must be answerable with a yes or no. Sarah's system of two blinks for yes and a single extended eye-closing as a no worked well and had gotten them through this morning's bath and a midday meal. Zohar himself had insisted on feeding her. She was mortified.

He placed the large wad of broth-soaked cloth in her mouth and pressed her lower jaw closed, squeezing the broth down her throat. "There now," he said and then opened her lower jaw, withdrawing the cloth to dip it back into the bone broth. "This smells good. I might try some." He grinned as he soaked the cloth again and placed it onto her tongue, pressing her jaw closed once more.

Sarah sat propped against a few pillows, shoulders high enough to keep her from choking but low enough to ensure the broth flowed down her throat. Zohar crouched over her in an awkward position for the tedious process, but at least she could see him by glancing straight down with her eyes.

What kind of man did such a thing for a woman—a woman not even his wife?

Zohar's expression changed to worry. "What, Sarah? Are you in pain? Why are tears forming?"

He'd forgotten his own rule of one yes-or-no question at a time. She closed her eyes, hoping to calm him. She heard a frustrated sigh and opened her eyes again.

"I know. One at a time. Are you in pain?"

She closed her eyes and waited.

"Are you afraid?"

She opened and closed them again.

"Then what's wrong?" When she opened her eyes, his brows were taut and lifted in concern.

She wished there was a way to reassure him. How could she ever repay his sacrifice? This sort of…love. Not romantic or tainted but rather pure and humble. Surely, when Abraham returned to find his longtime rival at Sarah's bedside, he would let gratitude untangle all the other emotions that might first erupt. The camp women's ululating signaled Abraham's arrival as if her thought had conjured him. *Oh, Zohar, please don't antagonize my husband. He'll already be weary and anxious.*

Zohar set aside the bone broth. "Does that mean someone has returned home?"

Sarah blinked twice.

"Isaac?"

She closed her eyes, wishing the women from camp would show the same excitement for her son as they did for the great Bedouin prince.

"Abraham then." The finality in his tone needed no affirmation. When she opened her eyes, Zohar was studying the wedding veil he'd laid across her neck. He'd placed it there after the maids bathed and dressed her in a fresh robe. Now, he slid his finger along its gold braiding, then brushed her cheek. "I fear this may be the last time I see you, so I'll say goodbye. You're a woman unlike any other, Sarah. I hope I've loved you well, my friend." He leaned up and kissed her forehead.

"Get away from my wife!" Abraham lunged toward Zohar, grabbing his robe, and dragged him out of Sarah's view.

Her husband's rage was a terrifying beast he kept carefully caged. She could do nothing to warn Zohar. Nothing to calm Abraham. Only listen while her husband panted in barely controlled fury.

Hurried footsteps shuffled into the tent. "Master, please!" Ketty said. "The maids just told me that Master Zohar saved Imma from an intruder and protected the camp while you and Isaac were gone. Please, Abraham, he's done so much to help."

"I saw what he's been doing." Abraham's accusation stung. "Sarah, how could you wear your wedding veil while another man seduced you?"

She closed her eyes, his words like a blow, while listening helplessly to more scuffling of sandals. *Please, Elohim, don't let them harm each other.* Stillness finally settled, and she opened her eyes. Trying to look right, she was still unable to see any of the three.

"You didn't even notice your wife can no longer move or speak." Zohar's tone was acrid. "While you and Isaac left Sarah completely unguarded, a thief came into her tent and stole her wedding veil. I placed it across her neck so she could celebrate its return when my guards recovered it. They've stayed to protect this camp while I've remained with your wife to calm and reassure her." He paused, then added. "I promised not to leave Sarah alone as her husband and son did."

"You're a manipulative snake!" Abraham roared.

"Stop!" Ketty's voice strained as if lifting something heavy. *Or holding two butting rams apart.*

Ketty heaved a sigh and said, "Abraham, please consider Master Zohar's kindness. He's protected this camp, apprehended a thief, and retrieved Imma's most-treasured jewelry."

When had Ketty started calling her master *Abraham?* She always used his formal title.

"I am grateful, Zohar," Abraham mumbled.

The Hittite's cynical huff was barely audible.

"Master Zohar," Ketty continued, "have you considered how difficult it was for Abraham and Isaac to leave Imma? Knowing she was seriously ill, they trusted Elohim to sustain her until they rescued me."

"Zohar has no idea," Abraham interrupted before Zohar could answer. "His gods are incapable of anything beyond human ability because they're made by human hands."

"My gods trust me to act on their behalf," Zohar said. "The same as your Elohim. The difference between you and me, Abraham, is that I don't use my gods to justify my selfishness and insecurity."

Another pause, and Sarah held her breath. *Please don't let Abraham unleash his fury, Elohim.*

"Leave." Abraham gritted out the word.

"I'll leave, but you're the reason I'll continue to protect Isaac when Sarah is gone." Shuffling of footsteps and the tent flap's shuddering proved Zohar had gone. Sarah mourned that her last memory of his voice would be an angry one.

"How can you be so tender and good in one moment," Ketty asked, "and so stubborn and blind in the next?" Her voice was small, wobbly, more like the daughter Sarah knew.

"I'm a flawed man, Keturah, like any other." Abraham's heavy footsteps rushed toward Sarah, but he stopped short of her line of sight. "Do you think she can hear—" His final word broke. He cleared his throat but remained silent. "I can't bear to see the wedding veil lying on her incorrectly. Take it away, Keturah."

"No, Abraham, I will not." Swift steps matched Ketty's terse tone, and Sarah glimpsed her daughter's back like a shield between Abraham and his wife. How had Ketty's new confidence found wings? "I'm beginning to think Zohar was right," the girl said. "Imma's hopes for my future led her to unselfishly obey Elohim's dream, regardless of damage to relationships or the fact that a younger wife might someday give her husband children. Have you ever considered all that Imma and Isaac overcame in Kiriath Arba during these years of separation while you remained in Beersheba?"

"I made sure they had everything they need—"

"They didn't have *you*."

"I was too angry to…" His words trailed into a long sigh.

"To what?" Ketty pressed. When silence drew out, she ended it with, "You were so focused on your jealousy of Master Zohar that you limited your visits to twice a year—hoping to avoid the hard work of repairing relationships."

"You know nothing about my relationships with Sarah and Isaac."

"I know them better than you do."

Abraham's breath hitched, and a familiar, painful sound followed. Sarah's husband walked away again. Out of the tent. Away from a life-altering conversation. The only question was, Had Ketty pushed him hard enough to send him all the way back to Beersheba—as Sarah had done after the Testing?

Elohim, please no!

All was silent except Ketty's quiet sniffs, and she finally settled beside Sarah's mat. If only they could fix this together. But Sarah couldn't help, and Abraham was gone. Only Elohim knew if he'd return, and only Elohim could mend the wounds, old and new.

"After the way he cared for me at Master Zohar's camp yesterday, the way he defended me to Isaac, and the relief on his face when he found me at the cave, I thought Elohim had actually moved Abraham's heart to love me. Or at least become fond of me." She sniffed again, and this time Sarah glimpsed a cloth in her periphery and knew Ketty was drying her tears. "It's no longer a question of whether Abraham would marry me, Imma, because I refuse to marry a man who can't—or won't—talk with me. I suppose Isaac spoiled me in that regard. I expect a man to at least try to convey his feelings as Isaac always has, even if he merely admits his inability to do so." Ketty continued sniffing while Sarah pondered the miraculous transformation.

Her daughter had spoken like a free woman—an equal—more boldly than she'd ever spoken before. It was the most beautiful thing Sarah had ever heard. What had caused her to finally realize her worth? She was a different woman than the daughter who had hastily packed her shoulder bag and run from the tent two nights ago, feeling as though she had no other options. Questions burned within, but because Ketty sat too far to her right, she could barely catch glimpses of her. Using her best hope of communication, Sarah began frantically moving her eyes up and down, up and down.

"Imma, what's wrong? What's happening?" Ketty leaned over her, face-to-face.

Sarah blinked twice. *Yes, stay here and talk to me.*

"What are you trying to say?" Ketty resumed her place on the cushion, and Sarah repeated the frantic call for her attention until the bright girl understood.

While hovering over Sarah, Ketty's expression lit with understanding. "Is this what Master Zohar was doing when Abraham first arrived in your tent?"

Sarah blinked twice, marveling again that she'd used Abraham's name with such familiarity.

Ketty's compassionate smile was like a balm to Sarah's soul. "Master Zohar was saying goodbye, wasn't he? Directly in front of your face." Two blinks again, then her eyes slid shut. "I'm sorry his departure was marred with unkindness between him and Abraham."

Sarah felt Ketty's comfort to the marrow of her bones. Now, how could she get the girl to tell her about Dirar? About the rescue? Sarah squeezed her eyes tightly closed and opened them wide, then repeated the motion several times.

"I can see you're adamant about something, but what?" Ketty forced a weary smile. "I praise Elohim for preserving you until we returned." She cradled Sarah's withered hand and pulled it to her chest. Then she leaned over so Sarah could look into her eyes as she spoke. "Abraham said they followed the donkey's tracks to find us, but Isaac took his men down the Ridge Road toward the Coastal Plain, so we don't know when they'll return. Master Zohar's archers killed Dirar and will collect the bounty for his daughter's dishonor."

Sarah blinked twice, affirming she understood, but what about Ketty and Abraham?

Her precious daughter held her gaze, eyes filling with moisture. "A week ago, I met Mistress Hagar, a woman who bore Abraham a child and was exiled to raise Ishmael alone. I know Elohim blessed them because they're an extension of Abraham's family. I wanted to believe your dream could be true, Imma, that I could also have children blessed as an extension of Abraham's family." She shook her head, eyes filling again. "But now I don't feel the same peace to marry him that I felt on our way home from the desert. The rage I saw in his eyes a few moments ago frightened me. I have few memories of my abba, but his anger is still vivid in my mind. I'd never seen Abraham so angry."

Sarah blinked twice, hoping she'd understand the meaning. *Abraham has learned—with Elohim's aid—to control his rage.* In that moment, Sarah realized with astounding clarity: *Abraham leaves to protect us from himself!* But how could she communicate it to Ketty?

The girl was fiddling with her hands. "All these years, he never once spoke my name, and now, within four days of hearing him say *Keturah*, my heart awakened to emotions it's never felt before. I'm afraid marrying him would be handing him the power to hurt me more than anyone else in my life." She pulled the soggy white cloth from her belt and dabbed at her cheeks. "When he refused to answer my questions and walked away, I felt—" Her voice broke. "He fought five armies with 318 men, yet he doesn't have the courage to fight for the hearts of those he loves." She shook her head and retreated from Sarah's view.

Frustration filled Sarah like new wine in an old wineskin until she thought she might pop. Indistinct sounds made the waiting even more impossible.

Finally, Ketty called out from a distance. "I'll remain with you until your last breath, Imma, and then I'll ask Master Zohar to let me serve somewhere in his camp. I'm sure he'll allow it if Isaac agrees—and Isaac will agree when I tell him how near I came to marrying his abba."

No, Ketty! Please! Sarah closed her eyes and gurgled, but the sound of retreating footsteps proved her daughter was leaving and hadn't seen the protest.

"I'll brew a cup of tea," Ketty said, "with the last of Dirar's special herb. Perhaps it will help restore you." The tent flap shuddered and then fell silent, Sarah's hopes with it.

CHAPTER TWENTY-FIVE

I remembered you, God, and I groaned....
You kept my eyes from closing;
I was too troubled to speak.
I thought about the former days,
the years of long ago....
My heart meditated and my spirit asked:
"Will the Lord reject forever?...
Has his promise failed for all time?"
—Psalm 77:3–8 (NIV)

Sarah's tent might as well have been a burial cave. She was already dead. Already alone. Helpless. Panic roiled in her belly. She could neither move nor cry out. A prisoner inside her own body. The horror was greater than any nightmare. Closing her eyes again, she tried to stave off the madness seeking to claim her.

Forcing her thoughts toward others, she wondered if Isaac would make it home before she died? *Home.* Would her son still call Kiriath Arba home after she died? *Elohim, what if Ketty refuses to marry Abraham—ever?* What if Abraham was already on his way back to Beersheba? No, he wouldn't leave without saying goodbye to Sarah. Would he? What if he'd changed his mind about her dream and now believed it only another of her emotional imaginings? But Elohim had confirmed the command to Abraham before he arrived. Her husband would obey. He would find a way to convince Ketty—and Isaac—after Sarah died.

Unless... What if her dream wasn't really from Elohim, and Abraham had simply played along to keep from upsetting her? Her eyes shot open, the thought too painful, like a dagger twisting in her chest. Hagar's face danced in her mind, not as she looked a few days ago, but radiant with Elohim's blessing—as she'd been the day she returned from her encounter in the wilderness. If Sarah's dream had been merely that—a dream—she would die without a personal encounter with the Most High God. Whenever she'd bemoaned the fact, Abraham had reminded her of that day the three visitors came to tell him that Sarah would bear his son exactly a year from that date. She'd remained in the tent and laughed at the preposterous prophecy—and been scolded. It hadn't been anything like Hagar's loving and reassuring encounter with the God Who Sees.

Her chest tightened even more, but she couldn't even wince. Like a dead fish on the shore, she could only gasp for breath and wait for death. Would she encounter Elohim today—in the afterlife? Of course, there would be no legends or wells named after the encounter—as had happened with Hagar's encounter—but the thought of finally meeting Elohim face-to-face was some comfort. Would He mind that she wore no cosmetics? She would have grinned at the thought if she could. Silly, to be sure, but perhaps no sillier than the importance she'd placed on such things while living all these years on earth. Why hadn't she spent more time reconciling with Abraham? More time urging him to reconcile with their son? Would she ever see either of them again? Would she see them in eternity?

Her throat tightened as the next thought formed. *Is eternity even real, or does Elohim exist only to comfort the living?*

She squeezed her eyes shut, and her spirit cried out, *Please, Elohim, come to me as You did to Hagar at Beer Lahai Roi!* For more than twenty winters, Isaac, Ketty, and Sarah had moved their whole camp from Kiriath Arba to the spring in the desert that Hagar named The Well of the God Who Sees. Each of them had high hopes for a divine sighting, but Elohim had never personally appeared to them in the desert or the hills.

Has my whole life been a lie, Elohim? Are You even real?

Silence met her plea and sent gooseflesh skittering over her whole body. *What if there is nothing waiting on the other side of death?* Swallowing hard, Sarah tried to keep fear from escalating to panic.

Where was Ketty? Why hadn't she returned with the tea? Only Zohar had seemed to understand Sarah's need to have someone close while she awaited her last breath. The awful memories of her imma's death flashed through her mind. Imma had thrashed and fought, fear and pagan practices tormenting her last moments with doubt and regret. Though her ethereal beauty hadn't been removed as Sarah's had, Imma's death mask became a frozen, twisted shriek, ugly and tortured.

Why had she wrestled with such fear when her divine beauty was an obvious gift from the one true God?

She served pagan gods with that beauty till the end.

The answer came quick and sure with a certainty beyond Sarah's reasoning. She remembered the same assurance after dreaming about Abraham and Ketty's wedding ceremony. This *knowing* wasn't something she'd conjured herself. It was a gift. Elohim had truly spoken—in the dream and about Imma's death. And she was certain His words about Imma held deep significance for her current struggle. What about Imma's fear and lingering beauty was instructive for Sarah's fear right now?

She waited, alert for another inner whisper from Elohim. None came. However, rather than doubting again, her thoughts reeled and shoved fear aside. Sarah had secretly succumbed to Imma's request and brought the pagan priest to her bedside. Her fear spiked after the priest left. He'd been the last person, besides Sarah, to see her alive. Swallowing down her lifelong guilt, Sarah remembered her pagan friend, Zohar, was the only one who had understood her angst at being alone. Had he perhaps witnessed deaths similar to Imma's—perhaps his wife's—who had been overwhelmed by fear in their final moments?

Sarah thought back to Abba Terah's death and remembered his final moments were entirely different than Imma's. He'd recited Elohim's eternal assurances, closed his eyes, and breathed out a long, slow breath. A palpable sense of peace had filled their domed mud house in Harran. It was a reverent moment. Though saddened by the finality of his earthly departure, Sarah felt no fear when his body no longer held the spark of life that was—well, uniquely Abba Terah. Abraham had hired mourners. He and Sarah grieved with Nahor, Milkah, Lot, and the rest of their family, but Sarah hadn't felt the hopelessness she remembered while grieving for Imma—or her brother Haran and his daughter, Iskah.

Perhaps Sarah's Imma and Zohar feared death because when standing at the yawning chasm of eternity—either as Imma did personally or Zohar with the wife he loved—they realized the pagan legends couldn't be true. The legends sprang up like weeds after Elohim scattered the tribes from the Tower of Babel. Countless tribes had settled for a definitive explanation about the afterlife—no matter how ridiculous—because it provided a visible idol and pleasurable worship. But the priest blathering about the goddess Inana at Imma's deathbed proved as reliable as grasping smoke. She'd needed truth. She'd needed Elohim.

Every afterlife legend—told from Ur to Harran to Egypt and all the lands Abraham and Sarah had traversed—were utterly fantastical. As Sarah thought through them one by one, she marveled at how much more faith each of them required than simply trusting that one God formed all the heavens and earth and waited to judge each soul in eternity. And to believe nothing waited beyond earthly existence when *something* must have created it was just as implausible.

Wait. Had she just reasoned out her own answer? *Elohim, are You real and waiting to greet me when I exhale my last breath on this earth?* Without hesitation she knew. Grinning inwardly, she blinked twice and shouted with her whole heart, *Yes, Elohim! I believe You!*

Realizing then that the pain and pressure in her chest were gone, she offered even more praise. How gracious her God had been to give her days to prepare for death. His preparations hadn't been for a single encounter but rather for the greater gift of eternity in His presence. What sort of glory was she about to experience? Though she didn't know exactly how eternity looked or the road to find it, she knew the Creator who would lead her there. Fear could no longer steal her joy. *Oh, Elohim Adonai, my Shepherd and Shield, I need only You to witness my last breath and beckon me into whatever afterlife You have waiting.* A gurgle erupted, and she undoubtedly drooled with it, but she gave it little thought. The Maker of the Universe had her full attention, and she had His.

Elohim had brought her into this place of revelation. Every moment since her physical beauty had fled was meant to benefit those she would leave behind. However, she no longer felt the need to go charging forward with her own plan like a brute beast, making its own way no matter who was trampled. Because her dream had most certainly been from Elohim, her sovereign God would find a way to bring Abraham and Ketty together in marriage. He would bless Ketty's children with favor, and Isaac would somehow find peace with their future. Reconciliation between the three was entirely left to their willingness to yield to Elohim's best for them.

A wave of peace washed over her like a cleansing flood. Why had she allowed fear, stubbornness, and her own selfish desires to bind her in a shroud for so much of her life? *Oh, Elohim, how frustrating I must have been—still struggling at 127 with the same issues I'd been fighting since I was a little girl!* Another gurgle, this one at the joyous release from her lifelong slavery to control. She wished she could have shared her new freedom with Abraham, Isaac, and Ketty. But celebrating it with her Deliverer was thrilling beyond compare.

El Roi, You see me! The realization stripped away decades of envy and the nagging insecurity that Abraham had respected Hagar's faith more than Sarah's. Elohim's presence surrounded her, filled her, consumed her. Eyelids heavy, she closed her eyes in the first real peace she'd felt since awaking four days ago to realize she was dying. *Take me anytime, Elohim. I am Yours forever.*

CHAPTER TWENTY-SIX

*A hot-tempered person stirs up conflict,
but the one who is patient calms a quarrel.*
—Proverbs 15:18 (NIV)

When Ketty left Imma's tent, she noted a huddle of maids gathered near the central fire, heads bent in whispers. Upon her approach, one of the women elbowed another, and they scattered like dust in sirocco winds. Too worried about Imma to wonder about gossip, Ketty ignored Cook, the only woman still at the fire. She reached for a clay cup to steep Imma's tea.

"Master Abraham rushed after the Hittite on his own," the woman announced. "We'd better pray he calms before he speaks to the chieftain, or the whole camp may join Mistress Sarah in paradise."

"What do you mean?" Ketty's hand stilled on a small pouch of herbs Dirar left behind. "Master Zohar and his men would never harm anyone in this camp."

She leveled her gaze at Ketty. "Men will do anything when seeking retribution."

"Retribution?" Ketty continued her tea preparation. As the camp's gossip hub, Cook tended toward exaggeration. "Master Abraham would never do anything to put this camp in danger."

The old woman huffed and handed Ketty the ladle. "I began cooking for Mistress Sarah when I was a girl in Harran, and I've witnessed Master Abraham's anger only twice. Once in Harran, when he discovered his brother had been with a prostitute in a pagan temple. The second time was when the Semite armies took his nephew, Lot, captive. His rage fueled the trained men of our househould—just 318 of them—to defeat five armies. The master's anger is a frightful thing, Ketty." She scraped chopped vegetables into the stew pot hanging over the fire and then pointed her knife toward the path leading to the Hittite camps. "If he's on his way to wreak the same kind of havoc on the Hittites, he'll bring down destruction on all our heads. Master Abraham is strong as a bull and a skilled fighter, but a rampage like I saw in Harran would destroy Master Isaac's alliance with Master Zohar. Mark my words, girl. The Hittites would eventually overpower Master Abraham and then come for us as retribution."

Ketty realized her hand had squeezed tighter around the clay cup as Cook prophesied their doom. "That's absurd," she said, demanding it to be so. But was it absurd? She set the cup on the ground so she could add a pinch of the special herb. Ketty had never seen Abraham truly angry until moments ago in Imma's tent when he'd barely bridled a trembling rage. She'd felt a stab of recognition, having lived with her abba's unpredictable outbursts for her first nine years of life. "How could Abraham have hidden his anger so long?" she wondered—then realized she'd spoken aloud.

"Why do you think we only see him twice a year?" Cook waved her hand as if trying to wipe away all she'd just revealed.

"Master Abraham is a good man. A great prince. He's Elohim's covenant bearer and has brought great blessing to many. But he is also a flawed man like any other, Ketty, so I'm telling you—" She chewed on her bottom lip, her eyes widening.

"What?"

"If you hold any sway over the master—if you could calm him—you must go to Master Zohar's camp and try to assuage both men's anger. The future of Kiriath Arba may rest on your shoulders."

Ketty exhaled sharply, dipping the ladle into the steaming water over the fire. What a ludicrous notion. The old woman was exaggerating again—or might the camp truly be in danger? *It can't be as bad as she claims.* Isaac had complained about his abba all their lives, but he'd never mentioned angry outbursts or frightening rage. As she emptied the steamy water over the herbs, the bitter, offensive odor reminded her of Dirar. "Has anyone heard from Isaac?" she asked, hoping to stall her decision. Why must she chase Abraham and Master Zohar into the forest?

"We've heard nothing, Ketty. There's no time to wait on Master Isaac."

She gripped the cup and bolted to her feet, spilling the burning liquid on her hand.

With Ketty's sharp inhale, Cook took the cup from her and cradled the pained hand. "Let me see." She examined it and patted it gently. "I think you'll be all right, but Master Abraham won't be unless you go to Master Zohar's camp. Please, Ketty. You must do it for us all."

With an inward groan, Ketty nodded. "I'll do it, but you must take care of Imma while I'm away. Give her the tea, and stay with her, Cook. Promise me." The thought of leaving Imma again nearly made her ill.

"I promise. Now go!" Cook nudged her away, grabbed the steaming cup of tea, and started toward Imma's tent.

Ketty hurried toward the forest before she changed her mind. The path she'd taken only two days ago was wider now and more clearly marked since the Hittites had tromped between Kiriath Arba and their camps for the past two days.

"Mistress Ketty."

She turned to face two of Isaac's shepherds rushing to catch up. "Mistress?" she scoffed. "You used to shoot me with pebbles from your slingshots when I brought messages to Isaac in the fields. When did I become *Mistress* Ketty?"

"Since we heard Master Abraham speak to you about becoming his wife," one of them said. They'd been part of the company that saved her.

The other one elbowed his partner, and both men bowed to one knee. "It's not proper for you to wander the forest alone, Mistress. We'd consider it an honor to protect Master Abraham's bride."

What could two shepherds do if Abraham flew into the kind of rage Cook described and started killing Hittite guards—or their chieftain? But she was touched by the shepherds' care and grateful for the company. "Thank you," she said and continued into the woods. The shepherds followed, letting her set the pace. Since she'd ridden the donkey part of the way home, her legs felt strong, and she was surprised at how much quicker she traveled in daylight than when she'd snuck through the woods alone at night. The day grew warmer as the sun rose overhead, and they traveled in silence, which allowed Ketty's thoughts to wander.

Long-buried memories emerged with the terror of a little girl hearing her name in a wild shriek from her abba's lips. *"Keturaaaahhhh!"* Even then, barely old enough to run, she'd known enough to hide. Others in their village also recognized Abba's temper and kept their distance. Only one old woman allowed Ketty to hide inside her thatched hut and gave her dried lentils to suck on while waiting for Abba's fury to pass. Ketty groaned at the raw memory and stopped, wiped both hands down her face.

"Are you well, Mistress?" one shepherd asked. The other offered his waterskin without a word. She took a quick gulp, passed it back, and resumed her hurried pace. The sooner they arrived at the Hittite camps, the sooner she could propose a reasonable solution to two rational men.

But memories of her abba's raging washed over her as if floodgates had been opened and nothing could shut them. The idea that Abraham could be capable of the same rage was impossible. Ketty couldn't reconcile that the kind and brave man who had followed her to Zohar's camp, then bravely rescued her from Dirar, was anything like the heartless abba who devolved into savagery when he became angry. Yet she couldn't deny a terrifying change in Abraham when he'd argued with Zohar in Imma's tent. He'd trembled from head to toe, and his eyes took on a wild glint—very much like the memories of an abba she'd successfully buried all these years.

"*He's a flawed man like any other,*" Cook had said, but she'd also pointed out that he only visited twice a year. When Ketty challenged him, he'd left. She'd accused him of staying away because of his selfishness and jealousy, challenging him to the point that he walked away. Hands clenched. Face the color of ripened grapes. Perhaps it wasn't selfishness that kept him away but rather concern that he couldn't control his anger if he lived too close to a man who picked at his rage like a child picks at a loose thread that then unravels the whole garment. Perhaps Abraham had stayed away so he didn't unravel the garment Isaac had been creating at Kiriath Arba.

Ketty began pondering the two incidents of Abraham's fury Cook had described and noted his righteous cause in each. Without more facts, she couldn't know if he'd sinned against God or man in his anger, but at least his anger had been rooted in the defense of Elohim and His ways. Ketty's stooped shoulders straightened, and her weary legs felt strengthened by the truth. Abraham was flawed, yes, but his flaws were bathed in a righteous zeal for the one true God that consumed his every decision. It had cost him dearly—in ways she could likely never fathom—but Abraham was not her abba.

Her legs now churned with new hope and purpose. Cook's warning was valid. Abraham's anger had been real. He'd seen a pagan chieftain—a man he'd suspected for years of trying to steal Sarah's heart—lying beside his helpless wife. His righteous indignation would be stirred to the core, and Ketty had no idea what the strong, skilled shepherd might do. *Elohim, I know Abraham will obey You. You're already with him. Speak Your command to Abraham, and he will obey.*

Finally, Ketty saw the outskirts of the first Hittite camp in the distance. Her thighs burned, and she wasn't sure she could walk another step. There was no sign of Abraham. She halted, bending to rest her hands on her knees and catch her breath. The two shepherds did the same. The sun had passed midday. Ketty hadn't slept since before Dirar took her captive yesterday morning.

"You should eat, Mistress, before we meet the guards." One of the shepherds gave her a piece of hard cheese. She nodded her thanks.

When all three finished their snack, she started toward the Hittite guards who were making their rounds. One of them raised a brow, seeming to recognize her from her last visit. "I doubt our chieftain will be inclined to see another Hebrew after he deals with Prince Abraham."

"I assure you," Ketty said, never breaking stride, "Master Zohar will wish to see me *while* he deals with Prince Abraham."

"Wait, I didn't—"

"My guards can accompany me to Master Zohar's encampment," Ketty shouted over her shoulder. "I remember the way." Her shepherds remained close at her right and left. None of them looked back, but Ketty heard both men release a sigh when they continued without additional footsteps behind them.

"You've never acted like the other slaves," one of the shepherds whispered. She turned her head, expecting a wry smile but seeing instead a look of respect on his features. "It came as no surprise when we heard both Mistress Sarah and Master Abraham had received word that Elohim had ordained your marriage to the great prince."

Ketty opened her mouth to reply, but she had no words. She pursed her lips and kept walking. *No surprise?* She nearly laughed aloud. Where had they been for the past four days? Hurrying through another camp and the king's pasture, they finally reached the king's encampment and approached the large, central tent. The chieftain's guards stood at their usual positions. Calm. All was quiet. No mayhem as Cook had predicted. *Thank You, Elohim.*

Feigning confidence, Ketty stopped only three paces from the tent's entrance and Zohar's guards. "I'll leave my men outside while I speak with my betrothed and your chieftain." Without awaiting comment or permission, she strode forward—and they opened the tent flap for her.

She ducked inside and straightened, finding both men standing, legs shoulder-width apart as if ready for battle. Facing each other, they were deep in a quiet conversation. Abraham faced the Hittite, his back to Ketty, so it was Master Zohar who glimpsed her over his visitor's shoulder.

"Look who else has come to force your God down my throat," he said, nodding toward her.

Abraham turned, his features a mixture of joy and pain when he saw her. "I came to apologize—sincerely—to Zohar and ask him to return to camp. I offered to let him stay in your tent since it's empty. I'm sure Sarah will appreciate having her friend close by during her last days. Zohar will have the privacy of his own tent and can come and go as he pleases."

"And…," Zohar coaxed, raising both bushy eyebrows.

"*And*," Abraham snapped, "we haven't come to an agreement on the second subject."

Zohar stepped around him. "If Isaac doesn't arrive back in time, Abraham wants me to speak some ancient blessing over the two of you at the wedding ceremony."

Ketty shot a surprised glance at Abraham. "You still wish to marry me?"

"I will always obey Elohim." His earnest answer pierced her. *Even if I don't want to.* Was that what he meant to say? "And you, Ketty?" he asked, taking a step toward her. "Sarah's dream hasn't changed, nor has the confirmation I received from Elohim. Will you obey Him and marry a man more than four times your age and more stubborn than a wild donkey?"

Master Zohar held a hand to his lips and whispered, "Run, girl. It's our only hope." Then he rolled his eyes at Abraham. "He won't allow me to speak your wedding blessing unless I renounce my gods and embrace only Elohim. Pfsssht. He walked into my tent, apologized for offending me, and then offended me again." He crossed his arms like a pouting child.

Ketty grinned at them both then focused on Master Zohar. "I assure you, Abraham meant no offense. In fact, the honor of speaking the wedding blessing is the greatest privilege that can be bestowed among our people. It is the seedbed of Creation's truth, and I would very much like to hear the blessing from your lips at my wedding." She glanced shyly at Abraham and thought she glimpsed pleasure on his stoic features. Turning back to Zohar, she added, "Besides, to know you've embraced Elohim as your God would be the greatest gift you've ever given Imma."

CHAPTER TWENTY-SEVEN

*May your fountain be blessed,
and may you rejoice in the wife of your youth.*
—Proverbs 5:18 (NIV)

Evening, Same Day

"Imma?"

Sarah felt someone shaking her.

"Imma, please. Open your eyes. Please, I can't lose you yet."

A wave of disappointment washed over Sarah at the realization that she remained on earth, but she needed to comfort her daughter. She channeled considerable strength to her eyelids, forcing them to open. She was rewarded with Ketty's palpable relief and sweet smile.

"You were sleeping so soundly. Are you all right?" Without even waiting for two affirmative blinks, Ketty covered Sarah with a ferocious hug. Sarah peered down and saw Abraham and Zohar standing at the foot of her mat, smiling like Egyptian cats in a granary full of mice.

Zohar nodded in Abraham's direction. "Your stubborn husband apologized and offered me a private tent so I can visit you as often as I'd like. I think the old geezer is finally softening."

"Zohar!" Ketty sat back on her heels. "You agreed not to rile her."

"She's not riled." He grinned at Sarah. "She's pleased."

She blinked twice and then worried what Abraham's reaction might be to their friendly banter. But when she focused on him, the same mischief on Zohar's features played on Abraham's too. "With your permission, my love, I'd like to marry your maid—well, your daughter." He turned to Ketty and held her gaze. "*Keturah.*"

The way Ketty's name escaped on a breath warmed Sarah's heart. Perhaps she hadn't awakened on earth. Maybe this was another dream. Or was she already in paradise? Had she somehow missed Elohim's greeting? Moving her eyes up and down, she scanned as much of her surroundings as possible. It was most certainly her familiar tent, not at all a dream. She need not pinch herself to know she was still locked inside her useless shell.

"Imma?" Ketty's worried voice broke into Sarah's pondering.

Abraham placed his hand on Ketty's shoulder. "Let me speak with her."

Ketty stood and backed away, reaching up to brush his hand before he bent to one knee beside Sarah's mat. The touch was casual and comfortable. Ketty had responded so naturally to Abraham's gentleness, it was as if they'd been closely knit for years.

When Abraham settled on the cushion beside Sarah, he leaned across her possessively, supporting himself with one hand on her other side. With his other hand, he traced his finger along the wedding veil still draped at her neck. "Would you like Ketty to wear this for the wedding ceremony?" His voice was low, having lost all trace of mischief.

Sarah blinked twice, quickly affirming.

He nodded once and lifted the treasure from her neck. Its departure was surprisingly painful, like the rending of a garment, the first act of mourning the death of someone dearly beloved. Their eyes met, and she knew he'd felt it too. Though his marriage to Ketty was exactly what she'd prayed for and was overjoyed to celebrate with them, it was like so many of life's blessings—a double-edged sword. Like the Hittites' best weapon, true blessings magnified life's pleasant and harsh realities. Sarah had loved only one man in her life. Elohim had given Abraham a second wife—a woman he could easily love. And Sarah *would* rejoice.

He kissed Sarah's forehead and stood, holding the wedding veil suspended between his two hands. Ketty's lips parted slightly, looking first at the glittering treasure and then alternating glances between Abraham and Sarah. "I feel as if I'm stealing Imma's greatest treasu—" Her voice broke, and she covered her face with both hands.

Abraham cradled her head and pulled her to his chest. "You aren't stealing anything, Keturah. Sarah and I are giving you our family's greatest treasure. This veil is woven of gold and set with glyptic gemstones from Abba Terah's own shop in Ur of the Chaldeans. It is priceless and unique, something created for a special purpose—just as you have been."

Ketty released a sob. Abraham released her, offering a cloth from his belt to dry her eyes. "I'm not worthy of any of this," she said. "I don't even know what 'glyptic' means."

Abraham's low chuckle even drew a smile from Zohar. "Let me show you." Abraham picked up an oil lamp in one hand and held the veil up with the other, allowing the gemstones to dangle from their delicate golden chains. "Abba and my two brothers, Nahor and Haran, were glyptic stone carvers. Before we left Ur, they had a thriving business of carving all sorts of images—mostly pagan gods—into gemstones. For Sarah's veil, however, Abba carved only the symbols representing the words of Great-Abba Adam's wedding blessing." He glanced over at Zohar. "So regardless of what our friend decides about his participation in tomorrow morning's ceremony, you will still be surrounded by Elohim's blessing."

What did Zohar have to do with tomorrow's ceremony of the wedding blessing? Before Sarah could find a way to garner anyone's attention, Abraham pressed the wedding veil into Ketty's hand.

"Take this with you tonight, and ask the other women in camp to prepare you for the ceremony tomorrow. We'll open one side of Sarah's tent completely, let the sunshine anoint our commitment, and trust Elohim to bring Isaac home in time to celebrate with us." He turned to Zohar. "Whether my son returns in time or not, you have a decision to make. Sarah would want to know what we've asked of you."

Zohar's eyes shot invisible arrows at Abraham. "Now who's the manipulative snake?"

Abraham smirked but didn't erupt into his usual defensive posture. How long had Sarah slept? A week? A month? What had transpired between these longtime rivals to provide this modicum of peace?

"Your husband is holding me hostage." Zohar's declaration wrenched Sarah from her musings. He knelt at the foot of her mat. "Abraham knows I want to please you, Sarah, especially now, so he's asked me to speak your God's wedding blessing at their ceremony if Isaac doesn't return in time—but he won't allow it unless I first renounce my gods and embrace Elohim." Searching her eyes, he waited as if she might overrule Abraham's wise restriction.

Sarah blinked twice, affirming her husband's wisdom. Zohar should realize Abraham was protecting him with the ultimatum. To speak the Creator's blessing without true belief in His being would be blasphemy and could bring judgment on them all.

Zohar dropped his head, exhaling his disappointment. "Well, you're no help," he said, chuckling. He looked up to face Ketty with a smile before he stood. "I brought something for you, my dear. Whether I speak the blessing over your marriage or not, I wish you all the happiness I shared with my wife for over sixty years." He reached into the satchel on his shoulder and pulled out a luxurious linen robe, as blue as a cloudless sky. "I had saved this for my daughter's wedding, but I want you to wear it, Ketty."

She covered a gasp and shook her head. "Zohar, I couldn't. It's too—"

"It's my gift to you, and you will take it." He bowed slightly, the robe draped over his two hands.

Abraham set aside the lamp and placed the jeweled veil into her hand. "Take this veil and Zohar's gift to Isaac's tent tonight and ask the women of camp to help you prepare for tomorrow's wedding. I'll have the men help me prepare Sarah's tent in the morning, and we'll be married at midday." He glanced at Sarah and back at the others. "Now, if you don't mind, I'd like to spend tonight alone with the wife of my youth."

Zohar nodded, waiting while Ketty kissed Sarah's cheek, and then escorted the soon-to-be bride out of the tent.

Abraham had remained where Sarah could see him, at her side, standing over her. She noticed the amber glow of dusk brighten her tent when Zohar and Ketty raised the flap to leave. Abraham turned slowly toward her, the subdued evening sounds of Kiriath Arba settling around them. He glanced toward her baskets and disappeared from view for a few moments. When he returned, he'd draped her favorite lightweight blanket over one arm. He dropped it into a pile beside her, untied his belt, and discarded his robe.

Sarah's eyes widened. *Abraham ben Terah! What are you—*

His boisterous laughter filled the tent as he knelt beside her wearing only his tunic. "I haven't seen you look this nervous since our wedding night." His eyes sparkled with mischief. "But our love will reach beyond physical pleasure tonight. I intend to hold you until we both feel comforted enough for me to marry another." He slid both arms around her, and then in one, fluid motion, Abraham rolled onto his back—holding her securely onto his chest.

Sarah's heart raced. She gurgled. Unable to laugh or express the absolute joy she felt, it sounded more like choking.

"Are you all right?" Abraham waited.

She stilled, hoping to offer her assurance. *Be at peace, my love.* With her ear pressed against his chest, she listened intently as his heartbeat began to slow. It was a heart that had beat for Elohim and for her all these years. Could he sense her joy? *Elohim, please—somehow—show my precious husband how happy he's made me.*

Abraham reached for the blanket he'd piled beside the mat and covered them. He smoothed every wrinkle on the sides and over her back. Then she realized he was simply caressing her. The deep baritone of a shepherd's tune vibrated beneath her cheek. Oh, how she adored hearing his singing—but this? Never before had she *felt* his voice, nor had their heartbeats risen and fallen in perfect rhythm while he praised Elohim for flocks and herds, for quiet streams, and even for rocky cliffs that made lush valleys seem greener. A harmony of sound and sensation, this was purest pleasure. The young had no idea what they were missing. Laughter leaked from her eyes in rapturous tears.

The singing stopped abruptly. "Sarah? You're crying!" He rolled over, staring down in horror. "Have I hurt you?" He tore away the blanket and began checking her frail arms and legs. "Oh my love, have I somehow..."

She gurgled frantically, trying to reassure him, but he was tortured by confusion. "Sarah, I can't understand you." He buried his head against her chest, weeping.

Please, Elohim. Comfort him. She sighed deeply and somehow a sound escaped her lips. "Zhzhzhzh." Almost a comforting hush.

Abraham's head snapped to attention, and her sound ceased. "How did you—" His gaze settled on her lips. "My head must have pressed your jaws together, so the sound escaped through your teeth." He grinned and caught one of her tears on his knuckle. "You were crying happy tears weren't you?"

She blinked twice.

"I'm happy too," he said, "but also a little unnerved." He lay beside her, this time ensuring he could still see her respond. "In all the years I'd visited Kiriath Arba, I'd never given Keturah a second thought until the day Elohim told me she was to be my wife. I agreed to obey, but I determined to live as you and I have lived since the Testing. Separate. Amiable. But without real affection or deep connection." He brushed Sarah's cheek. "I'm sorry for that, my love. I told myself the separation was something you wanted, so I never pressed for more. In truth, I was a coward. I feared more conflict might take you and Isaac from me completely, so I settled for less, fearful of losing all."

Thinking of all the years they'd wasted, Sarah shed more tears. This time, Abraham didn't ask what caused them. Surely he knew her as she knew him. They'd both been at fault. She, too, had been cowardly, justifying their separation as a necessity for her and Isaac's growing faith. Looking back, she now understood that Elohim could have proven faithful if they'd remained together, strengthening their relationships with open and transparent communication. But rather than lament their poor choices and missed blessings, Sarah would focus on the good things to come in her short time left.

"I've only really started to know Keturah," Abraham was saying, "but I believe Elohim has already started knitting our hearts together. I never thought I could love anyone but you."

The words sobered her. She'd sensed their connection, but to hear him admit it was harder than she'd expected.

Abraham studied her, his brows pinched. "Did I hurt you by telling you?"

She closed her eyes. *No.* The depth of his sharing was like a fresh wind over her soul, and she wanted him to continue for as long as she had breath.

"I hope Isaac returns in time to speak the blessing, but perhaps Elohim will use the opportunity to win Zohar's heart."

She blinked twice, the thought of Abraham speaking a kind word about Zohar still beyond her wildest dreams.

"I realize you have limited capacity to communicate, my love, but you seem exceedingly calm considering all that's happened during the past few days. You were sleeping so peacefully earlier when Keturah tried to wake you—more soundly than I've seen you sleep in years." He paused, studying her intensely. "Has Elohim spoken to you again?"

She blinked rapidly. *Yes, my love. Yes!* Oh, if only he knew how completely enamored she was with Elohim and downright giddy with the expectation of meeting Him face-to-face. Soon, she would leave this earth and embrace eternity—whatever it held. How could she communicate all that?

Abraham chuckled. "I see He has spoken." Then he placed a hand against her chest. "Your heart is pounding, woman!" His big, bold laughter swelled as he pulled her into his arms. "I don't know what He said to you, my love, but it seems to have changed your outlook on life and eternity. I'm so relieved.

We'll be able to celebrate tomorrow's wedding as more proof of His faithfulness." He yawned ferociously and settled his chin atop her head.

Sarah lay in the warmth and comfort of her husband's embrace, completely content. If eternity felt anything like this, she would thrive there forever.

CHAPTER TWENTY-EIGHT

Abraham looked up and there in a thicket he saw a ram caught by its horns. He went over and took the ram and sacrificed it as a burnt offering instead of his son. So Abraham called that place The LORD Will Provide. And to this day it is said, "On the mountain of the LORD it will be provided."
—Genesis 22:13–14 (NIV)

Next Morning - 7th Ajaru (April)

The slow awareness of being held, of strong arms around her, drew Sarah from deep slumber. How long had it been since Abraham had held her through the night? If she could speak, would he understand that the way he shared his soul last night felt more intimate than sharing their bodies? A contented sigh escaped, as the utter rapture of it washed over her anew. She opened her eyes to the glow of a new day and her husband's tender compassion.

"Good morning, my love." Deep creases rumpled his brow. Concern had replaced his carefree smile. "Elohim spoke to me in the night," he said without preamble. "I cannot marry Keturah unless Isaac is here to speak the wedding blessing. His command was given through your dream and must be obeyed in its every detail—just as He chose Mount Moriah to sacrifice our son and the eighth day for every male circumcision. Our obedience must be as precise as the God who rewards it with lavish blessing."

A thousand objections raced through Sarah's mind while Abraham stared down at her, waiting for her only form of communication. But how could she blink? How could she steal Ketty's joy when it seemed like Elohim Himself had ordained it? Hadn't He softened Ketty's heart? Couldn't He bring Zohar to the truth by making him renounce his false gods? It all seemed so right!

No! She closed her eyes, and her stomach tightened. Leaving them closed, so there would be no mistaking her message, Sarah resisted the memory of Elohim's dream—but the vision came as vividly as it had the first time. Abraham faced Ketty and gently drew aside the glittering, gemstone veil. His affection for her was unmistakable—as was the identity of the man who pronounced the blessing over them. Not Zohar. It was Isaac. He spoke Great-Abba Adam's words with conviction and joy, then began humming a shepherd's tune.

With a sudden pang of conscience, she realized it was Abraham humming the tune beside her—not Isaac in the vision. Her husband had pulled her closer, choosing calm rather than arguing with his dying wife. How disappointed he must be in her. She'd reacted as she always did, chosen her own way to fulfill Elohim's plan instead of allowing God to work His way in His time. If she believed Elohim had finally come to her, fulfilling years of longing for a personal encounter, how could she *not* obey every detail of her dream and visions?

Forgive me, El Shaddai, for falling so easily into old habits. Now, help me communicate my changed heart to Abraham. She began with the only sound she could make.

Abraham's humming ceased immediately, and he gazed down at her, his cheeks wet with tears. "I'm so sorry, my love, but do you understand now why I couldn't tell you the morning I left to sacrifice Isaac?" He gasped in a sob and released her, sitting up and turning away.

No, Abraham! Please! Talk to me! She gurgled again, hoping—praying—he'd have the courage to speak with the same transparency he'd shared last night. *Elohim, only You can help us communicate what needs to be said in these difficult moments.*

As she finished the prayer, Abraham turned and leaned over her on one elbow. "Sarah, only Elohim can help us communicate fully all that needs to be said in this difficult moment. I've asked Him to help you understand all that I'm about to say."

Her heart nearly leaped from her chest, but two immediate blinks was the only way she could show him her ready approval.

His brow rose, seeming somewhat surprised. "Good. Thank you for being willing to listen. I—"

"Imma!" The tent shuddered as Isaac burst inside. "Imma, are you—" He stood out of her line of sight, but he panted as if he'd run all the way from Egypt.

Abraham bolted to his feet. "She's alive, Son, but..."

"But what?" Isaac fell on his knees beside her but not close enough that she could see him. "Imma, look at me."

"Isaac, she can only see directly in front of her," Abraham whispered. "And she can no longer speak."

"Imma?" Her son leaned into view. His hair was tied back, his whole body filthy from travel. "Can you hear me?"

She blinked twice as Abraham explained the patterns of communication they'd established.

Tears streamed down Isaac's cheeks. "I couldn't find her, Imma. I'm so sorry."

"I found her, Son."

He gasped. "Is she—?"

"She's safe and well." Abraham moved to the foot of Sarah's mat, standing over her so she could now see both her men. "Zohar's archers killed Dirar for the bounty. Evidently, Dirar had promised the Hittite maiden enough to steal her innocence."

"Did he also steal Ketty's?"

"No, Son. Elohim protected my bride."

Isaac's jaw clenched like a vise, his glare equally severe. "You will not have my sister."

Abraham glanced at Sarah, then back at his son. "I was just about to explain to your imma why Keturah and I couldn't proceed with the wedding we had planned for today. Would you also like to hear the reason?"

"You would have married her without my approval?" Isaac's menacing tone proved the wisdom of Elohim's overnight warning to Abraham.

"May I come in?" Zohar shouted from outside.

Isaac's eyes widened when Abraham invited him in. Isaac leaped to his feet, leaving Sarah's view, but she could imagine his posture by the immediate apology he offered for Dirar's behavior. "I owe you my deepest regret for the pain Dirar caused you and your household, my friend. I don't know how I can make it up to you, but I will."

"You've already made it up to me, boy, by returning before the ceremony. Abraham would have made me renounce my gods to speak the wedding blessing over him and Ketty. At least now I can decide on my own time if I believe Elohim is the only real God."

"I…I don't…what do you—"

"Let's all sit down where Sarah can see us and be part of our conversation." Abraham moved toward her left side and motioned Zohar to sit at the foot of her mat while Isaac took his place at her right side. When the three men settled, Abraham focused on Sarah. "You and I have discussed much that these two don't know about, haven't we, my love?" He grinned and turned to Isaac first. "Keturah and I have spoken and both agree that our hearts have become softened toward each other. Elohim has blessed His command not only with a willing obedience but also with affection between us, Isaac. Because Sarah's condition worsened significantly in the short time we were away from her, we decided to have the wedding today at midday whether you had returned or not. We asked Zohar to pronounce the blessing—only if he would renounce his gods and embrace Elohim."

"But he would never…" Isaac looked at his friend and mentor. "Would you?"

Zohar shrugged. "Maybe, maybe not. I'd never really considered it until your abba and Ketty presented me with the ultimatum."

"Well, I'm grateful for their ultimatum then." Isaac released a small huff and turned to his abba. "And I'm grateful Elohim brought me home in time to stop this wedding ceremony."

Without flinching, Abraham said, "I was wrong to rush the wedding ceremony, Isaac. Will you forgive me, Son?"

Isaac glanced at Zohar and then Sarah, suspicion clouding his features, before he asked his abba, "What do you mean?"

"I've wronged you," Abraham said. "I'm apologizing."

Zohar leaned toward Isaac. "He apologized to me yesterday. I wasn't quite sure what to make of it either, and I still don't trust him." He turned to Abraham. "Especially if you're about to renege on your promise to marry Ketty."

"Oh no," Abraham said. "I'll still marry Keturah, but not until Elohim convinces my son to approve of the match." When he turned to Isaac, he added, "I was just about to explain to your imma the way Elohim made it very clear to me last night that we must obey her dream in every detail—including the part where it's you, Isaac, who speaks the wedding blessing over Keturah and me."

"I will never—"

"I'm a weak man, Isaac. *That's* the reason I never told anyone where we were going the morning we left for Mount Moriah. Elohim told me I was to sacrifice my son, my only son, which made absolutely no sense. If I had told anyone—the servants, you, your imma—and any one of you had asked aloud the same questions going through my mind, I'm not sure I could have obeyed my God. And my decision to rush this wedding is another example of the same weakness."

Isaac's eyes narrowed. "I don't understand how the two relate."

"I knew your imma desperately wanted to see her dream fulfilled before she left this earth. Keturah and I wanted to be married. Even though your imma clearly said it was you who pronounced the blessing in her dream, I believed the small deviation of Zohar pronouncing the blessing could be overlooked because of the positive outcome of Zohar's conversion."

"I still don't see your point."

"Nor do I." Zohar leaned forward. "Are you saying my contribution wouldn't have been good enough for your god?"

"Yes, Zohar, but it's because Elohim called *Isaac* to pronounce the blessing. That means only Isaac's obedience is good enough." Abraham turned to his son. "My desire to please your imma, Ketty, and myself clouded my decision to obey Elohim. If I had told anyone that morning, when we left for Mount Moriah, what God had commanded me in the night, I could have easily been swayed to adjust what I'd heard from Elohim to what other people said. But we serve a precise God, Isaac. You were born on the exact day the three visitors predicted and circumcised on the eighth day—not the seventh or the ninth."

Zohar scoffed. "Why would I chain myself to such an obdurate master?"

Abraham drew breath, but Isaac answered too quickly. "Because when He speaks clearly—as He does to Abba—obedience is lavishly rewarded and faith becomes as natural as your next breath, Zohar." Though speaking to the Hittite, he'd stared at his abba. "But Elohim refuses to speak to me, so I'll continue to wait for my personal encounter before I let anyone take Ketty from me."

Sarah heard Abraham gasp, recognizing their realization came at the same moment. Isaac was experiencing his own Mount Moriah, but Ketty was to be his sacrifice. "Oh, Isaac," Abraham whispered. "If I hadn't heard personally from Elohim, I never could have been willing to sacrifice one of the two people I loved most."

Isaac released a small huff as if the truth hit him like a blow. As the color drained from his face, he turned to Sarah. "I thought you made up the dream, hoping when Abba took Ketty away, I'd be forced to turn to a Semite wife for comfort."

No. She closed her eyes. A lifetime of trying to control God's plans had done more damage than she'd realized.

When she opened her eyes again, Isaac was watching her. "Do you agree with Abba? Is Ketty my sacrifice? My Testing?"

Sarah blinked twice.

"That means—"

"Yes," Isaac interrupted. "I know." He dropped his head. Abraham and Sarah exchanged a glance.

Zohar struggled to his feet. "I think I should go and return after you've settled your family squabble." He winced as he straightened his back and then looked down at Sarah. "Don't die yet, my friend, not if you want to hear my decision about your God. I'm still considering." He winked at her and left.

She blinked twice, though she knew he couldn't see.

"I'm going too." Isaac bolted to his feet. "I need to think. Pray."

"And bathe." Abraham grinned at him.

Isaac allowed himself a reluctant smile. "Yes, Abba, and bathe."

Abraham's laughter filled the tent, and their son finally released a full smile. Sarah blinked so rapidly her eyelashes fluttered to signal her adamant agreement. Their son rolled his eyes and turned to go.

"Isaac, wait!" Abraham said.

Their son turned.

"Look for the ram. The Lord will provide for your sacrifice."

Isaac nodded once and ducked out of the tent.

Abraham sighed heavily and lay on his side next to Sarah. He leaned over to kiss her cheek and then propped his head on one hand. "I suppose that went about as well as we could have expected."

Sarah blinked twice. It went better than she'd hoped. Her two men had opened their hearts and shared more about the Testing than ever before. Who could have known that the events of the past few days would have so closely coincided with Abraham's emotions of that fateful event that had completely changed their lives? *You knew, Elohim. Your ways are so far above our ways. Why have I ever doubted You?*

"The only one left to tell is Keturah." Abraham looked down at Sarah and sighed again. "I wish you could tell me what to expect. Will she weep? You know I can't bear a woman's tears. I'd rather she shout." A deep crease formed between his brows. "I can't picture Keturah shouting." His eyes grew distant, and Sarah knew he was thinking of his new bride.

This time, there was no pang of envy or sadness. Only a deep and abiding peace that their marriage would be a happy one. Whether she witnessed their wedding on this earth or was somehow aware of it in eternity suddenly made little difference. The eventful morning had made her weary, and her eyelids began to droop. She felt a gentle kiss on her cheek and the bend of her husband's frame around hers. His strong arm lay across her middle, and she knew he'd decided to nap before sharing the new developments with Ketty. Perhaps Elohim would give him wisdom for the conversation as he rested.

Jireh—Provider...on the mountain of the Lord it will be provided.

CHAPTER TWENTY-NINE

Abraham took the wood for the burnt offering and placed it on his son Isaac, and he himself carried the fire and the knife. As the two of them went on together, Isaac spoke up and said to his father Abraham...

"The fire and wood are here," Isaac said, "but where is the lamb for the burnt offering?" Abraham answered, "God himself will provide the lamb for the burnt offering...." And the two of them went on together.
—Genesis 22:6–8 (NIV)

The predawn air was brisk, sending an invigorating chill through Keturah the moment she stepped out of Isaac's tent. Cook led them toward the east forest, a small torch in hand. She and two older women had insisted on staying with Ketty on the night before her wedding, scrubbing her from head to toe and bathing her in scented oils. Except her hands and feet. "We'll decorate your hands and feet with henna after you help us prepare the morning meal," Cook had announced as firmly as she massaged the oil into Ketty's calves. "How are we supposed to prepare a wedding feast by midday?" she'd asked the other women. "Did Master Abraham think of the food, the seating, the musicians? Humph! Of course not. Men don't think of such things. Only women know what must be done to prepare for a wedding." The other two hens joined her clucking, obviously enjoying their fussing. Ketty listened helplessly, knowing if Imma were there, she would have spoken a profound word of wisdom to encourage them, yet silence the negativity.

"We'll fetch the firewood while the others start the morning gruel and put the wedding lamb on the spit." Cook peered over her shoulder, leading Ketty toward the forest's woodpiles. "You're not allowed to sweat, you know. A bride mustn't sweat on her wedding day. You can help with small tasks but nothing too strenuous. You must save your strength for the wedding night. Master Abraham will surely be as kind as my dear Elias—though he's a long sight more handsome!" Cackling, she continued out of the camp, chattering like a sparrow.

Ketty had never seen Cook so excited. She'd been up before the sun and had shaken the other two women awake, barking assignments like an army commander. Ketty was already dressed in her work robe. She'd lain awake all night, praying for Isaac to return before the ceremony. Though she desperately hoped Master Zohar would embrace Elohim, the idea of marrying Abraham without Isaac's blessing felt wrong—almost deceitful—as if they were rushing to it before Isaac could protest. She'd agreed to the plan in a moment of excitement. Now, she didn't want to break her promise to marry Abraham today and disappoint him and Imma—or Cook and the other women who, despite their complaining, were so excited about this day. But every time she closed her eyes, she saw what she imagined

Isaac's reaction would be when he learned they had wed in his absence.

Shock. Betrayal. Anger. Would it progress to hatred? *Elohim, please no.* But to know she was about to cause pain and ask Elohim to fix it was like jumping off a cliff and asking God to save her from injury. It was worse than irresponsible—it was abusing her relationship with the Creator. *Forgive me, Elohim.*

"Jonah!" Cook waved at a man already gathering wood. "I didn't realize you'd returned!"

Ketty's heart leaped to her throat. Jonah had accompanied Isaac.

"We've only just. Master Isaac went directly to Mistress Sarah's tent to see—" He looked at Ketty. "Is she…"

Ketty nodded. "She's still with us, though she can no longer move or speak."

With a relieved sigh, he offered Ketty a kind smile. "Master Isaac will be pleased he returned in time, and he'll be especially happy to see you safe and well, Ketty."

"It's *Mistress Keturah*," Cook said. "She marries Master Abraham at midday."

Jonah's smile died. "Does Master Isaac know yet?"

Ketty swallowed the lump forming in her throat. "I suspect if he went to his imma's tent, he knows now."

Jonah collected a few more pieces of wood, suddenly in a hurry. "Congratulations, Mistress Keturah. I should get back to my tent before the wife sends our children out to look for me." Head down, he nodded a hurried greeting, "Shalom."

Shalom? Ketty mused. There would likely be little peace when Isaac discovered what had been planned in his absence.

Cook placed her torch in the leather strap on the nearby tree. "All right," she said, "hold out your arms, and I'll load the wood." One by one, she loaded Ketty's arms with enough firewood to feed the central fire for this morning's gruel. Someone would need to fetch more to keep the spit roasting—if there was still to be a wedding.

"Perhaps we should have the shepherds wait to slaughter the lamb for the spit," Ketty said as Cook added the final log to her arms.

The old woman leveled a warning glare. "We will have a wedding today, girl. Master Abraham has looked at only one other woman the way he looks at you. Only Elohim could open his heart to you, Ketty, and we must trust Him to do the same with Master Isaac." She grabbed the torch from its holster and nudged Ketty's shoulder. "Come on. We have food to prepare and then a bride to make ready. And remember, no sweating!"

The last command would be a bit trickier now that Ketty's arms were full of firewood. The eastern horizon was aglow, but the forest was dense enough with its blossoms and leaves that Cook's torch was still needed to make their way back to camp. This time they walked side by side, Cook lifting the torch with one hand while the other hand supported Ketty's elbow to steady her heavy load on the uneven ground.

Concentrating on her footing, Ketty was startled when she heard a man call her name.

She halted and looked up, but Cook spoke first. "Master Isaac, you're home!"

He stood like a tent post, ten paces from them, the low light of dawn casting haunting shadows through the trees. Or was it his expression that was haunting? He still hadn't spoken.

"Isaac?" Ketty said softly.

"That day, when we reached Mount Moriah, Abba carried the torch, and I carried the wood," he said. "I asked him, 'Where is the lamb for the offering?' and he said, 'God Himself will provide the lamb.' Abba was right, Ketty. You're my sacrifice." His face twisted with emotion as he fell to his knees.

Ketty dropped the wood. "Return to camp, Cook. Now. Don't speak of this to anyone." She started toward Isaac and nudged the old woman past him.

"But the wood!" Cook said. "I need it for the—"

"Borrow wood or send someone else to get it," Ketty snapped, kneeling beside Isaac.

"Of course, of course." Cook's brow knit with concern. "I just…" She loved Isaac and had helped care for him as a child.

"It's all right, Cook," Ketty assured her. "Elohim does good work through hard things."

Cook's expression softened. "Indeed, *Mistress,* He does." The woman inclined her head and walked away, leaving Ketty to comfort her brother.

He was obviously dealing with memories from the Testing, but what had caused it? And why had he called her *his sacrifice?* "Isaac," she said, leaning over him, "talk to me. What happened in Imma's tent? Did they tell you—" She couldn't even say the words.

He wiped both hands down his face, leaving streaks from the travel dirt he wore. "Abba said Elohim has given both of you true affection for one another and that you had agreed to let Zohar speak the wedding blessing if he embraced Elohim as his God."

"It's true, but I reconsidered overnight."

"As did Abba."

The news struck like a blow. Had Abraham's feelings toward her changed? Startled at how much pain the thought caused her, she whispered, "Well then. You're relieved, I'm sure." She bowed her head to hide the sudden rush of tears, but the last word had broken as surely as her heart.

Isaac's knuckle curled under her chin, nudging it upward, but she couldn't face him. How could she explain such strong feelings for a man her brother had distrusted most of his life—when she herself couldn't even rationalize them?

"Please, Ketty. Look at me."

"I don't want to make you more upset," she said, wiping stubborn tears.

"Then look at me and help me reason out what Elohim is doing." His plea snared her attention, and she gazed into his intense brown eyes. "I made the same demand, Ketty, that Elohim would prove Imma's dream was truly His command by affirming it to me personally. Abba likened my struggle to give you up to his inner struggle to sacrifice me on Mount Moriah."

"How could I be—"

"You're one of the people I love most in the world. I truly believed Imma contrived her dream so Abba would take you away and I'd be forced to rely on a Semite wife for comfort."

"Isaac," Ketty chided. "Imma wouldn't lie about hearing from Elohim."

He combed both hands through his dusty brown hair and pulled out the leather tie. "I believe she had a dream, but I wanted Elohim to tell *me* before I could make such a sacrifice." His eyes met hers. "Abba finally understood. He said he couldn't have taken me to Mount Moriah unless he'd personally heard from Elohim. Then he assured me that Elohim always provides and said I should be watching for the ram—as Elohim provided on the mountain for Abba's sacrifice the moment before his dagger bit into my throat."

"Oh, Isaac." Ketty reached for his hands. "Then Elohim spoke to you when you saw me with the wood and Cook with the torch. I saw it on your face."

"No, it was just a memory." He pulled his hands from hers. "Before Abba and I climbed the mountain, I was carrying the wood. He carried the torch and knife. The memory came so strong that I knew what Abba had said to me in Imma's tent was right—that you were my sacrifice. Now, I must wait for the substitutionary 'ram' to come before I give you to Abba."

Ketty felt a distinct unease at his interpretation. His jaw was clenched, muscles flexing. *Elohim, give me wisdom and courage.* Somehow, she knew her brother had slid from sincerely questioning to dangerously resisting their God. "You've told me the events of that day several times, Isaac, but may I ask you a few questions?"

Eyes narrowing, he nodded.

"You'd seen enough sacrifices on the altar in Hebron by that time to recognize the necessary components and realize your abba intended to make an offering to Elohim, right?"

"Yes."

"And you knew the lamb was missing because you asked him about it." He nodded.

"Yet you followed him up the mountain anyway because both you and your abba *believed* Elohim was *Jireh,* the perfect Provider." Isaac gave no indication he'd heard or agreed. "You climbed that mountain, Isaac, and you dropped the wood. You let your abba bind your wrists and ankles and then you worked together with him to position yourself atop that altar. on top of you. Isn't that what you've always told me?"

"Yes." A sheen of moisture gathered on his forehead despite the morning chill.

"Here's the most important question, Brother. In those moments, did you still believe Elohim would provide another lamb?"

He was shaking now, his whole body rigid. "No," he said, blinking tears down his cheeks.

"Then what kept you on that altar?" Ketty wiped his cheeks and hers.

"I wanted Abba to see that my faith was as strong as his." He scoffed and tipped his head up to a brightening sky. "Neither Abba nor Elohim seemed to notice."

Ketty's heart twisted at the brokenness so evident in her beloved brother. "Look at me, Isaac." Determination surged through her with the love she'd always felt for him. "You've lived for others' approval long enough. Elohim made you His covenant bearer before you did anything right or wrong. He created you the way *He* wants you and has given you the skill and heart He wants you to use for Him. Do you think your weaknesses are too severe for God to overcome? Are you the one person on earth the Creator can't communicate with? Is His arm too short to reach you? His ears too dull to hear you?"

"Stop it, Ketty." Isaac stood and dusted off his robe.

"No, I won't stop." She shoved his arm, demanding his attention. "You continued up the mountain with your abba because you trusted *Jireh*, the Provider. Your faith was tested and proved that day, Isaac, whether polluted by seeking approval or not. Today, you asked Elohim to personally speak to you. He did that."

"He didn't!"

"He did!" she shouted. "When you saw me carrying the wood."

"That was just a memory," he said.

"Do you expect an angel or a voice from heaven?"

"I deserve it!" he shouted, his face turning crimson. Just as suddenly, he seemed to realize his hubris. "I didn't mean—"

"How long will you charge Elohim and your abba with the debt of your heroism?" Ketty crossed her arms, compassion at an end. "Stop being a victim, Isaac, and embrace the valor of your birthright. If I am your sacrifice, you must place me on the altar before Jireh gives you the ram." She hurried away, desperate to remove her things from Isaac's tent. At least

Abraham and Imma already knew the wedding would be postponed.

The wedding. Imma's dream. It had seemed impossible from the first moment she'd told Ketty about it. *But You are my Provider, Elohim.* She would keep walking up the mountain even without her lamb for the sacrifice and wait for Elohim to fulfill His promise.

CHAPTER THIRTY

At once I was in the Spirit, and there before me was a throne in heaven.... And the one who sat there had the appearance of jasper and ruby. A rainbow that shone like an emerald encircled the throne.
—Revelation 4:2–3 (NIV)

Zohar sat at the end of Sarah's mat, pouring his heart out about his daughter. He'd never even mentioned the girl before. How Sarah wished she could have met her before Dirar ruined her future with his lies. "But one of my guards," Zohar was saying, "actually the one who collected the bounty, has asked to make her his concubine."

Sarah vehemently squeezed her eyes closed. No woman should have to settle for being a man's cast-off lover.

Zohar's bushy brows shot up. "I see you're opposed to the idea, but what else can she hope for? Who would marry her after she gave herself to a slave?" He roared his frustration and turned away, swiping at the corner of his eyes. The heart of an abba, breaking.

She knew well the lines between masters and slaves, rulers and ruled, but she'd also seen what Elohim had done to open Abraham's heart to Ketty. And Sarah knew personally how she and Abraham had loved Ishmael—the son of a slave—and raised him as their own until Elohim announced she would bear Isaac from her own body. *Thank You for letting me see Ishmael and make peace with Hagar before my last breath, Elohim.*

"Have I upset you, my friend?" Zohar laid his hand on her foot. He'd been cautious to remain at a distance since he and Abraham had somehow struck their truce.

She closed her eyes. *No.* He hadn't upset her. Far from it. He'd been good company and a kind distraction after Isaac returned, washed and in a clean robe, and asked to speak with Abraham outside. Time had lost all meaning, but it seemed like ages ago to Sarah.

"What will you miss most about your life on earth?" Zohar asked with a crooked smile. "I don't know what your Elohim promises for the afterlife, but I assume you expect to be reunited with loved ones—as most promise. So, besides your family and me, of course"—he flashed a dashing smile—"will you miss living in tents?"

Eyes closed. *Definitely not.*

"No, well, neither will I. What about livestock, birds, animals?"

Sarah had never considered it. Had Elohim created creatures for paradise? She widened her eyes to show the wonder she felt at the thought.

Zohar laughed, and as he drew breath to ask another question, the tent shuddered and drew his attention. "Well, it's about time you returned. I was running out of distractions."

Distractions?

"Isaac and I will open up the tent," Abraham said from her right side, out of her view. "Place some pillows against that center pole, and you can settle there with Sarah. Be sure she's seated upright so she can see everything."

See everything? A sudden rush of daylight dazzled her, and she squinted. Zohar disappeared from view, and footsteps shuffled all around her. What was happening? In the noise and confusion, Sarah's chest began to seize. Pain forced a gurgle from her lips, and her eyes closed tight.

"Imma? Imma, I'm here."

Sarah opened her eyes and wondered if she was having another version of her vision. This time Ketty knelt before her in the golden veil, gemstones tinkling, but the expression behind them was frightened.

"Imma, can you hear me?"

Sarah blinked twice.

"Are you in pain?"

Two more blinks.

"All right." Ketty turned and shouted, "Isaac, get Imma some tea and bring me the poppy seed powder. I'll add it—"

Sarah's frantic gurgling halted her. *No!* She squeezed her eyes tight. *No poppy in my tea.* If this was real, she certainly wasn't going to sleep through Elohim's miracle! Eyes locked with her daughter, they spoke with their hearts and understood more in that moment than mere words could have conveyed.

Sarah looked up and gasped. The bright midday sun reflected off the gemstones in Ketty's veil, casting rainbows of color onto the tent walls. *"Be fruitful and multiply,"* Elohim had said to Noah and his family when they left the ark. Then He'd given them the rainbow as a covenant promise of His protection.

When Sarah looked at Ketty, her daughter was staring at the rainbows, swaying her head and watching them move on the walls around them. "Elohim set his rainbow in the sky as a lasting covenant with Noah, his descendants, and all living creatures, that He would never again destroy the earth with floodwaters." She looked down at Sarah. "Elohim is my protection, Imma, as surely as the rainbow covers the earth."

Two blinks, and the pain in her chest was gone. Isaac arrived with the tea, but Sarah didn't need it now. Peace filled her as Zohar placed her on the pillows he'd prepared at the center tent pole. But it was the Hittite chieftain she leaned on. His arm slid around her shoulders unapologetically as Abraham and Ketty stood five paces in front of them, Isaac on the other side. The rest of the camp gathered behind Isaac, dressed in clean robes, their faces radiant.

"Abba," Isaac said, "I entrust to you Keturah, my sister and closest friend, because Elohim has promised me another comforter will come. So, I will continue up the mountain until I see the ram from Jireh, my Provider." A cheer rose behind him, and Sarah thought she saw her son stand a little taller. "Now, El Elyon made Great-Imma Eve from the rib He had taken out of Great-Abba Adam, and He brought her to Adam, who said, 'You are now bone of my bones and flesh of my flesh.'" He placed his right hand on Abraham's head and his left hand on Ketty's. "May Elohim bless you, and may His covenant bear fruit through us all."

As if bolts of lightning had shot from his hands, Sarah was blinded for a moment. Blinking a few times, she opened her eyes to discover she was standing. With a gasp, she looked down at her pure white robe, then her flawless hands. No longer wrinkled or marred by raised blue veins, they looked even younger than before she came to Canaan.

Sarah.

The voice reverberated in her chest, gentle power that drew her attention to an elevated golden throne—surrounded by every color of the gemstones Abba Terah had cut into her bridal veil. Jasper, ruby, emerald. Colors never seen and beyond description.

Sarah, my girl. The One on the throne opened His arms and beckoned her to come.

"Elohim!" The Name erupted from her chest with more than mere voice. It filled her being, this place, the heavens. "Elohim. I am Yours." Her legs moved. She danced. She flew. She was in His arms, and that was everything.

EPILOGUE

Abraham rose from beside his dead wife and spoke to the Hittites. He said, "I am a foreigner and stranger among you. Sell me some property for a burial site here so I can bury my dead." The Hittites replied to Abraham... "You are a mighty prince among us. Bury your dead in the choicest of our tombs...." Then Abraham rose and bowed down.... "Intercede with Ephron son of Zohar on my behalf so he will sell me the cave of Machpelah, which belongs to him and is at the end of his field. Ask him to sell it to me for the full price...."
Ephron the Hittite was sitting among his people and he replied to Abraham...
"No, my lord.... I give you the field.... The land is worth four hundred shekels of silver, but what is that between you and me? Bury your dead."
Abraham agreed to Ephron's terms and weighed out for him the price he had named in the hearing of the Hittites: four hundred shekels of silver....
So Ephron's field in Machpelah near Mamre—both the field and the cave in it, and all the trees within the borders of the field— was deeded to Abraham as his property in the presence of all the Hittites.... Afterward Abraham buried his wife Sarah in the cave in

the field of Machpelah near Mamre (which is at Hebron) in the land of Canaan. So the field and the cave in it were deeded to Abraham by the Hittites as a burial site.
—Genesis 23:3–11, 15–20 (NIV)

AUTHOR'S NOTE

The following are a few examples of how I placed fact and fiction on the foundation of biblical truth in *Beauty Surrendered: Sarah's Story*.

The Sages and the Tower of Babel

Ancient Mesopotamia covered the whole land of Shem's tribes—the son Noah blessed and who, according to the Book of Jasher (a rabbinic text), started schools for young men in his tribe to pass down knowledge of the Most High God.

Ancient Mesopotamian records describe "seven sages" in their history, revering them as semidivine beings highly esteemed for their extraordinary wisdom. These seven men are mentioned in the ancient record of Gilgamesh. If I were writing a dissertation, I might have gone deeper into study. However, I'm writing biblical fiction and instead saw a correlation in Shem's descendants:

> Two years after the flood, when **Shem** was 100 years old, he became the father of Arphaxad. And after he became the father of Arphaxad, Shem lived 500 years and had **other sons and daughters**. When **Arphaxad** had lived 35 years, he became the father of Shelah.

And after he became the father of Shelah,
Arphaxad lived 403 years and had **other sons and daughters**.
When **Shelah** had lived 30 years, he became the father of Eber.
And after he became the father of Eber,
Shelah lived 403 years and had **other sons and daughters**.
When **Eber** had lived 34 years, he became the father of Peleg.
And after he became the father of Peleg,
Eber lived 430 years and had **other sons and daughters**.
When **Peleg** had lived 30 years, he became the father of Reu.
And after he became the father of Reu,
Peleg lived 209 years and had **other sons and daughters**.
When **Reu** had lived 32 years, he became the father of Serug.
And after he became the father of Serug,
Reu lived 207 years and had **other sons and daughters**.
When **Serug** had lived 30 years, he became the father of **Nahor**.
—Genesis 11:10–22 (NIV)
(**emphasis** mine)

Nahor, Abram's grandfather, was the first descendant mentioned in Genesis 11 who died before he reached the age of two hundred. Before Nahor, there were *seven* men from Shem's blessed tribe who lived extraordinarily long lives. Because I write *fiction*, I chose to consider Shem's descendants the ancient Mesopotamian sages whose mission was to remind the scattered tribes (after the Tower of Babel) of the one true God.

Each of the seven men mentioned in Shem's biblical lineage had "other sons and daughters." Did they also have equally long lives? We don't know, because the Bible doesn't tell us. What we do know is this: Terah, the son of Nahor—the first man who died before he reached 200—was called to leave Shem's tribal region. Yes, it was Abram's father, *Terah*, who was originally called to leave Ur and go to Canaan.

> Terah took his son Abram, his grandson Lot son of Haran,
> and his daughter-in-law Sarai, the wife of his son Abram,
> and together they set out from Ur of the Chaldeans
> to go to Canaan.
> But when they came to Harran, they settled there.
> Terah lived 205 years, and he died in Harran.
> —Genesis 11:31–32 (NIV)

The Tower of Babel

Have you ever heard of a ziggurat? It's a strange name for a towering ancient temple, built by people who hoped to somehow use human effort to reach godlike status. Sound familiar? It's a common goal for us humans—starting with the Garden:

> "You will not certainly die," the serpent said to the woman.
> "For God knows that when you eat from it your eyes will be opened, and you will be like God, knowing good and evil."
> —Genesis 3:4–5 (NIV)

We humans are a stubborn lot, however, and as they moved eastward, they tried to reach God by their own efforts again, building a tower on "a plain in Shinar." If you check the footnote, you might see it explained as *Babylonia*, which is the empire built right in the middle of Shem's tribal territory.

Genesis 11:8 then tells us God scattered the people over the whole earth and confused their languages. They even "stopped building the city." Does that mean they stopped building the city *forever*? Not likely, or there couldn't have been a Babylonian empire. Here's the really interesting part. There are remains of a ziggurat still *today* on the ancient site of Babylon that archaeologists believe may date back to the Tower of Babel!

In this novel, I've stationed Shem and his grandson as the two powerful sages still living in "the shadow of the Tower of Babel" to remind those who remain that Elohim is the only true God. It's *fiction*, but I hope you saw the significant biblical truths and historical facts that were interwoven to make it a plausible *might-have-been*.

Hebron/Kiriath Arba

Though I couldn't find any specific dates on exactly when the name of Hebron changed to Kiriath Arba, Scripture seems to indicate that the area in the hill country southwest of Jerusalem was called Hebron while it was occupied by Mamre and his Amorite clans.

> So Abram went to live near the great trees
> of Mamre at Hebron,
> where he pitched his tents. There
> he built an altar to the Lord.
> —Genesis 13:18 (NIV)

After Sarah's death, Abraham negotiates with Hittite owners to purchase a burial cave for his wife:

> [Sarah] died at Kiriath Arba (that is,
> Hebron) in the land of Canaan....
> Then Abraham rose from beside his dead wife
> and spoke to the Hittites....
> "Intercede with Ephron son of Zohar on my behalf
> so he will sell me the cave of Machpelah."
> —Genesis 23:2–3, 8–9 (NIV)

Kiriath Arba does, in fact, mean *four cities*, so I added that Zohar gave the conquered hilltop the name and divided it into four cities to build a world readers could visualize.

Afterlife

There seems to be no clear indication of what the patriarchs knew or believed about the afterlife, which seems odd since the pagan pantheons had complex theories on levels of pleasure (or punishment) after death. Since Job's writings are likely dated during this period or soon after, I looked to his writings for biblical truth to support Abraham and Sarah's beliefs on what awaited after death.

> "I know that my redeemer lives,
> and that in the end he will stand on the earth.
> And after my skin has been destroyed,
> yet in my flesh I will see God;

> I myself will see him
> with my own eyes—I, and not another.
> How my heart yearns within me!"
> —Job 19:25–27 (NIV)

Sarah's Heart

As with every story I write, Sarah's story has changed me. Searching both the scriptures and the historical data about this extraordinary woman of the Bible has challenged my tendencies toward control and strengthened my yearning to see my God face-to-face. This world can become overwhelming if I focus on current events or let my imagination project too far into the what-ifs of modern society. However, keeping my focus on eternity—regardless of how many days I have left on this earth—has been a soothing balm for my soul.

It's my hope—for both you and me—that this story about Sarah's last days can make the rest of our days more peaceful, with our focus on the God who still proves faithful and true.

Signed,

Mesu Andrews

A SCHOLAR'S VIEW OF ABRAHAM AND SARAH

The account of Abraham and Sarah is one that has inspired many people for thousands of years. How an ordinary man and woman could become the ancestors of enough descendants to be "as numerous as the stars in the sky and as the sand on the seashore" (Genesis 22:17) is unimaginable—especially considering that by the time they became parents, they were around ninety and one hundred years old! But by faith, Abraham and Sarah believed that the God who called them into the Promised Land would fulfill His promises to them, including the promise of an heir.

What did Abraham and Sarah's world look like? When Abraham's father, Terah, moved his family out of Ur of the Chaldees and into the land of Harran (Genesis 11:31), the family lived in a metropolitan setting. Ur was a city in southern Babylonia, and Harran in Mesopotamia. Harran was a major trading center that boasted protection from the Mesopotamian moon god Sin. Abraham had been called out of Ur by the living God, and yet he and his family settled in a land that was just as plagued by false deities.

Ancient texts from surrounding areas describe a group of seminomadic tribes in the area surrounding the city of Harran, so while Abraham and Sarah lived within the city's walls, the nomadic lifestyle they were to embark on was not wholly unfamiliar to them.

Although the land of Canaan was made up agricultural societies, the geographical landscape and climate posed great challenges. Water supply varied greatly—from rainfall to freshwater pools and springs, manmade wells and cisterns, and dew—and this supply was often seasonal and dependent upon region. In the land of Canaan, a type of seminomadism took place in which the flocks and herds were moved from one location to another for part of the year so that herders with specialized skills could care for the livestock during the summer and winter months.

Abraham owned no property within the land of Canaan, even though it was promised to his descendants. Rather he moved from place to place, following the food supply. This likely explains Abraham's two camps—one in Hebron, and the other in Beersheba.

TERAH

Abraham's father, Terah, is a bit of a mystery. What does Scripture teach us about this man, and what information can be gleaned from other sources? The Bible doesn't say much about him. A short description of Terah is found in Genesis 11:24–32. Here are the biblical facts about the father of Israel's great patriarch:

- He was a descendant of Shem, Noah's son (11:10–25)
- He was the father of Abram (Abraham), Nahor, and Haran, and the grandfather of Lot (11:26–27)

- He lost his son Haran (11:28)
- He set out for the land of Canaan with his son Abraham, daughter-in-law Sarah, and nephew Lot but settled in the land of Harran (11:31)
- He died at the age of 205 in the land of Harran (11:32)

Some Jewish texts describe Terah as an idol worshiper, and some even describe him as a priest of idolatry. In Jewish tradition, Abraham was the first of his family to worship Yahweh as the one true God, and he was the one who encouraged his father to walk away from idol worship. In fact, some interpretations of the origins of Terah's name speculate that the name is related to the moon, taking into consideration that lunar worship was common throughout the region, and others in the family had names that may have also been associated with such worship.

SHEM

As with Terah, there is little biographical information to be found about Abraham's ancestor Shem. It is known that he was one of three sons of Noah; that he and his wife were travelers on the ark; that he and his brother Japheth preserved their father's dignity when their brother Ham found him drunk and naked, passed out; and that while Ham was cursed, Shem was blessed. The name *Shem* is the Hebrew word for *name*, and many attempts have been made to connect the name with great significance. One scholar notes the contrast between the account in Genesis 11:1–9, which features the builders of the tower of Babel who tried to make a "name" for themselves, and the genealogy in Genesis 11:10-26, which features God's chosen line, beginning with the man whose name literally means "Name."

Scripture portrays Shem as a man of great character, who was blessed for his handling of his father's nakedness. It was through Shem's line that Abraham would come, and through Abraham's seed would come the Messiah. In later Jewish traditions, Shem was described as "Shem the Great" and depicted as a priest of God. The "tents" of Shem were viewed as places where many could come and study the Torah. A little bit of biblical math shows that Shem was likely still alive when Abraham left Ur for the land of Canaan.

SARAH'S BEAUTY

What can be said of Sarah? Scripture describes her as childless almost immediately upon her introduction. It is stated in Genesis that she is both Terah's daughter-in-law, as well as his daughter, making her the half sister of her husband, Abraham. By the time God made His covenant with Abraham, he and Sarah were both old, and the idea that she would give birth to his heir was laughable to her (Genesis 18:12). After leaving their homeland and a lifetime of barrenness, Abraham and Sarah must have struggled to believe that God would fulfill His promises, but their faith carried them through their lives.

The idea of Sarah inheriting a supernatural beauty from Eve that only left her as death drew near is a work of fiction, however Scripture does state that Sarah was a beautiful woman. Genesis 12:10–20 and 20:1–18 contain similar stories of Abraham and Sarah seeking refuge in foreign lands. Abraham asked Sarah to tell both the Pharaoh in Egypt and the king in Gerar that she was his sister, because he feared that when they saw how beautiful she was, they would kill him and take her into their harems. Both kings did take her into their palaces, but when Pharaoh's household was stricken with disease, and when the king of Gerar was warned in a dream not to touch Sarah, Abraham's ruse was quickly discovered.

The Bible doesn't often comment on physical appearance. In places where one might expect a comment on someone's attractiveness or lack thereof, Scripture says that God looks beyond outward appearance (1 Samuel 16:7). The fact that Sarah's beauty is mentioned at all tells readers that it was great indeed. Whether it was supernatural or not? The reader can decide.

GOD'S FAVOR

The story of Abraham and Sarah is one of God's favor and faithfulness. Did He place His favor on this couple because of anything they had to offer Him? No, rather He blessed them because He loved them and swore to be their God from that time forward, and to remain faithful to their descendants forever. Moses wrote, "The LORD did not set his affection on you and choose you because you were more numerous than other peoples, for you were the fewest of all peoples. But it was because the LORD loved you and kept the oath he swore to your ancestors that he brought you out with a mighty hand and redeemed you from the land of slavery, from the power of

Pharaoh king of Egypt. Know therefore that the LORD your God is God; he is the faithful God, keeping his covenant of love to a thousand generations of those who love him and keep his commandments" (Deuteronomy 7:7–9 NIV). Abraham and Sarah's faith and obedience, with God's love and covenant, led to the Blessing of all the ages.

Fiction Author
MESU ANDREWS

Mesu Andrews is a Christy Award–winning author whose deep understanding of and love for God's Word brings the biblical world alive for readers. Andrews lives in North Carolina with her husband, Roy. She stays connected with readers through newsy emails, fun blog posts, and social media communities.

Nonfiction Author
CAROLINE E. CILENTO
MA Biblical Studies

Caroline E. Cilento is a lifelong reader and writer. She has been a student of the Bible and passionate about the Word of God from a young age, which led to graduate studies in the Bible. She lives in New York, NY, and serves in her church, as well as teaching ballet. Her friends, family, and pets mean the world to her. In her spare time she enjoys exercising, playing the piano, and binge-watching old sitcoms.

Read on for a sneak peek of another exciting story in the Extraordinary Women of the Bible series!

THE WOMAN WARRIOR: DEBORAH'S STORY

BY VIRGINIA SMITH

The sun beat down on the baked clay roof and rendered the air inside Deborah's house sweltering and nearly unbreathable. She knelt before the quern and applied the millstone to a handful of grain, singing in a low voice and doing her best to ignore the sweat trickling its way down her face. Her daughter, Sabra, sat in the doorway, hoping to catch a stray breeze, and applied a needle to patch a section of ripped fabric. Such heat was unusual so early in the year, as if the earth itself joined in the laments of Yahweh's people. She fervently hoped the earth's weather would resume its normal pattern soon.

"I do not see why I must mend Tivon's tunic when he will only rip it again." A whine of complaint saturated Sabra's voice, a tone that Deborah had noticed all too often of late.

She stopped singing and answered with a laugh in her voice. "You would have him work the fields without benefit of clothing?"

"I would have him take greater care," the girl replied. "And perhaps show a bit of gratitude." She pulled a stitch tight.

"Perhaps if he had to mend his own tunic he would be more appreciative."

Deborah did not answer. Sabra's thirteenth birthday drew near, and it seemed every day she grew more impatient with her brother. And with her mother, truth be told. *Yahweh, she is nearly grown. Only You know what her future holds. Bless her with a happy life.*

Her daughter's life had been laid out since shortly after her birth. She was to marry a cousin, the eldest son of Lappidoth's brother in Shechem. Three years past, Shechem was attacked by a band of Canaanites, and the boy was killed along with many others. The tragedy had devastated them all.

The grain on the quern had become a fine powder beneath her stone. She swept it into a jar and reached for another handful of grain.

Sabra stood abruptly. "We have a visitor." Excitement colored her tone. She tossed her brother's tunic aside and hurried toward the storage room, announcing as she went, "I will bring a cool drink to refresh her."

Deborah didn't bother to hide a knowing smile. A visitor meant a break in routine, something her daughter relished. Anything to take her away from chores she found tedious.

A woman appeared in the open doorway and peered inside. "Deborah?"

"Ophira." Deborah sat back on her heels. "Come inside."

The woman entered and lowered her head covering to her shoulders. "I do not wish to interrupt."

"Join me." Deborah waved her over. "We can talk while I work."

If she stopped work for every visitor, nothing would ever get done. It had begun with one woman from a neighboring farm coming to Deborah for advice. Before she knew what had happened, her reputation in the village as a wise woman spread. Even older women came to seek her guidance. Deborah never failed to acknowledge the Source of her wisdom or to give thanks to Yahweh for each woman He allowed her to help.

Ophira left her shoes by the door and settled on a woven mat near the quern. Deborah retrieved the millstone and once again began to methodically reduce the grain to powder. Ophira watched silently. From the corner of her eye Deborah noted the younger woman's tense shoulders and tightly drawn features.

Yahweh, something disturbs her. Help me put her at ease.

A question fell from her lips almost without thought. "Have you had word from your *abba*?"

She was not surprised when the young woman drew in a quick breath. "How did y—"

Her words stopped when Sabra appeared from the storage room carrying a tray. She crossed the distance slowly and set the tray on the floor opposite Deborah, then lowered herself to another mat.

"I've brought water to cool you from the heat."

She handed a mug to Ophira, who took it with a smile of thanks. The smile dissolved a moment later, the woman's gaze sliding to Deborah.

"Thank you, daughter," Deborah said, accepting her own mug.

Taking the third mug from the tray, Sabra settled herself comfortably and then fixed a gaze on Ophira. "Is your husband well?"

Ophira had recently married the eldest son of a potter in the village. She sipped from her mug, then gave a quick nod. "Reuben is well."

"And his *imma*?" Sabra asked. "Have you settled into a peaceful routine?"

"We work well together."

Deborah watched her daughter attempt to draw their guest into polite conversation. Could she not see Ophira's discomfort? Was it not obvious that she wanted to speak privately with Deborah?

"Sabra, I believe the goats needs tending," Deborah said. "Would you see that they have food and fresh water?"

Resentment flashed onto her young features. Her chest inflated with a quick breath, but Deborah spoke again before she could voice an argument.

"The heat is fierce today, and there isn't much shade for the poor things." She held Sabra's gaze and arched her eyebrows in a silent command.

Sabra understood. Her chest deflated with a breath blown through her nose that was almost, but not quite, a frustrated snort.

"Yes, Imma."

She set her mug on the tray and rose. With a quick nod at Ophira, she left the house. Moments later they heard her singsong voice drifting through the open door from the direction of the courtyard where they housed their animals.

"She's nearly grown," Deborah told her visitor, "and wants badly to be thought of as such."

Ophira gave a distracted nod, her expression still pinched. She gulped from the mug and then clutched it in her lap with both hands. "Why did you ask if I have heard from my abba?"

Deborah pondered her answer. Finally, she admitted, "I do not know. The question came to mind and felt right to ask."

She might have gone on to explain that Yahweh's wisdom often came to her like that, as a thought that did not feel like her own, or an urge to speak words without pausing to wonder why.

"I received a scroll from Jericho. Asif read it to me for two coins."

Deborah kept her expression blank. Asif, whose family ran the village's only olive press, served as a scribe for those not fortunate enough to have been taught to read or write. Though he had been taught by priests and was widely regarded as wise, Deborah found him to be a harsh man. He never failed to find fault with the beeswax wicks she fashioned and supplied for the lamps in the Tabernacle in Shiloh.

"I hope all is well in Jericho," she said.

"It is. That is to say, Abba did not say otherwise." Her head drooped forward.

Deborah prompted her to continue. "Your abba had a request for you?"

Ophira looked up then, misery in the eyes that fixed on Deborah. "He wants to send my brother here, to be apprenticed along with my husband as a potter."

It was unusual for a man, even a father, to make such a request of his daughter. The letter should have been sent to Yosef himself, the potter.

"Have you relayed the request to Yosef?" she asked.

Ophira shook her head. "I have not told Reuben either," she added, clearly miserable.

Was she afraid of her husband and of his abba? No, that did not feel right. But if not, then what troubled the young woman? *Yahweh?*

The answer came as clearly as spring water.

"Tell me about your brother."

Words poured from Ophira's lips then, as if a dam had broken. "Tyrek is wild. Even as a child he caused more mischief than anyone else in Jericho. The teachers of the Law cast him out, saying he caused disruption among the young men. Abba gave him watch over our sheep with instructions to take them into the hillside, thinking lonely nights would tame him. But he took a wineskin and drank it dry and fell asleep." She leaped to her feet and began to pace. "A wolf attacked and killed a ewe who was near to birthing a lamb. The rest of the flock scattered. Tyrek left with fifteen and returned with four."

Deborah shut her eyes against a flood of sympathy. Such a loss could devastate a family.

Ophira's pacing quickened. She reached the back window, whirled, and returned. "Then Abba set him to tending the wheat field. But Tyrek said the work did not suit him. Instead, he left Jericho to become a fisherman." She stopped beside Deborah. "That was before my marriage to Reuben. Abba's message said Tyrek has returned, claiming that fishing was not to his liking."

"And now your abba wishes to send him to Yosef to see if he can become a potter."

"Yosef is a kind man." Ophira's eyes filled with tears. "He will welcome my brother if I ask. But Tyrek will cause trouble, as he always does." She dropped cross-legged onto the mat and buried her face in her hands. "Tyrek has no regard for Yahweh. He will bring strife into the household."

Deborah rose to her knees, picked up her millstone, and began grinding the grain again.

Yahweh, Ophira is right. This young man will disrupt the peace of not only Yosef's household, but of the entire village. There are already too many of Your children who have turned away from You here. One more, and a mischief maker at that, will cause even more disorder.

The familiar sounds of the stone crushing grain filled her ears. A gentle comfort settled in her soul. Without words, even without thought, Deborah knew Yahweh's answer.

"Do you know the words of the covenant Yahweh gave to Moses, the *aseret ha'devarim* that are carved into the stone tablets in the Tabernacle in Shiloh?"

The young woman lifted her face. "Yes, I do."

"Of those ten *mitzvah*, only one that comes with a promise. Do you know which that is?"

Ophira's eyes became distant with thought. Deborah continued her work with the stone.

"*Honor your father and your mother, that your days may be long in the land that Yahweh is giving you.*"

Deborah nodded. "You cannot compel your brother to change his attitude or his actions, and Yahweh does not expect that of you. But He does expect you to obey Him."

"But what if Tyrek becomes a burden to my husband's family?"

Deborah allowed a smile. "Oh, he will. For a while. But Yahweh has plans for Tyrek, plans that can only come to fruition if he is here. Not in Jericho."

Ophira tilted her head, her features filled with skepticism. "How do you know?"

A chuckle rumbled through Deborah's chest. "Because Yahweh knows. You came for advice, and here it is. When you honor your abba by relaying his request, tell your husband and Yosef what you have told me. The decision will be theirs. And then commit your brother to Yahweh's care."

Ophira shook her head. "Tyrek does not know Yahweh."

"But Yahweh knows him. And you. You can trust Yahweh."

"Thank you." For the first time since her arrival, Ophira's features relaxed. "What can I do for you in return for your advice?"

Deborah laughed. "Give your praise to Yahweh, the source of all wisdom."

The young woman rose and went to the doorway to slip on her sandals. She pulled her head covering up over her head.

"One more thing," Deborah said, and Ophira turned. "If you receive further messages, I will gladly read them for you and take no coin in return."

With a final grateful smile, Ophira left.

The afternoon brought no respite from the heat. Deborah sent Sabra to start a fire with kindling and dung in the outdoor *tannur* while she mixed dough for the evening's bread. After twenty years of marriage to Lappidoth and keeping his house, the task was so familiar she barely paid attention to the work of her hands. Her thoughts drifted to a passage from *Torah*, from Yahweh's instruction to Moses in urging Pharoah to release His people from enslavement. *And the river shall bring forth frogs abundantly, which shall go up and come into thine house, and into thy bedchamber, and upon thy bed, and into the house of thy servants, and upon thy people, and into thine ovens, and into thy kneading troughs.* A chuckle rumbled in her throat as it always did when she thought of that passage. How startled Egyptian housewives must have been while performing this same task that occupied Deborah now, only to have a plague of frogs leap into their bowls.

"Imma." Deborah looked up to find Sabra standing in the doorway. "We have visitors."

The girl wore an oddly hesitant expression.

Deborah continued to mix the warm dough. "Show them in."

"But—"

A woman pushed past her. "Deborah, I need you to settle an argument."

"Tima." Deborah forced a smile of welcome, though truth be told, she had always found the woman to be harsh and not a little difficult. "You've caught me in the middle—"

She fell silent when Tima gestured for two more people to enter. Her sons. No wonder Sabra hesitated to admit them. It was considered unseemly for a woman to entertain a man in her home in her husband's absence.

After patting the dough into a ball in the kneading trough, she rubbed her hands together to dislodge the residue. "Perhaps we should go outside. Sabra, would you finish for me?"

She started to rise, but Tima jerked an impatient gesture in her direction. "There is no reason for that. This will only take a moment." Her eyes narrowed and she cast a meaningful look at Sabra. "It is a *private* matter."

Sabra's gaze slid to Deborah, who gave a tiny nod. Turning with a huff, she stomped out of the house.

Tima stared after her. "You had best get a handle on that girl, Deborah. Before you turn around twice she will be an unruly wench, and then what will you do?"

With an effort, Deborah maintained a calm demeanor. "Thank you for your advice, Tima."

The woman preened, obviously pleased that her warning had been received as advice by the one famous for giving advice.

Deborah glanced at the two young men, who both managed to look flustered. Though she should insist on exiting the house, these two were Tima's sons. Surely no one would call her to task for entertaining them and their mother in her home.

"Haran." She nodded at the first, who shifted his weight from one foot to the other. "Joel." The younger dropped his head and did not meet her gaze. She looked again at Tima. "What help can I provide?"

"You can instruct my youngest son as to the care of his widowed mother." Tima's jaw jutted forward.

Deborah glanced at Joel, who had not raised his head.

Haran took a half step forward. "My brother insists on leaving half of our harvest lying on the field to be picked up by *Gentiles*." He spat the last word.

"By *Gentiles*," Tima repeated, mimicking her oldest son's tone.

Scripture filtered through Deborah's mind. Lessons from Torah she had been privileged to learn as a young person, to memorize and hold close in her heart. Still, she held her tongue.

"Joel!" His mother snapped the name. "Tell her."

The young man's head dipped lower. "There is a Moabite woman."

"Moabite!" Tima shrieked the word. "A Moabite, Deborah. A Gentile of the worst kind."

Deborah did not take her eyes from the young man. "Go on, please."

Joel's chest inflated. "She is a widow."

"*I* am a widow!" Tima screeched.

The young man winced. "She is a widow without means of provision. She has no property, no family. And she reveres Yahweh. Her husband was Hebrew and died in a skirmish with the Canaanites." The young man lifted his head to lock Deborah's gaze. "If we do not help her, she will die."

"He lusts after her." Haran turned his head and spat upon the packed-dirt floor.

Deborah would have admonished him, but she held her tongue. Yahweh's wisdom had begun to stir her soul. The Lord her God had a word to share, though at this point she knew not what it might be.

"Not so." Joel's head shot upright, anger plain in his voice. "I have compassion for her. Does not Yahweh urge us to have compassion for the less fortunate?"

"*I* am the less fortunate." Tima beat a fist upon her breast. "Am I not a widow dependent on the kindness of my family?"

Deborah had to lower her own head, to hide a secret smile. Joel spoke Yahweh's heart. But how to phrase the judgment so Tima and Haran could accept it?

She closed her eyes. *Yahweh, what is Your judgment here? Give me Your wisdom.*

After a long moment, she looked up and locked gazes with Joel. "Are you giving this widow more than her share?" She paused and held his gaze for a long moment. "Are you leaving more than a tithe's portion for her to glean?"

His eyelids fluttered down, and he once again lowered his head. "Perhaps I am."

A song erupted in Deborah's soul. In an instant she *knew*. It was as though Yahweh allowed her a brief glimpse into Joel's soul. A wave of compassion washed over her at the tenderness she found in the young man's heart.

"You see?" Tima glared at her youngest. "He forces his imma to go without while feeding the mouth of a pagan Moabite."

A question rose up in Deborah's spirit. "Are you truly without, Tima? Are you starving? Do your sons not care for their widowed mother?"

In the face of such a direct question, Tima's shoulders drooped. Her glance slid toward Haran before she answered, "My sons are dutiful. I am not in want."

Lord, let Your wisdom shine through me.

Deborah smiled, trusting that she had opened herself up to Yahweh's wisdom for this situation. She straightened to her full height, which attained the height of neither of the men before her. "Do you know what Torah says regarding widows?"

Joel's head shot upward. "It says we should take care of widows, and also that we should allow widows to glean from the fields." His head lowered for a moment. "Honestly I do not know where that passage is, but I know it is there."

Tima took steps toward him. "I am a widow, my son. Would you put that harlot on the same level as I am?"

The struggle on the young man's face wrenched in Deborah's stomach.

"No, Imma," he whispered. "But she is not a harlot. She is merely hungry."

A passage from Torah rose in Deborah's mind. She could not stop her smile. Joel was right. She paused a moment, in which her kinship with the younger son grew, and she warmed to his cause.

"Joel is correct," she announced. She poured the authority given her by Yahweh into her voice, and the Lord her God answered by pouring power through her words. "Yahweh says: You shall not ill-treat any widow or orphan. If you do mistreat them, I will heed their outcry as soon as they cry out to Me, and My anger shall blaze forth and I will put you to the sword, and your own wives shall become widows and your children orphans."

She paused to let that sink in. The color drained from Haran's ruddy cheeks. He had taken a wife a few years ago, and the couple recently welcomed their second child.

Watching Tima's face, she continued. "Elsewhere Yahweh instructs: When thou cuttest down thine harvest in thy field, and hast forgot a sheaf in the field, thou shalt not go again to fetch it: it shall be for the stranger, for the fatherless, and for the widow: that the Lord thy God may bless thee in all the work of thine hands." She caught and held Tima's gaze. "Yahweh does not differentiate between an Israelite widow and a Gentile widow. If you are not in need, perhaps you should rejoice that your son has found a way to bless a Gentile and thus exemplify the power of Yahweh."

"She is a *Moabite*!" Tima said. "Does Torah not also say that we must destroy the foreigners who dwell in the land Yahweh promised our forefathers?"

Deborah struggled to maintain a calm expression, for she knew full well that Tima had not joined the rest of the villages in the pilgrimage feasts to the tabernacle in Shiloh. It was whispered that she had even been observed offering sacrifices to Baal.

"As our ancestors claimed our birthright, yes. But we dare not forget that we were foreigners in Egypt. We must always remember. Yahweh also commands, *'You shall not oppress a stranger, for you know the feelings of the stranger, having yourselves been gerim in the land of Egypt.'*"

"But that—that is—" Tima's lips clamped shut into a hard line.

Deborah softened her tone. "It is a hard teaching, I know."

Haran spoke up then. "But the one passage contradicts the other." He threw his hands into the air. "How are we to understand the will of Yahweh in the face of such inconsistency?"

After a long moment, during which Deborah sought Yahweh's answer, she nodded. "I confess I struggle to understand as well. Until I remember that Yahweh loves the fatherless and the widow and gives them food and clothing. Are we to do less?"

"This is worthless." Tima threw her hands into the air. "How can we follow the teaching of a God who asks us to take food from our children's mouths and give it to harlots?" She whirled and stomped out of the house.

Haran hesitated, his gaze fixed on Deborah as though testing her. After a long moment, he followed his imma, leaving Deborah alone with Joel.

"Thank you," the young man said. "I am sorry for the trouble my family has caused this day."

He started to turn away, but Deborah stopped him. "There is another teaching in Torah concerning the foreigners among us that I would have you consider."

Caution stole over his expression. He nodded for her to continue.

"*You shall not intermarry with them.*" She watched him flinch. "*You shall not give your daughter to his son, and you shall not take his daughter for your son. For he will turn away your son from following Me, and they will worship the gods of others, and the wrath of the Lord will be kindled against you, and He will quickly destroy you.*"

He shook his head in protest. "I will not turn away from the God of my fathers."

How clearly this young man's heart showed upon his face. Even in his protest, he admitted the feelings Deborah had glimpsed in his heart. He loved this Moabite widow. And yet in Joel she discerned something she had not seen in his brother or his imma. Joel revered Yahweh. In a time when so many had forgotten the God of their fathers and turned to idols, such devotion was rare.

"I am sorry," she said. "We are a people set apart since our father Abraham's covenant. Our lives are to be committed to Yahweh." She poured as much compassion into her voice as she could manage. "It is not always easy to serve the King of the universe."

She wanted to close her eyes against the pain she saw in his. But after a moment, he gave a silent nod.

"My advice is this: continue to have compassion on the Moabite widow, but do not leave for her more than you should. Give your imma and your brother no cause to fault you." She ducked her head to catch his eye. "You may one day persuade them to strengthen their own devotion to Yahweh."

A snort, full of scorn, blasted from his nostrils. "We will sooner see manna from heaven covering the fields than witness either of them worshipping Yahweh in more than word."

Deborah grinned. "It has happened before."

That did elicit a slight smile from the young man. A motherly rush of fondness washed over her. He would make a fine husband one day. Maybe even for...

"Come," she told him. "Let us go outside. Have you met my daughter, Sabra?"

At the doorway Joel paused for Deborah to exit first. She did, stepping over the bricks that separated their home from the surrounding pen where their animals were housed. For a moment the sun dazzled her eyes, and she blinked. When her vision cleared, her gaze fell on a passerby, a man wearing a shawl of draped linen over an inner tunic. In a flash she recognized Asif.

His gaze slid from hers to a point behind her, and settled on Joel. His eyes narrowed, and a wave of palpable animosity rushed toward her. Before she could call a greeting, or an explanation, he jerked his face away and hurried down the packed-dirt path.

Deborah drew in a breath. She had just been seen leaving her house with a man. Never mind that the man was young enough to be her son. He was a man, and she had entertained him alone in her house.

She would hear more of this. Of that she was certain.

A Note from
THE EDITORS

We hope you enjoyed another exciting volume in the Extraordinary Women of the Bible series, published by Guideposts. For over seventy-five years, Guideposts, a nonprofit organization, has been driven by a vision of a world filled with hope. We aspire to be the voice of a trusted friend, a friend who makes you feel more hopeful and connected.

By making a purchase from Guideposts, you join our community in touching millions of lives, inspiring them to believe that all things are possible through faith, hope, and prayer. Your continued support allows us to provide uplifting resources to those in need. Whether through our communities, websites, apps, or publications, we inspire our audiences, bring them together, and comfort, uplift, entertain, and guide them. Visit us at guideposts.org to learn more.

We would love to hear from you. Write us at Guideposts, P.O. Box 5815, Harlan, Iowa 51593 or call us at (800) 932-2145. Did you love *Beauty's Surrender: Sarah's Story?* Leave a review for this product on guideposts.org/shop. Your feedback helps others in our community find relevant products.

Find inspiration, find faith, find Guideposts.

Shop our best sellers and favorites at **guideposts.org/shop**

Or scan the QR code to go directly to our Shop

Find more inspiring stories in these best-loved Guideposts fiction series!

Mysteries of Lancaster County
Follow the Classen sisters as they unravel clues and uncover hidden secrets in Mysteries of Lancaster County. As you get to know these women and their friends, you'll see how God brings each of them together for a fresh start in life.

Secrets of Wayfarers Inn
Retired schoolteachers find themselves owners of an old warehouse-turned-inn that is filled with hidden passages, buried secrets, and stunning surprises that will set them on a course to puzzling mysteries from the Underground Railroad.

Tearoom Mysteries Series
Mix one stately Victorian home, a charming lakeside town in Maine, and two adventurous cousins with a passion for tea and hospitality. Add a large scoop of intriguing mystery, and sprinkle generously with faith, family, and friends, and you have the recipe for *Tearoom Mysteries*.

Ordinary Women of the Bible
Richly imagined stories—based on facts from the Bible—have all the plot twists and suspense of a great mystery, while bringing you fascinating insights on what it was like to be a woman living in the ancient world.

To learn more about these books, visit Guideposts.org/Shop